# ABITUR 2015

Prüfungsaufgaben
mit Lösungen

## Englisch

Erhöhtes Anforderungsniveau
Gymnasium • Berufliches Gymnasium
Niedersachsen

2011 – 2014



STARK

ISBN 978-3-8490-1051-5


10. neu bearbeitete und ergänzte Auflage
www.stark-verlag.de

# Inhalt

Jeweils zu Beginn des neuen Schuljahres erscheinen die
neuen Ausgaben der Abitur-Prüfungsaufgaben mit Lösungen.

**Autoren:**

Christian Fischer (Übungsaufgabe 1: komplett; 4, 6: Sprachmittlung; Lösungen der Abituraufgaben 2013)
Ahlke Gerdes (Übungsaufgabe 2: Leseverstehen)
Karl Große Kracht (Übungsaufgabe 2: Textaufgabe)
Rainer Jacob (Kurzinterpretationen)
Arnd Nadolny (Übungsaufgaben 3, 4: Textaufgabe; 5, 6: Textaufgabe; Lösungen der Abituraufgaben 2012)
Christoph Neuerer / Johannes Schmidt-Wellenburg (Lösung der Abituraufgabe 2014: Sprachmittlung)
Heike Ortscheid (Übungsaufgabe 5: Sprachmittlung; Lösungen der Abituraufgaben 2014: Textaufgaben)
Petra Schulze Wierling (Lösungen der Abituraufgaben 2011)

# Vorwort

**Liebe Schülerinnen, liebe Schüler,**

bald werden Sie Ihre Abiturprüfung im Fach Englisch ablegen. Wir möchten Sie gerne auf Ihrem Weg zu einem guten Abschluss begleiten und Ihnen helfen, sich mit den Anforderungen des Zentralabiturs in Niedersachsen vertraut zu machen.

Mithilfe der folgenden Aufgaben und Lösungsvorschläge haben Sie die Möglichkeit, gezielt und umfassend in Ihre (nähere) Zukunft zu investieren. Der erste Teil des Buches enthält sechs Beispiele für **konkrete Aufgabenstellungen** im Stil der **kombinierten Abiturprüfung** mit Aufgaben zu **Leseverstehen** bzw. **Sprachmittlung** und zur **Textaufgabe**. Außerdem enthält dieser Band die **Original-Prüfungsaufgaben** der Jahrgänge **2011 bis 2014**. Anhand von **Musterlösungen** können Sie herausfinden, in welchen Teilbereichen Sie Ihre Kompetenzen weiter verbessern müssen. Der Band umfasst zudem **Kurzinterpretationen**, die Ihnen bei der Wiederholung und Vertiefung der **Pflichtlektüren** nützlich sein werden.

Bevor Sie mit den Beispielklausuren beginnen und eigene Lösungen formulieren, sollten Sie die Besonderheiten der Abiturprüfung in Niedersachsen analysieren. Unsere **Hinweise** zu diesen Fragen werden Ihnen helfen, Inhalt und Form der Beispielklausuren besser zu verstehen und aus ihnen zu lernen. Das Kapitel **Hinweise und Tipps** enthält zusätzlich viele wichtige Informationen zur Vorbereitung auf die **länderübergreifende Abiturprüfung** (Prüfungsteil Sprachmittlung).

Sollten nach Erscheinen dieses Bandes noch **wichtige Änderungen** im Zentralabitur 2015 vom Kultusministerium Niedersachsen bekannt gegeben werden, finden Sie aktuelle Informationen dazu im Internet unter:
www.stark-verlag.de/pruefung-aktuell

Schon jetzt wünschen wir Ihnen viel Erfolg bei Ihrem Zentralabitur.

# Stichwortverzeichnis

## Points of Special Interest

## Literature



## Stylistic Devices and Composition

# Tipps und Hinweise zum Zentralabitur Englisch in Niedersachsen

## Die zentrale Abiturprüfung in Niedersachsen

In Niedersachsen findet die Abiturprüfung in Form des Zentralabiturs statt. Das bedeutet, dass die Aufgaben für alle Fächer einheitlich vom Kultusministerium gestellt werden. Im Fach Englisch ist seit dem Abitur 2013 eine kombinierte Aufgabe vorgesehen. Diese setzt sich zusammen aus einem sprachpraktischen Teil (Leseverstehen oder Sprachmittlung) und einer verkürzten Textaufgabe. Seit dem Abitur 2014 wird dieselbe **Sprachmittlungsaufgabe länderübergreifend** in mehreren Bundesländern gestellt. Die Textaufgabe dagegen wird vom niedersächsischen Kultusministerium ausgewählt. Als Prüfling können Sie dabei aus zwei unterschiedlichen Texten wählen.

Die Abiturvorbereitung im Englischunterricht stützt sich auf das Kerncurriculum, das wesentliche Unterrichtsinhalte und -methoden festlegt. Folgende Themenfelder werden danach in der Oberstufe behandelt und sind Grundlage für das Abitur:

- *Beliefs, values and norms in Western societies: Tradition and change (the British way/Britishness, the American experience)*
- *Individual and society (individual identity, roles and role conflicts, outsiders and counter cultures)*
- *National identity and ethnic/cultural/language diversities (migration, postcolonial experiences)*
- *The Media (media: forms and function, the influence of the media on public opinion and personal life)*
- *Globalisation (a global market and the world of work, effects on ways of life)*
- *Science and technology (chances and risks)*
- *Shakespeare (the world that made him, his universal appeal)*

Ergänzend veröffentlicht das Kultusministerium eine Liste mit verbindlichen Materialien, die im Unterricht behandelt werden müssen und die Grundlage für die Abiturprüfung bilden. Die Abiturtextaufgaben entstammen nicht diesen **Pflichtlektüren**. Sie müssen vielmehr diesen Text zu den verbindlichen Materialien in Bezug setzen, wenn es die Aufgabenstellung verlangt. Zu den verpflichtenden Lektüren und Filmen für die Abiturprüfung 2015 finden Sie in diesem Band **Kurzinterpretationen**.

**Verbindliche Materialien für das Abitur 2015 (erhöhtes Anforderungsniveau)**

- Roman: F. Scott Fitzgerald, *The Great Gatsby*
- Biografie: Auszüge aus Ben Mezrich, *The Accidental Billionaires*
- Kurzgeschichte: Hanif Kureishi, "My Son the Fanatic"
- Drama: Auszüge aus William Shakespeare, *The Merchant of Venice* oder *Romeo and Juliet*
- Drama: Arthur Miller, *The Crucible* (für allgemeinbildende Gymnasien)/*Death of a Salesman* (für Berufliche Gymnasien)
- Film: *Outsourced*
- Film: *Billy Elliot*

## Wie sieht die kombinierte Abiturprüfungsaufgabe aus?

Wie eine Abiturprüfungsaufgabe auszusehen hat, ist in den „Bildungsstandards der Kultusministerkonferenz (KMK) für die Allgemeine Hochschulreife" geregelt, die auf den „Einheitlichen Prüfungsanforderungen in der Abiturprüfung Englisch (EPA)" basieren. Sie gelten verbindlich für ganz Deutschland und beinhalten eine große Zahl möglicher Aufgabentypen. Tatsächlich haben Sie aber nur Aufgabenformen zu erwarten, die in den niedersächsischen Vorgaben vorgesehen sind. Seit 2013 werden nur noch zweigeteilte Abiturprüfungen zugelassen. Der erste Teil kann entweder aus einem Leseverstehen *(reading comprehension)* oder einer Sprachmittlung *(mediation)* bestehen. Für das Jahr 2015 ist im Rahmen der **länderübergreifenden Aufgabe** eine **Sprachmittlung** vorgesehen. Für diesen Teilbereich der Prüfung haben Sie eine Stunde Zeit. Es besteht keine Wahlmöglichkeit. Für die Sprachmittlung stehen Ihnen sowohl ein einsprachiges als auch ein zweisprachiges Wörterbuch zur Verfügung.
Nach Abgabe des ersten Prüfungsteils werden Sie zwei **Textaufgaben** vor sich haben, von denen Sie eine auswählen können. Für die Auswahl der Aufgabe stehen Ihnen bis zu 20 Minuten zusätzlich zur eigentlichen Bearbeitungszeit (240 Minuten) zu. Sie dürfen ein einsprachiges und zweisprachiges Wörterbuch benutzen. Der zweite Prüfungsteil basiert in jedem Fall auf einem **Text**, der nicht Teil einer Unterrichtslektüre ist und der möglicherweise durch einen Cartoon, ein Foto oder eine Statistik ergänzt wird. Dieser Text dient als Grundlage für die mehrteilige Aufgabenstellung.

## Welche Aufgabentypen gibt es?

Beide Prüfungsteile zusammen müssen so gestaltet sein, dass sie die drei folgenden, in den EPA näher beschriebenen „Anforderungsbereiche" abdecken. Eine thematische Verbindung zwischen den beiden Einzelteilen ist nicht zwingend erforderlich.
Bei den Aufgaben im **Anforderungsbereich 1** sollen Sie darlegen, **was** im Text gesagt wird. Dieser Bereich bezieht sich vor allem auf die Bereiche Sprachmittlung oder Leseverstehen. Beide Formate können sich aber auch schon auf den **Aufgabenbereich 2** erstrecken.
Die folgenden beiden Anforderungsbereiche finden vor allem für die Bearbeitung der Textaufgabe Verwendung: Aufgaben im **Anforderungsbereich 2** zielen darauf ab,

**wie** die Textaussage vermittelt wird. Es kann z. B. nach der Struktur, nach der Textsorte (z. B. Zeitungsartikel) oder nach der Wirkung auf den Leser gefragt werden.
Bei den Aufgaben im **Anforderungsbereich 3** sind Sie **persönlich gefragt**. Hier wird entweder eine begründete Meinungsäußerung oder eine kreative Leistung gefordert. Diese kann beispielsweise darin bestehen, dass Sie einen Brief oder Dialog verfassen oder dass Sie sich einen alternativen Schluss bzw. eine Fortsetzung zu einer Geschichte ausdenken.

Im Folgenden werden die drei prüfungsrelevanten Bereiche mit für sie typischen Aufgabenformen beschrieben:

### Sprachmittlung

Die Sprachmittlung basiert auf einem oder zwei deutschen Ausgangstext(en) (siehe Übungsaufgaben 4–6 und Abituraufgabe 2014-1 f.). Aufgabe des Prüflings ist es, **die wichtigsten Informationen des Textes bzw. der beiden Texte** von der Ausgangssprache **in die Zielsprache zu übertragen**, d. h. vom Deutschen ins Englische. Zwei mögliche Aufgabenstellungen könnten folgendermaßen lauten: "Write a letter asking your member of parliament to take immediate action to stop cyber mobbing by following the advice given in the German newspaper" oder "Based on this comment on exchange programmes, write an article for the homepage of your partner school in England."
Obwohl bisher die Textsorte des Artikels in den Aufgabenstellungen dominierte, bietet es sich an, auch die Merkmale bestimmter **Textsorten** zu wiederholen. In der Regel sind Sprachmittlungsaufgaben in konkrete Situationen eingebettet. Gebräuchlich sind *comment, e-mail, formal letter, personal letter, report, review, speech* und *summary.*

### Leseverstehen

Alternativ kann die Sprachmittlung durch ein Leseverstehen ersetzt werden. Dieser Kompetenzbereich (Anforderungsbereich 1 bzw. 2) wird meist anhand mehrerer Texte überprüft, die inhaltlich den Themenfeldern des Kerncurriculums zugeordnet werden können (siehe Abituraufgabe 2013). Es können **geschlossene** bzw. **halboffene Aufgabenformate** vorkommen, z. B. *multiple choice,* Zuordnung *(multiple matching, sequencing), short answer questions* oder Aufgaben des Typs *true/false/ give evidence.* Fragen nach dem **Globalverständnis** zielen darauf ab, herauszufinden, ob ein Text in seiner Gesamtaussage erfasst wurde. Eine mögliche Aufgabe könnte sein, zu erkennen, welche Zusammenfassung von einer Auswahl an verschiedenen Zusammenfassungen für den vorliegenden Text am besten geeignet ist. Das **Detailverständnis** bezieht sich auf Einzelheiten des Textes, z. B. könnte eine Tabelle vervollständigt werden *(table completion)*, in der die Kategorien vorgegeben sind. Beim **inferierenden Lesen** werden Informationen gesucht, die nicht explizit im Text zu finden sind. Die Informationen des Textes müssen also weiterverarbeitet werden. So kann z. B. nach Textbelegen gefragt werden, die die Intention des Autors verdeutlichen.

**Textaufgabe**

Die Textaufgaben beziehen sich auf den Prüfungstext bzw. die zugehörigen Materialien. Dieser Bezug muss auch dann hergestellt werden, wenn die Aufgaben auf Sachverhalte zurückgreifen, die im Unterricht behandelt wurden. Aufgrund der vorgeschalteten sprachpraktischen Aufgabe fällt die Textaufgabe weniger umfangreich aus als in den vorhergehenden Jahren. Seit dem Abitur 2012 wird die Textaufgabe in einen situativen Rahmen eingebettet. Lassen Sie sich davon nicht verwirren. Sie können z. B. eine auf den Kontext bezogene Einleitung schreiben, bevor Sie mit Teilaufgabe 1 beginnen. Denkbar sind auch kontextbezogene Überleitungen zwischen den Teilaufgaben sowie Zwischenüberschriften.
Damit die Aufgabenstellungen in der Abiturprüfung eindeutig sind, wurde für die Formulierung der Teilaufgaben ein bestimmtes Format festgelegt, das Ihre Englischlehrerin oder Ihr Englischlehrer bereits in den Kursklausuren anwenden kann. Bei diesen Aufgabenstellungen handelt es sich nicht um Fragen *(What is Frank's attitude towards his job?)*, sondern um „Arbeitsaufträge" *(Describe Frank's attitude towards his job)*. Folgende Arbeitsaufträge, auch **Operatoren** genannt, kommen häufig vor:

**Anforderungsbereich I**

| Operator | Definition | Beispiele | Nützliche Wendungen |
|---|---|---|---|
| **describe** | Dieser Arbeitsauftrag fordert eine exakte Darstellung einer Sache oder eines Sachverhalts. | *Describe Biff's feelings after he has unsuccessfully tried to see Bill Oliver.* | • *to portray the situation of*<br>• *to depict various sides of*<br>• *to give a short description of*<br>• *to give an account of* |
| **outline** | Der Auftrag *outline* zielt auf die Nennung der Hauptmerkmale eines bestimmten Sachverhalts. | *Outline the author's views on the role of the family.* | • *to give an outline of the main points*<br>• *to sketch*<br>• *to describe briefly* |
| **state, point out** | Bei diesen Arbeitsaufträgen geht es (ähnlich wie bei *outline*) um eine klare und knappe Darstellung. | *State briefly the main developments in the Loman family after Biff failed his maths exam.* | • *to express briefly*<br>• *to give a short abstract of*<br>• *to mention the central aspects of*<br>• *to present the main ideas about* |
| **summarise, write a summary** | Hier wird eine knappe und prägnante Zusammenfassung des Originaltextes erwartet. | *Summarise the text in your own words.* | • *to give an account of the central aspects of the text*<br>• *to sum up the main points*<br>• *to refer to the core points made by the author* |

**Anforderungsbereich II**

| Operator | Definition | Beispiele | Nützliche Wendungen |
|---|---|---|---|
| **analyse, examine** | Hier wird eine detaillierte Beschreibung bestimmter Aspekte des Textes verlangt. | *Analyse Frank's and Rita's views on education. Examine the author's use of language.* | • *to study (thoroughly) the different aspects of*<br>• *to give a detailed analysis/ examination of*<br>• *to draw a distinction between … and …* |
| **characterize** | Hier wird gefragt, wie der Autor die Charaktere mit bestimmten Eigenschaften und Wesenszügen versieht. | *Examine how Willy Loman is characterized through the way he talks to Charley. Analyse the author's method of characterizing Willy's sons.* | • *to portray the dominant features of*<br>• *to describe the characteristic features of*<br>• *to present the characteristics of*<br>• *to identify the typical features of* |
| **compare** | Hier geht es darum, Parallelen und Unterschiede aufzuzeigen. | *Compare X's and Y's views on moral standards in business.* | • *to make/draw a comparison between … and …*<br>• *to point out the similarities/differences between …*<br>• *to show parallels between … and …*<br>• *to state the resemblances of … and …* |
| **contrast** | Im Gegensatz zu *compare* wird bei *contrast* Wert auf die Herausarbeitung von Unterschieden gelegt. | *Contrast Willy Loman's relationship to his sons with that of other characters from your classroom reading.* | • *to weigh/balance/measure the differences between …*<br>• *to differentiate between …*<br>• *to draw a contrast between …*<br>• *to juxtapose … and …* |
| **explain** | Hier ist die Beschreibung eines Sachverhalts und seiner Ursachen gefordert. | *Explain the Willy Loman's aggressive behaviour towards his wife.* | • *to give an explanation of*<br>• *to unfold the question of*<br>• *to show clearly* |

**Anforderungsbereich III**

| Operator | Definition | Beispiele | Nützliche Wendungen |
|---|---|---|---|
| **assess, evaluate** | Dieser Arbeitsauftrag fordert die ausgewogene Betrachtung und Einschätzung eines Sachverhalts. | *Assess the role of the peer group in a child's upbringing.* | • *to give an assessment of*<br>• *to evaluate the nature of*<br>• *to arrive at a decision about/at the personal conclusion that*<br>• *to make up one's mind about*<br>• *to make a judgement about* |
| **comment** | Das ist der klassische Arbeitsauftrag für eine persönliche Stellungnahme; gefordert wird eine klare Meinungsäußerung mit nachvollziehbarer Begründung. | *Comment on Howard's view that 'business is business' and that 'everybody has to pull his own weight'.* | • *I would like to make/give a comment on/about*<br>• *It is worthwhile commenting on*<br>• *I would like to give my personal opinion on*<br>• *I would like to make a statement concerning*<br>• *I would like to make some personal remarks about* |
| **discuss** | Hier wird eine Gegenüberstellung von Pro- und Contra-Argumenten verlangt. | *Discuss the implications of globalisation as presented in this text.* | • *to weigh the pros and cons of*<br>• *to give a balanced description of*<br>• *to show the different ideas/opinions about*<br>• *to juxtapose the different/contrasting ideas about* |
| **justify** | Hier wird eine nachvollziehbare Begründung für ein Verhalten/eine Entscheidung gefordert. | *You are the principal of a school. Justify your decision to forbid smoking on the school premises.* | • *to give a justification of/an explanation for*<br>• *to give reasons/grounds for*<br>• *to explain in detail*<br>• *to defend a position* |

## Allgemeines zur sprachpraktischen Aufgabe

Für sprachpraktische Aufgaben ist ein großer Wortschatz in der Fremdsprache die zentrale Voraussetzung für ein gutes Abschneiden. Dadurch, dass Sie sich **regelmäßig mit der englischen Sprache beschäftigen**, verbessert sich automatisch Ihre Fähigkeit, den Sinngehalt von Aussagen in der Fremdsprache zu erfassen, auch wenn Ihnen nicht jedes einzelne Wort bekannt ist. Ob Sie Ihr Sprachvermögen am liebsten mit englischsprachigen Filmen, Büchern, Zeitschriften oder Songtexten trainieren, bleibt Ihnen überlassen. Konkret lassen sich beispielsweise Informationen über bestimmte Charaktere oder deren Entwicklung im Laufe der Handlung auf Englisch (Training für Leseverstehen und Sprachmittlung) zusammentragen. Gerade für die Sprachmittlung empfiehlt es sich auch, deutsche Zeitungsartikel für (imaginäre) englische Bekannte zusammenzufassen.

## Konkrete Vorgehensweise bei der Sprachmittlung

Da Ihnen für die Aufgabe lediglich eine Stunde zur Verfügung steht, sollten Sie sich die Regeln für das Abfassen einer Sprachmittlung noch einmal vergegenwärtigen, damit die einzelnen Arbeitsschritte reibungslos ablaufen können und keine wertvolle Zeit verloren geht. Wiederholen Sie die Reihenfolge der einzelnen Schritte aber nicht wie ein Kochrezept, sondern machen Sie sich klar, welchen Sinn eine Sprachmittlung eigentlich hat: Sie dient dazu, einem Leser oder Zuhörer die wichtigsten Informationen aus einem ihm unbekannten bzw. sprachlich unverständlichen längeren Text nahezubringen, sodass ein korrekter Eindruck vom Inhalt des Originals entsteht. Die Fähigkeit, eine gute Sprachmittlung anzufertigen, kommt Ihnen nicht nur in der Schule zugute, sondern hilft Ihnen auch in Ihrem späteren Beruf und im Alltag – immer dann, wenn umfassende Sachverhalte in eine andere Sprache übertragen und präzise auf den Punkt gebracht werden sollen.

Versuchen Sie es selbst einmal. Lesen Sie einen Artikel auf der Homepage einer deutschen Tageszeitung. Versuchen Sie, einem imaginären englischsprachigen Zuhörer/Leser in einem knappen Vortrag die Kernaussagen des Artikels zu vermitteln. Fassen Sie die relevanten Informationen auf Englisch zusammen. Bemühen Sie sich darüber hinaus auf Ihren Adressaten, seinen Kenntnisstand und die Situation, in der diese Inhaltswiedergabe stattfindet, einzugehen. Schließlich macht es einen Unterschied, ob Sie gebeten werden, für Ihre sportbegeisterte englische E-Mail-Partnerin die wichtigsten Informationen zu einem Zeitungsartikel über das Champions League Finale auf *Spiegel Online* wiederzugeben oder einen Brief an den Gouverneur von Texas zu schreiben, in dem Sie sich für die Abschaffung der Todesstrafe aussprechen. Legen Sie dazu jetzt (!) dieses Buch zur Seite; lesen Sie also zunächst nicht weiter!

Wenn Sie Ihre Sache gut gemacht haben, sind Sie folgendermaßen vorgegangen:

- Zuerst haben Sie die zentrale Aussage des Textes bestimmt.
- Diese zentrale Aussage haben Sie anschließend in Ihren *umbrella sentence* integriert. Mit diesem Satz informiert Ihre *mediation* den Zuhörer/Leser über den inhaltlichen Kern und den situativen Rahmen des Ausgangstextes – inklusive Quellenangabe.
- Die wesentlichen Aspekte (z. B. Textstellen, die Ihre Kernaussage stützen) wurden von Ihnen um den Informationskern arrangiert.
- Sie haben sich auf das Wesentliche beschränkt und unwichtige Details weggelassen. Logische und zeitliche Bezüge haben Sie durch Konjunktionen hergestellt.
- Sie haben den Kontext der Sprachmittlung berücksichtigt, d. h. die Umstände, unter denen sie stattfindet bzw. die Personen, an die sie sich richtet.
- Unbekannte Wörter und Wendungen haben Sie so umschrieben, dass ihr Gegenüber den Sinn der Aussage dennoch verstehen konnte.
- Sprachliche und soziale Besonderheiten der Ausgangs- und Zielsprache wurden von Ihnen berücksichtigt (keine Umgangssprache in Ihrem Vortrag etc.)
- Ihre *mediation* ist wesentlich kürzer als das Original.
- Sie haben den Ausgangstext nicht wortwörtlich ins Englische übersetzt, sondern nur die Hauptaussagen wiedergegeben; der Bezug zur Aufgabenstellung ist klar.

## Textaufgabe

Da die Textaufgabe im Vergleich zur sprachpraktischen Aufgabe deutlich mehr Gewicht hat (70 %), sollte sie insgesamt auch besonders intensiv eingeübt werden. Häufig ist aber zu beobachten, dass Schülerinnen und Schüler die inhaltliche Vorbereitung wichtiger nehmen als die sprachliche. Es wird überlegt, was man alles noch einmal lesen und evtl. auswendig lernen sollte, anstatt nach den Möglichkeiten zur Verbesserung des angewandten Englisch zu fragen.

### Sprachliche Vorbereitung

Nach langen Jahren Englischunterricht hat jeder Schüler und jede Schülerin mittlerweile ein sehr individuelles Profil von Stärken und Schwächen entwickelt. Wirklicher Lernfortschritt lässt sich nur noch durch ein individuelles Lernprogramm erzielen und das können Sie am besten selbst.

Ein guter Ansatzpunkt dafür sind Ihre korrigierten Klausuren. Spätestens mit Beginn Ihres letzten Schuljahres sollten Sie diese kopieren und sorgfältig aufbewahren. Als Vorbereitung auf die nächste Klausur und natürlich insbesondere auf die Abiturprüfung setzen Sie sich am besten noch einmal intensiv mit Ihren „gesammelten Werken“ auseinander. Machen Sie sich dabei noch einmal klar, was Ihre häufigsten Fehler sind, und treffen Sie eine realistische Auswahl von Problemfeldern, auf die Sie sich in der kommenden Klausur besonders konzentrieren wollen. Prüfen Sie anschließend auch kritisch, in welchem Maß Sie Ihre guten Vorsätze hinsichtlich der Verbesserung der sprachlichen Qualität auch tatsächlich umsetzen konnten.

Zudem lassen sich natürlich auch vorhandene Kenntnisse weiter verbessern. Auch wenn Sie im Bereich „Sprache“ üblicherweise gute Ergebnisse erzielen, sollten Sie sich mit einigen Strukturen, die Sie mit hoher Wahrscheinlichkeit in Ihrer Prüfungsarbeit benötigen werden, noch einmal intensiv befassen. Dazu gehören:

- ***if-clauses:*** Häufig werden Sie in einer Teilaufgabe dazu aufgefordert, sich in eine Rolle oder eine Situation hineinzuversetzen und zu erklären, was Sie tun, sagen oder denken würden. Beispiel: *Explain what you would do if you were one of the characters in the story.*
- ***reported speech:*** Diese Konstruktion benötigen Sie, wenn Sie wiedergeben müssen, was jemand sagt oder denkt. Beispiel: *In his speech George W. Bush points out that ....* Wenn Sie in Ihrer Prüfungsarbeit die indirekte Rede anwenden müssen, machen Sie sich vorher genau klar, ob Sie in der Vergangenheit oder in der Gegenwart schreiben.
- ***past tense/present perfect:*** Da diese beiden Zeiten im Englischen anders verwendet werden als im Deutschen, bestehen häufig Unsicherheiten bezüglich ihrer Unterscheidung. Beispiele: *The last time I saw him was two years ago. I bought the latest Harry Potter volume when I was in England.*
- ***modal verbs:*** Die deutschen Verben „müssen“ und „sollen“ werden im Englischen je nach Zusammenhang unterschiedlich wiedergegeben *(shall, ought, be supposed to; must, have to, need to).*

Entdecken Sie hinsichtlich dieser Grammatikbereiche Wissenslücken, empfehlen wir das „Abitur-Training Englisch: Grammatikübungen“ (Best.-Nr. 82452) des Stark Verlags.

**Inhaltliche Vorbereitung**

Bei der Vorbereitung auf den inhaltlichen Teil der Textaufgabe sollten Sie sich noch einmal vergegenwärtigen, wie die Aufgabenstellung aufgebaut ist. Im Mittelpunkt steht das Material (Text, evtl. Bilder), das Sie in der Prüfung erstmalig zu Gesicht bekommen und auf dessen Erschließung sich die Aufgabenstellung bezieht. Damit ist umgekehrt auch klar, was Sie nicht erwarten müssen, nämlich Aufgaben, in denen lediglich Wissen abgefragt wird, das Sie im Unterricht erworben haben.

Die Verbindung zwischen Aufgabenstellung und Unterricht ergibt sich vielmehr daraus, dass im Abitur Themen und Probleme angesprochen werden, über die Sie sich im Unterricht schon einmal Gedanken gemacht haben und die Sie deshalb sprachlich und inhaltlich bewältigen können. Darüber hinaus kann die Aufgabenstellung auch ausdrücklich Bezüge zwischen den Prüfungsmaterialien und einzelnen Unterrichtsthemen herstellen. Sie wird aber kein umfangreiches und detailliertes Sachwissen (wie z. B. Jahreszahlen oder Inhaltsangaben gelesener Literatur) abfragen.

Im Zuge der inhaltlichen Prüfungsvorbereitung sollten Sie daher Folgendes tun:

- Auf die **Pflichtlektüren** können Sie sich anhand der **Kurzinterpretationen in diesem Band** vorbereiten. Vergegenwärtigen Sie sich noch einmal die Inhalte der Werke sowie die darin auftretenden Themen und Probleme. Wiederholen Sie Vokabeln, die Sie in diesem Zusammenhang neu gelernt haben.
- Stellen Sie sicher, dass Sie von den im Unterricht gelesenen Werken die Titel sowie die Namen der Autoren und der Hauptcharaktere kennen und richtig schreiben können. Solche Schreibfehler kommen im Abitur tatsächlich vor und hinterlassen einen wenig vorteilhaften Eindruck.

## Das Anfertigen der Prüfungsarbeit

Achten Sie darauf, dass Sie sich die Ihnen zur Verfügung stehende Zeit gut einteilen. In der ersten Phase der Beschäftigung mit der Aufgabenstellung machen viele Prüflinge den Fehler, sich zu lange und zu intensiv mit dem inhaltlichen Verständnis der Texte und der Zusatzmaterialien zu befassen und die eigentliche Aufgabenstellung zu spät ins Blickfeld zu rücken. Gerade den **ersten Teil der Prüfung** sollten Sie zügig angehen, da Sie ihn vor der Bearbeitung des zweiten Teils abgeben müssen.
Widmen Sie sich nach dem flüchtigen Lesen des bzw. der jeweiligen Texte zunächst der **Aufgabenstellung** und Ihrer Systematik. Stellen Sie sicher, dass Sie die Aufgabe verstehen. Damit schaffen Sie sich einen „Filter", der Ihnen hilft, bei der anschließenden intensiven Beschäftigung mit dem Text das Wichtige vom Unwichtigen zu unterscheiden und sofort die relevanten Passagen mithilfe bestimmter Kennzeichnungen (Farben, Aufgabennummern am Rand) zu markieren.

Für die Auswahl der Textaufgabe **im zweiten Teil der Prüfung** haben Sie insgesamt 20 Minuten Zeit – sollten Sie sich nicht entscheiden können, ist dies ein Hinweis darauf, dass Ihnen beide Aufgaben gleichermaßen liegen und Sie sich nicht allzu sehr den Kopf zerbrechen müssen. In der ersten Aufgabe empfiehlt es sich, Angaben wie z. B. Autor, Titel des Textes und das Publikationsdatum zu Beginn der Ausführungen zu nennen. Ein kurzer Kernsatz zum Inhalt bietet sich gerade bei der Analyse der Struktur und/oder Sprache des Textes an. Die Erfahrung zeigt, dass in jeder Teilaufgabe mindestens drei und höchstens fünf Stichpunkte angesprochen werden sollten. Wenn Sie diese festgelegt haben, nehmen Sie sich ein wenig Zeit, um die Reihenfolge der einzelnen Aspekte zu bestimmen. Dann können Sie mit der Reinschrift beginnen.
Vermeiden Sie dabei folgende problematische Vorgehensweisen:

- Zu ausführliche Konzeptarbeit: Konzept und Reinschrift unterscheiden sich nur minimal. Es wird wertvolle Arbeitszeit vertan.
- Ungleiche Gewichtung der Aufgaben durch falsche Zeiteinteilung: Häufig wird die erste Aufgabe sehr sorgfältig bearbeitet, während die Bearbeitung des zweiten Arbeitsauftrags – offenbar aus Zeitmangel – oft oberflächlicher ausfällt. Versuchen Sie sich einen Zeitplan zu machen, indem Sie etwa die letzten 45 Minuten Ihrer Arbeitszeit für die Überprüfung einplanen und die reine Schreibzeit gleichmäßig auf die Einzelaufgaben verteilen.

- Nichtbeachtung des Themas: Wird eine Aufgabe als schwierig empfunden, dann neigen Prüflinge häufig dazu, den Text in unnötig langatmiger Darstellung noch einmal wiederzugeben. Bei Fragestellungen mit Bezug zur Unterrichtslektüre wird oft einfach nur deren Inhalt nacherzählt, anstatt die Verbindung zur Aufgabe und zum Prüfungstext aufzuzeigen.

Gerade im Zentralabitur bringen Sie den Korrektor in eine sehr missliche Lage, wenn Sie sich nicht an die Aufgabenstellung halten – für jede Aufgabe ist vorgegeben, was vom Prüfling inhaltlich erwartet wird und wie seine Leistung zu benoten ist. Wenn Sie also völlig an der Aufgabe vorbeischreiben und keines der verlangten Elemente in Ihrer Bearbeitung auftaucht, kann man Ihren Text, gleichgültig wie lang er ist, nur mit null Punkten bewerten. Verfassen Sie hingegen einen kurzen, aber zumindest auf das Thema bezogenen Text, dann können Sie evtl. noch Punkte sammeln.

## Bewertung der Prüfungsarbeit

Um zu einer Gesamtnote für Ihre Prüfungsarbeit zu kommen, werden der erste und zweite Prüfungsteil getrennt bewertet. Während der erste Prüfungsteil mit 30 % in die Gesamtbewertung eingeht, zählt der zweite Teil 70 %.

Die Bewertung des **Leseverstehens** erfolgt über Rohpunkte, wobei pro richtige Antwort *(item)* ein sogenannter Rohpunkt vergeben wird. Für eine ausreichende Leistung (5 Notenpunkte) ist das Erreichen von 60 % der Rohpunkte notwendig. Für nicht eindeutig zugeordnete oder zweideutige *items* kann kein Punkt vergeben werden.

In der **Sprachmittlung** werden sowohl Inhalt als auch Sprache bewertet. Folgende Kriterien sind ausschlaggebend für die Benotung:
- Beachtung der Aufgabenstellung (Nennen der wesentlichen Aspekte)
- Adressaten- und Situationsbezug
- Inhaltliche und sprachliche Korrektheit

Für die **Textaufgabe** werden Sprache und Inhalt zunächst getrennt voneinander bewertet. Hinsichtlich der **sprachlichen Qualität** geht es darum, dass Sie in flüssiger Ausdrucksweise einen möglichst fehlerfreien Text erstellen und dabei das passende Vokabular verwenden.
Fehler, die das Verständnis Ihres Textes erschweren, mit störender Häufigkeit auftreten oder darauf schließen lassen, dass Sie elementare Regeln der englischen Grammatik nicht beherrschen, schlagen natürlich negativ zu Buche. Unterlaufen Ihnen dagegen nur wenige Flüchtigkeitsfehler, so kann Ihre Arbeit immer noch recht positiv bewertet werden, wenn Ihr sprachlicher Ausdruck flüssig und abwechslungsreich wirkt und Ihr Text klar gegliedert ist. Für die Qualität der sprachlichen Leistung wird eine einzige Note vergeben; nach Sprachrichtigkeit und Ausdrucksvermögen getrennte Teilnoten gibt es nicht.
Die **inhaltliche Qualität** Ihrer Arbeit hängt davon ab, wie genau Sie die Aufgabenstellung befolgt haben und inwieweit Ihr Text klar gegliedert und schlüssig ist. Jede Teilaufgabe wird einzeln bewertet; aus der Summe der Ergebnisse ergibt sich die Ge-

samtnote für den Inhalt. Um das Endergebnis für den Prüfungsteil Textaufgabe zu ermitteln, wird die sprachliche Note mit 60 % und die inhaltliche Note mit 40 % gewertet. Die Teilaufgaben im Bereich Inhalt werden einzeln benotet und anschließend nach den Lösungsvorgaben des Kultusministeriums noch prozentual gewichtet. Diese prozentuale Gewichtung wird bei jeder Abiturprüfungsaufgabe vom Kultusministerium individuell festgelegt, kann also jedes Mal unterschiedlich sein.
Ein Beispiel: Nehmen wir einmal an, Sie haben für Ihre Arbeit im Bereich „Sprache“ 11 Punkte bekommen. Im Bereich „Inhalt“ ergibt sich für Sie bei zwei Aufgaben und prozentualer Gewichtung ein Mittelwert von 9,2 Punkten. Für das Endergebnis multiplizieren Sie Ihre sprachliche Note mit 0,6 und die inhaltliche Note mit 0,4 und addieren dann beide Ergebnisse. Es ergibt sich 10,28 – dieser Prüfungsteil wird also mit „noch gut (10 Punkte)“ bewertet.

## Hinweise zur Arbeit mit diesem Band

Dieses Buch enthält **Übungsaufgaben** wie sie Ihnen im **Abitur** begegnen könnten. Sie sollen Ihnen vor allem ermöglichen, sich auf die Art der Aufgabenstellung vorzubereiten und die im Unterricht vermittelten Methoden zu üben. Für den Fall, dass Sie nicht sicher sind, ob Sie die Aufgabenstellung richtig verstehen, gibt es zusätzliche **Hinweise und Tipps**, die Ihnen bei der Bearbeitung helfen sollen. Außerdem finden Sie zu jeder Aufgabe auch eine **Musterlösung**, mit der Sie Ihre Texte vergleichen können. Neben den Übungsaufgaben enthält dieser Band die **Original-Prüfungsaufgaben** der Jahrgänge 2011–2014 des Zentralabiturs auf erhöhtem Anforderungsniveau, natürlich ebenfalls mit ausführlichen Musterlösungen und Hinweisen. Anhand der alten Prüfungsaufgaben (2011 sowie 2012) können Sie sich umfassend auf den zweiten Prüfungsteil des kombinierten Abiturs vorbereiten und lernen Ihr eigenes Arbeitstempo besser einzuschätzen. Die Prüfungsaufgaben 2013 und 2014 können Ihnen eine realistische Vorstellung vom Anspruch der sprachpraktischen Aufgaben und vom Umfang der verkürzten Textaufgabe vermitteln. Das Kapitel „**Kurzinterpretationen**“ ermöglicht es Ihnen, sich inhaltlich auf den Prüfungsteil Textaufgabe vorzubereiten.

# Kurzinterpretationen zu den Pflichtlektüren

## Stephen Daldry / Lee Hall, *Billy Elliot* (2000)

*Billy Elliot* is a comedy written by Lee Hall. Stephen Daldry directed the film. It was released in 2000 and won several awards. Hall (born 1966) began his career as a playwright after leaving Cambridge University, where he studied English Literature. The inspiration to write the story for *Billy Elliot* came to him when he was writing about his own childhood. The film company Working Title, the producers of such successes as *Notting Hill* and *Four Weddings and a Funeral*, engaged Stephen Daldry (born 1960), who had made a name for himself as one of England's leading theatre directors, to turn the script into a film. Later, Daldry also directed the stage musical version, with music by Elton John and lyrics by Lee Hall. The musical became an instant hit in London's West End and opened on Broadway in New York in 2008.

### Contents

The film tells the story of 11-year-old Billy Elliot, who wants to become a ballet dancer. It is set in the mining village Everington (County Durham) in North Eastern England during the UK miners' strike (1984/1985).
Billy Elliot lives in a modest house together with his father Jackie, his older brother Tony and his invalid grandmother. His mother has been dead for some time. Billy's father and brother, both miners, are out on strike and take their post at the picket line to prevent strike breakers (so-called "scabs") from resuming work. Every week Billy is given 50 pence for boxing lessons in the hall of the boys club of the village. The boy is not too enthusiastic about boxing and clearly lacks talent. One day the young boxers have to share the hall with the ballet class of Mrs Wilkinson, because the downstairs hall is being used as a soup kitchen for the striking miners. Billy watches with interest and eventually joins the lesson, encouraged by Debbie, the young daughter of the ballet teacher. He becomes so fascinated with dancing that he practises at home as well and steals a book from the library to teach himself special movements such as the pirouette. Having realised Billy's talent, Mrs Wilkinson drives him hard to improve his routines.
Meanwhile, things come to a head: The miners' strike has been going on for several months now and the clashes with the police are getting more violent. Tony gets more

and more involved. Moreover, Mr Elliot learns from Billy's boxing trainer that his son has not turned up for boxing sessions for months. Mr Elliot is furious when he finds out that Billy spends his time dancing instead of boxing and forbids him to join the dancing classes. After an argument with his father, Billy, who wants to continue dancing, runs away to Mrs Wilkinson, who encourages him to go to an audition in Newcastle to apply for a place at the Royal Ballet School in London. To prepare the boy for the audition, she secretly gives him private lessons.
The tension at home increases, as Mr Elliot wants to stop Tony from getting further into trouble with the police. Billy finds it hard to concentrate on the dancing lessons. One day Billy witnesses the police arrest Tony, who is one of the union leaders behind the miners' strike and consequently has to spend a night in prison. Billy misses the important audition in Newcastle as he and his father have to fetch Tony from court.
Time passes and as a result of the long-lasting strike the family's financial situation gets worse. During Christmas holidays, Billy takes his friend Michael, who confesses that he is gay, to the hall where he practices dancing and shows him a few routines. His father, who unexpectedly turns up, is amazed by Billy's talent and decides to support Billy in his efforts from that moment on. To give Billy a chance and earn the necessary money for the trip to another audition, Mr Elliot is even prepared to go back to work. At the last minute Tony can stop his father from breaking the strike, promising to find some other way of raising money for Billy. Friends and neighbours organise collections and raffles, and Mr Elliot sells the jewellery of his deceased wife. Some time later father and son travel to London for the audition at the Royal School of Ballet, where Billy presents an unusual high-energy dance number. Eventually, the letter of acceptance arrives. When Mr Elliot breaks the good news to his colleagues, he learns that the strike has ended with the defeat of the union. In the end, Billy leaves his family and friends to be trained as a professional dancer. The final scene of the film shows Mr Elliot and Tony in London several years later: They are watching a performance of *Swan Lake* with Billy as one of the lead dancers.

### Characters

**Billy Elliot** is a young boy of 11 years of age, who grows up in an all-male household in a mining town in England's north. His mother is dead and the family is in financial trouble because both father and brother are out on a miners' strike, trying to make ends meet on the meagre strike pay. Billy does not take much notice of the employment troubles because he himself is in a **deep crisis**: he **does not want to** follow in his father's and forefathers' footsteps and **become a miner**. Neither does he want to do boxing in his free-time. Instead, he discovers his **talent for dancing**. Supported by his teacher, Mrs Wilkinson, Billy eventually persuades his father to let him audition for the Royal Ballet School in London. In order to achieve this end, he puts up with a lot of pressure both from his **initially disapproving family** and a community which regards male dancers with suspicion.

**Jackie Elliot:** Billy's father is a miner, who has to cope with many problems in his family and his job. As a **widower**, he is struggling to raise his sons and look after his late wife's mother who is not in the best of mental health. Times are rough and income is low as the **miners are on strike**. They protest against Prime Minister Margaret Thatcher's decision to close down several mines. Although Jackie Elliot supports the strike, he is afraid that his elder son Tony will get into serious trouble with the police. Furthermore, he **finds it difficult to accept that Billy** does not want to continue the family tradition of working down in the pit, but **has decided to become a professional dancer** instead. Jackie Elliot is a **loving father**, a bit rough on the outside, but deep down he **tries hard to support both his sons**. He is even prepared to put up with the humiliation of being disgraced as a strike breaker to earn money for Billy's training. In front of the committee of the Royal Ballet School in London he firmly backs his son's decision to become a dancer.

**Tony**, Billy's older brother, is a miner like his father and grandfather. As a leading member of the union he is **deeply involved in the industrial action of the miners** and **determined to make the strike a success**. The livelihood of the majority of people in the town depends on coal mining. Consequently, he is devastated when he sees that his father is about to become a "scab" and return to work as money is needed for Billy's ballet audition in London. The emotional confrontation with his Dad makes Tony give up his opposition to Billy's dancing and he **helps to organise the support of the mining community to "give the kid a chance."**

**Mrs Wilkinson** is an **energetic, rigorous**, chain-smoking dance instructress, who discovers Billy's extraordinary gift for dancing. She believes so firmly in the boy's talent that she **wants Billy to study at the Royal Ballet School** in London. She even offers to put up the money for the trip which Billy's father proudly declines. Under Mrs Wilkinson's **strict guidance** Billy prepares for a successful audition.

## Themes and Interpretation

**The miners' strike (1984/1985):** The story is set against the turbulent background of the mid-1980s' miners' strike in North East England. The Prime Minister at that time was the Conservative Margaret Thatcher (1925–2013), perhaps the most influential British political leader since Winston Churchill (1874–1965). Her Tory government embarked on a radical free-market programme that became known as "**Thatcherism**". Thatcher's determination to **close inefficient mines** and, at the same time, **crush the power of the trade unions** provoked a bitter strike in 1984. The British National Union of Mineworkers (NUM) went on **strike to save jobs in the coal industry**. The strike lasted one year and was a hard time for the miners' families who had to survive on low strike pay and donations. Billy's father also has to scrape together the weekly 50 pence of his son's boxing training. In the course of the strike riot police increased their drastic measures against union members and Billy's brother Tony is arrested. To break the resistance of the miners, the government imported coal from Eastern Europe. The **defeat of the striking miners** was not only a turning point for Britain's mining industry (numerous mines were closed), but also **the end of the powerful trade union movement**.

**Father-son conflict:** As a member of the working class Billy's father is shocked when he discovers that Billy skips boxing for dancing. To him ballet is unmanly, and he assumes that **any boy interested in ballet must be gay** (= "a poof"). Therefore he uses his authority as a father to quench the boy's interest, banning him not only from dancing but also from boxing and ordering him to stay at home and look after his grandmother. **Billy is deeply frustrated and feels deserted by his father**. His love turns to hate. The turning point is reached as **Mr Elliot witnesses his son dancing and realises how talented Billy is. From then on he gives up his opposition and supports Billy**. He is even prepared to sacrifice his good name in the mining community and the respect and love of his elder son Tony by joining the strike breakers. Billy, in turn, appreciates what his father is doing for him. To some critics the change in Jackie Elliot's attitude seemed a little unrealistic: "I can believe a coal miner supporting his son's dancing dreams, but anyone who believes he would become a scab to raise the money doesn't know much about union miners."[1]

**Growing up – The difficulties of adolescence:** The term adolescence is generally used to describe the **transition period between childhood and adulthood**. Although potentially an adult, the young individual still plays the role of an inexperienced child bound and restricted by the culture in which he lives. Many instances show that **Billy is still treated like a child**: He is not allowed to borrow adult books from the library and has to accept what he is being told by adults (his father, the boxing trainer, the ballet teacher, his elder brother). However, **rebellion starts as Billy discovers his own personality and ambition**. Consequently, sparks fly when he tells his father about his devotion to dancing and resists Mrs Wilkinson's pressure. Billy's story is typical of the problems of an adolescent who has trouble finding his identity (e. g. Who am I?; What do I want to do with my life?), while having to adapt to the requirements of society. In Billy's case, finding a compromise is especially difficult as he grows up in a **restrictive environment**, in which youngsters are expected to follow the pattern laid out for them by their elders. The film shows that Billy eventually succeeds because **the others** (father, brother and the community as a whole) **accept his decision and support him in the end**.

## F. Scott Fitzgerald, *The Great Gatsby* (1925)

### Author

The American novelist F. Scott Fitzgerald was born in 1896 in St. Paul, Minnesota, and grew up mainly in New York and Minnesota. Having attended Princeton University in New Jersey, he joined the army and was stationed in Montgomery, Alabama, where he met his future wife Zelda Sayre, who became the model of the "flapper" – the young, easy-going woman of the 1920s. Scott Fitzgerald's first novel, *This Side of Paradise* (1920), made him instantly famous and wealthy, and together with Zelda he embarked on a life of big spending and heavy drinking. The effects of their wild and extravagant lifestyle soon made themselves evident first in Zelda, who suffered a

1 cf. Roger Ebert, http://www.rogerebert.com/reviews/billy-elliot-2000

mental breakdown from which she never recovered, and later in Scott Fitzgerald. He ran into financial difficulties and spent the last years of his life in poor health in Hollywood working as a screenwriter. Scott Fitzgerald died from a heart attack in 1940, leaving his last novel, *The Last Tycoon* (1941), unfinished. His works include *Flappers and Philosophers* (1920), *The Beautiful and Damned* (1922), *Tales of the Jazz Age* (1922) and *The Great Gatsby* (1925).

## Contents

Francis Scott Fitzgerald's novel *The Great Gatsby*, which he dedicated to his wife ("Once again to Zelda"), comprises nine chapters. The action is set in the 1920s and tells the story of Jay Gatsby (called "The Great Gatsby") through the eyes of the narrator Nick Carraway. Gatsby has accumulated wealth with illegal methods and now, as a rich man, tries to win back his early love Daisy, who has in the meantime got married to rich Tom Buchanan.

**Chapter I** (pp. 5–34)[2]: In the summer of 1922 Nick Carraway decides to leave the comfortable Middle West where his well-to-do family has lived for three generations and move east to work in New York's financial sector. He rents a run-down bungalow in West Egg, a commuting town on Long Island, where the "new rich" live. Next to Nick's house is a huge mansion owned by Mr Gatsby, whom Nick does not yet know. One evening he is invited to dinner by the Buchanans, who live across the bay in East Egg, a fashionable place inhabited by people with "old" money. Nick knows Tom Buchanan from college days in New Haven and Tom's wife Daisy is a cousin of Nick's ("Großkusine"). In the impressive home of the Buchanans he meets the attractive Jordan Baker, a friend of Daisy's and a professional golf player. During the evening Nick learns that Tom has an affair with a woman in New York. When Nick returns home, he sees his neighbour Mr Gatsby stretching out his arms across the bay where a green light blinking in the distance can be seen.

**Chapter II** (pp. 34–56): A few days later, Nicks gets to know Tom Buchanan's mistress, Myrtle Wilson. She lives with her husband, garage owner George Wilson, in an area halfway between West Egg and New York. It is known as the "valley of ashes", watched over by the gigantic eyes of Doctor T. J. Eckleburg, who is portrayed on a huge advertisement poster put up by an optician in Queens. Tom takes Nick and Myrtle to an apartment in New York, which he has rented for the purpose of his secret rendezvous with Wilson's wife. Myrtle's sister Catherine and a couple from the floor below join them, drink heavily and start talking about Nick's neighbour, the mysterious Mr Gatsby. Catherine tells Nick that Tom and Myrtle both hate their spouses, but that Tom will never divorce Daisy. Towards midnight Tom forbids Myrtle to mention Daisy's name and when, out of spite, she teases him, hits her so hard that he breaks her nose. Nick makes his way back to Pennsylvania Station in the morning.

2 Page numbers refer to: F. Scott Fitzgerald, *The Great Gatsby*. Reclam: Stuttgart 1995.

**Chapter III** (pp. 56–84): Throughout the summer extravagant parties take place in Mr Gatsby's mansion, which many people attend, mostly uninvited. As none of the guests seems to know anything about their host, rumours and gossip about Jay Gatsby abound. One day Nick receives an invitation and is picked up by Gatsby's driver. When he arrives he cannot find Gatsby, but sees Jordan Baker and meets an owl-eyed man looking at the books in the library in awe. Nick eventually makes the acquaintance of his mysterious neighbour, who does not take part in the revelries. He just watches the crowd approvingly. Later in the summer Nick starts going out with Jordan. He remembers that she was once involved in a scandal because she cheated at her first big golf tournament. He also notices that Jordan is a bad driver and urges her not to drive at all. He breaks off a relationship he kept with a girl back in Chicago, because he wants to play honest.

**Chapter IV** (pp. 84–111): Late in July Nick is picked up by Gatsby to have lunch in New York. During the drive to the city Gatsby tells Nick a few details about his personal background and later introduces him to his business partner Meyer Wolfshiem[3], who, Gatsby tells him, is "the man who fixed the World's Series in 1919" (p. 102), the annual baseball championships. Nick learns from Jordan, whom he meets later, that in 1917 Gatsby fell in love with 18-year-old Daisy Fay, one of the most popular girls in Louisville. But Gatsby, then a young officer, soon had to leave for the war. In 1919 Daisy married rich Tom Buchanan, who soon after the wedding had an affair with a chambermaid. Jordan tells Nick that Gatsby bought his house in West Egg merely to be close to Daisy and arranged the luxurious parties in the hope that she would drop by one day. Nick is asked to arrange a casual (by-chance) meeting between Daisy and Gatsby.

**Chapter V** (pp. 111–131): Nick offers Gatsby to arrange a meeting with Daisy at his house. In return, Gatsby offers Nick a job, but Nick turns it down, pretending he is too busy at the moment. A few days later the meeting takes place and Gatsby and Daisy see each other again for the first time in five years. Gatsby is extremely nervous and the reunion with Daisy does not go too well at first, but eventually the couple rediscover their love. Gatsby wants to impress Daisy and takes her and Nick on a tour of his house to show them all his valuable possessions. He tells Daisy that he has been watching the green light on the other side of the bay that belongs to the dock of her house. Gatsby summons Klipspringer, a man who lives in his house, to play the piano. Nick is aware that Gatsby and Daisy no longer take any notice of his presence and leaves the two of them alone.

**Chapter VI** (pp. 131–150): A reporter makes inquiries about rumours that Gatsby is involved in bootlegging (= smuggling alcohol). At this point Nick includes information about Gatsby's past. His real name is James Gatz, the son of farm people from North Dakota. At the age of 17, Gatsby began his career working for millionaire Dan Cody and changed his name to Jay Gatsby. Nick doesn't see Gatsby for a few weeks. One Saturday night Tom and Daisy come to a party at Gatsby's mansion. Daisy does

**3** Scott Fitzgerald's original spelling; his editor Edmund Wilson later changed it to "Wolfsheim".

not have a good time and Tom, who looks upon the famous people there with disdain, suspects that Gatsby made his money by bootlegging, like a "lot of these newly rich" (p. 146). After the party Gatsby tells Nick that he is disappointed that Daisy did not tell Tom she does not love him, but Nick warns him that the past cannot be recreated.

**Chapter VII** (pp. 151–191): Gatsby has reunited with Daisy again and stops arranging parties in his house. On the hottest day of the summer Tom, Daisy, Nick, Jordan and Gatsby meet for lunch at the Buchanan's and later drive to the Plaza Hotel in New York. While Tom, Nick and Jordan take Gatsby's yellow car, Gatsby and Daisy follow in Tom's blue coupé. On the way to New York, Tom stops over at Wilson's garage for some petrol and is seen by Myrtle. Wilson tells them that he intends to move westwards with his wife soon. He seems to have found out about Myrtle having an affair although he does not suspect Tom. At the Plaza Hotel, the atmosphere becomes very tense: Tom and Gatsby start a heated argument. Tom has made investigations about Gatsby, whom he calls "Mr Nobody from Nowhere" (p. 172). He accuses Gatsby of not being an Oxford man. Gatsby retaliates by telling Tom that Daisy will leave him, because she only loves him, Gatsby. However, Daisy claims she loved Tom when she married him. As Tom reveals that Gatsby made his money with bootlegging alcohol, Daisy wants the unpleasant confrontation to end and go back home. This time, Daisy and Gatsby leave in Gatsby's car; Tom, Nick and Jordan follow later in Tom Buchanan's coupé. On their drive home they pass the scene of an accident. A yellow car is said to have killed George Wilson's wife Myrtle. Tom suspects that Gatsby is responsible for Myrtle's death, but Nick learns from Gatsby that Daisy was driving. However, Gatsby wants to take the blame for the fatal accident. He insists on staying close to Daisy's house the whole night in case she is having an argument with Tom and needs protection.

**Chapter VIII** (pp. 191–210): The next morning Nick goes over to Gatsby's place and advises him to go away for a couple of days, but Gatsby rejects. He tells Nick how he fell in love with Daisy ("the first 'nice' girl he had ever known", p. 192) and lost her due to the war. He now hopes to rebuild a life with her. At work Nick has a telephone conversation with Jordan and realises that he is not really interested in her anymore. Nick then relates what happened at the garage the night of the accident: The devastated George Wilson is convinced that Myrtle was run over by her lover and sets out to track the man down and take revenge. In the afternoon Nick finds Gatsby's body floating in the swimming pool, and Wilson's corpse nearby in the grass.

**Chapter IX** (pp. 211–233): The Chicago newspapers print reports of Gatsby's death. Nick tries to contact Tom and Daisy, but they have gone away without leaving an address, and neither Meyer Wolfshiem nor Klipspringer want to get involved. Only Nick, Mr Gatz, Jay Gatsby's father, who has read about his son's death in the newspaper, and a few servants attend the funeral.
Nick ends his relationship with Jordan. Later in the year he runs into Tom, who confesses that he told Wilson that Gatsby had run over Myrtle. Before returning to the Midwest, Nick goes over once more to Gatsby's house, remembering Gatsby as the man who chased a dream without realising that it was already behind him.

## Characters

**Nick Carraway** is the first-person narrator of the story. Nick is 29 years old, when he arrives in West Egg. He comes from a well-to-do family in Minnesota, studied at Yale University and served as a soldier in World War I. He buys books to teach himself the "bond business" (p. 8). As **Gatsby's neighbour** and Daisy's cousin he observes and comments the events from a distance, **enabling the reader to judge** the behaviour of **the main characters**. Nick feels quite **sympathetic towards Gatsby** and cares for him, but is **disgusted by** the superficiality of the people at Gatsby's parties and **the emptiness of Eastern lifestyle**. Disillusioned he returns back home.

**Jay Gatsby** is the **typical American self-made man**. Born James Gatz from a humble background, he works himself to the top financially, though using doubtful and illegal means (e. g. bootlegging alcohol). He assembles his wealth to **win back his lost love Daisy**. **Jay Gatsby lives the American Dream**, achieving success through hard work, but **his reckless methods symbolise the corruption of that ideal**. Despite the public attention Gatsby receives, he seems to be quite lonely and only has Nick Carraway as a real friend he can talk to.

**Daisy**, the love of Gatsby's life, was born named Daisy Fay in Louisville, Kentucky, and is Nick's cousin. Although she loved Jay Gatsby, she married the rich Tom Buchanan, because Gatsby had to leave her to serve in the war. Daisy chose Tom, as she values wealth and security more than real love. She is **torn between her greed for money** (in the novel symbolically connected with the colour gold, e. g. Daisy has a golden pencil) **and true love** (Daisy as the white fairy queen, pure in her whiteness). Gatsby expresses the nature of this mixture when he describes Daisy's voice: "Her voice is full of money" (p. 160). Despite all the trouble she has put Gatsby in, Daisy does not even seem to care enough about him to attend his funeral.

**Tom Buchanan**, Daisy's husband, is a former football player whom Nick knows from Yale University. Being the oldest son of an extremely wealthy and successful East Egg family, Tom Buchanan **represents America's "old money"**. A **loudmouth**, he is **egoistic, violent** and expresses **sexist and racist** views (e. g. he talks of the downfall of civilisation because of the rise of inferior races). He is **hypocritical**, because he protests against Daisy having an affair with Gatsby, while he himself has been unfaithful to her throughout his marriage. Tom does not seem to regret that he told George Wilson that Gatsby's car ran over Myrtle, thus also implying that Gatsby had an affair with Wilson's wife. Instead of facing responsibility for his rival's death, he tells Nick **cold-blooded and careless** that Gatsby "had it coming to him" anyway (p. 231).

Attractive young **Jordan Baker** is a friend of Daisy's from Louisville who spends her days gossiping, drinking and golfing. She is **cynical, critical of others, independent** and, above all, **determined to succeed**. This is why she cheated at a tournament. She enters into a **flirtatious** relationship with Nick, who merely feels a "tender curiosity" for her (p. 82). Jordan Baker **represents the flapper**, a type of woman that emerged in the 1920s: a fashionable party girl **disregarding traditional behaviour**.

**George Wilson** owns a run-down garage in the valley of ashes, halfway between West Egg and New York. He is a **simple ordinary man**, who **adores his wife**. He is unaware that she betrays him with Tom Buchanan, who looks down on Wilson, saying to Nick: "He's so dumb he doesn't know he's alive" (p. 40). **Myrtle's death in the accident devastates him** and drives him to kill Jay Gatsby.

**Myrtle Wilson** is George Wilson's wife. She is in her mid-thirties and has an affair with Tom Buchanan. She has **more energy than her husband** and hopes Buchanan will divorce his wife and get her out of her **empty boring life** in the valley of ashes.

**Meyer Wolfshiem**, Gatsby's business partner and friend, is a **shady character**. The main interest of the small, middle-aged Jew is making money. He is **involved in organized crime** (i. e. the bootlegging of alcohol) and there are rumours that he fixed the 1919 World's Series (= was involved in a massive bribing scandal). He is **uneducated**, e. g. he believes that Gatsby went to "Oggsford College in England" – a place which does not exist, contrary to Oxford. His **cold-hearted business nature** becomes evident, when he refuses to attend Gatsby's funeral. His flawed character is already hinted at by the cuff links he wears: they are made of human teeth (cf. p. 101).

## Themes and Interpretation

**The Roaring Twenties:** F. Scott Fitzgerald has become widely known as the chronicler of the "**Jazz Age**", the years following World War I (1914–1918). As a result of the Great War the economies of the European countries were destroyed, but America entered an era of unprecedented prosperity and material excess. On the other hand, the dreadful experiences during the war and the destructions it brought, as depicted by William Faulkner (*Soldiers' Pay*, 1926) and Ernest Hemingway (*A Farewell to Arms*, 1929) set an end to the optimistic views of the pioneer days and the industrialisation of the 19th century. A disillusioned generation concentrated on worldly pleasures and developed a new lifestyle which F. Scott Fitzgerald shows and criticises in *The Great Gatsby* – although he himself took part in it. The **years between World War I and the Great Depression** of the late 1920s became known as the "Roaring Twenties", **a time of wild partying and lax morality among the rich upper class**. Since **Prohibition** laws passed in 1920 forbid the manufacture and sale of alcohol, people arranged parties to enjoy **illegally produced alcoholic beverages**. Jay Gatsby is one of the profiteers of bootlegging alcohol. Like Gatsby, many people acquired wealth – some not through their own hands' work, but through speculation at the stock exchange – and their **moral standards dropped**, as the extramarital affairs of Tom Buchanan, Myrtle and Daisy show. The party was over when Wall Street crashed on Black Friday 1929.

**The American Dream:** A major theme in Scott Fitzgerald's novel is the illustration of the failure or corruption of the American Dream. The original concept, which was first spoken of in the 19th century, is the **ideal of individual independence in an open society which offers opportunities for all**. Every person, regardless of his origins, can succeed in life through his own abilities and hard work. Scott Fitzgerald shows the **corruption of the American Dream**, because in the 1920s the old social and moral values were replaced by **materialism, greed** and the **pursuit of fame, glamour and pleasure**. The **decay of moral values** becomes evident in the characters of the flapper Jordan Baker, who cheated at the golf tournament, and Meyer Wolfshiem, whose wealth is based on criminal business methods. Scott Fitzgerald makes him the disgusting symbol of ruthlessness – even his outer appearance arouses feelings of aversion. Gatsby himself is so determined to get rich that he does not have second thoughts about profiting from Meyer Wolfshiem's criminal activities. Nick feels he is surrounded by liars and cheaters and comes to the conclusion that he himself is one of the few honest people he knows. At the end of the novel he turns his back on this degenerate world dominated by liars and cheaters and returns to the Midwest.

**Class and inequality:** Social Class is another important theme in *The Great Gatsby*. On the one hand, there are the representatives of "**Old Money**", the heirs of fortunes which were assembled generations ago. Nick, Tom and Daisy come from well-established and influential families. On the other hand, there are those who strive to make it to the top and become rich by taking advantage of the boom years after World War I. It is the group of people called "**New Money**" to which Gatsby belongs. The rivalry between these *nouveau riche* (= newly rich), who show off their acquired wealth, and the rich with a traditional background is illustrated by the fight between Gatsby and Buchanan for Daisy's love. People like George and Myrtle Wilson, who live in dire poverty in the horrible valley of ashes, belong to a third group of people. Scott Fitzgerald highlights the **inequality of American society** in the Roaring Twenties by contrasting the decadent partygoers in Gatsby's mansion with the hardworking mechanic Wilson in his filthy garage. In 2013, an influential economic adviser of US President Obama, Alan Krueger, coined the term "**The Great Gatsby Curve**" to describe the fact that the US today is still a land of social immobility and inequality caused by an uneven distribution of wealth passed on from generation to generation.

## John Jeffcoat/George Wing, *Outsourced* (2006)

*Outsourced* is a comedy, written by George Wing and John Jeffcoat, who also directed the film. It was released in 2006 and won several awards. In the commentary to his film Jeffcoat pointed out that many scenes are based on his own experiences when he travelled around the Indian subcontinent. Following the success of the movie, a TV series was developed in 2010 to which Jeffcoat contributed as a writer. *Outsourced* is currently Jeffcoat's most successful film. Apart from directing, Jeffcoat works as an editor, writer and producer. After finishing his studies at New York University, screen writer George Wing worked for a law firm in New York and also took part in vaccination campaigns in Latin American countries. His first film *50 First Dates* (2004) was a big success.

**Contents**

Todd Anderson works in Seattle for Western Novelty, an American firm that sells "patriotic knickknack", such as silly hats to wear at sporting events or mini-irons for branding hamburgers. Todd is the manager of the call centre, where agents accept customers' orders. One day his boss Dave announces that the management has decided to restructure order fulfilment, which requires moving Todd's department. The jobs of the Seattle employees are being outsourced, and Todd is to go to India to train his own replacement manager. At first, Todd refuses to accept, but is put under pressure by Dave threatening him with unemployment and a life without health insurance – so Todd flies to Mumbai, India, in the end. At the airport he misses the person who is supposed to collect him because his name is misspelt. He has to make his own way to the village of Gharapuri, where he meets Puro, his replacement.

Todd makes all the mistakes typical of an inexperienced Western tourist to Asia: he buys a fruit drink with ice ("Gola") from a street vendor or eats with his left hand. Consequently, he suffers from an upset stomach and feels completely exhausted. In addition, he is dissatisfied with the performance of the workers in the call centre, which is housed in a half-finished concrete building outside Gharapuri. The agents spend about twelve minutes on average on the phone with the customers. Todd has been ordered to reduce the time to six minutes. The training sessions with his staff also reveal the clash of cultures. Due to various reasons, Todd feels completely frustrated and depressed: there is the pressure Dave puts on him, the inefficiency of the employees, the exotic and polluted environment and the unfamiliar food. To forget about his unhappiness he phones his ex-girlfriend Julie back home, only to find out that she is in a new relationship. In a fast food restaurant in Mumbai he meets another American who tells him that reducing phone time to six minutes is impossible in India. He advises Todd not to resist India, but to give in to this way of life.

The following day, Todd overlooks a notice warning him not to go out today. It is the day of the Hindu festival Holi, when people throw coloured powder at each other. At first, Todd tries to hide and run away, but then decides to join the fun together with Puro who came to his rescue. In the course of the festival, his mobile phone is stolen by a small boy from the slums and he even has a bath in the local reservoir. When he arrives late at work, Asha, the most outspoken employee, has taken charge. Todd promotes her to assistant manager and asks the team how their workday could be improved. In the end, the employees bring in pictures of their families, decorate their work bays to their taste, wear traditional clothes and the most popular products of the Western Novelty catalogue are ordered as incentives for the fastest workers. As a result, the work atmosphere improves and Todd is finally accepted.

But the shipload with Western Novelty articles is sent to a different Indian village of the same name. Bringing it back requires a couple of hours' journey by car and ferry. Asha offers to accompany Todd. Because of a fire on the ferry they cannot return the same day and have to share the only hotel room left – a honeymoon suite. Both find the situation rather awkward and embarrassing, but end up making love. Asha appeals to Todd to keep quiet about the whole incident as she has been engaged to be married

since she was four. To keep in touch she gives him a mobile with her personal ringtone.
Todd's boss Dave arrives to check on him and repeats Todd's mistakes (e. g. drinking Gola, drawing poor comparisons between the Indian and the US workforce). When they arrive at the call centre they find the floor completely flooded after a fault in the irrigation system of a neighbouring farm. Todd tells the team to move the equipment up to the roof and rewire the whole place. Everything works out fine and the agents even manage to break the six minute mark. Todd is informed that Western Novelty has been acquired by the largest direct marketing firm in the US and will outsource 4,000 call centre jobs to China. Therefore, the Indian call centre is no longer needed. The workers are not too unhappy about their dismissal because they are now well-trained and will quickly find a new job. Only Puro is worried as he will find it harder to get employment and cannot marry without any income. Although he is offered extra bonuses for moving to Shanghai, Todd refuses to accept. He passes his job on to Puro and returns to the US. Back in Seattle, his mobile rings – the ringtone sounds like Asha's.

## Characters

**Todd Anderson:** He is the **typical young American manager** who earns good money as long as his firm is prospering. His own **well-being** – his salary, social security, health insurance and pension – is **closely connected with his employer's success**. Therefore, he is forced to comply with the management's orders. Todd is thrown into an unfamiliar environment and has to learn a lot about India, its culture and traditions, but also about himself. A new world opens up for him and, in the end, he benefits from his experience as he is now able to **reject the financially attractive offer**. On seeing his successor Puro off to Shanghai, he thanks the Indian for saving his life by teaching him that there is more to life than just making money.

**Asha:** The young Indian woman is the **best worker** in the call centre. She always speaks her mind and seems quite **sure of herself**. Having accepted her situation without complaining, she **questions the traditional Indian ways** for the first time when she falls in love with Todd. Although Todd asks her to go back to Seattle with him, Asha cannot imagine life without her family and decides to marry the husband her parents chose for her long ago.

**Puro:** He is a very **friendly, helpful** and **obliging** person who is looking forward to his promotion to the manager of an American firm's call centre. He is **deeply rooted in Indian culture** and hardly understands Western attitudes. He tries very hard to fulfill his boss's demands and happily accepts his new position in Shanghai.

**Dave:** Todd's boss is a stereotypically **ruthless** and **narrow-minded executive** whose mind is set on **making profit**. For the success of the company, he is willing to fire anybody who does not comply. He underestimates the efficiency and creativity of the Indian workers in the call centre.

## Themes and Interpretation

**Culture clash:** Only the first and the last scene of the film are set in the US, the rest of the action takes place in India. This country is so very different from Todd Anderson's world that he experiences a **culture shock** as he is used to Western standards and therefore confronted with a complete change in the way of life. Not knowing anything about the culture of this foreign and strange land, he judges everything from his Western point of view and only gradually adjusts his perspective. He begins to focus on new values such as **tolerance, personal relations**, **solidarity** and **love**. In the film, India also provides a backdrop to expose Western follies. Whereas people in the industrialised world waste money on useless items (such as those sold by Western Novelty), people in the Third World fight scarcity with **inventive genius** (e. g. a hub cap used as a frying pan) and display remarkable **stamina** (e. g. the employees are prepared to work day and night at the call centre). Despite poverty they have preserved their **dignity, generosity** and **enthusiasm**. One of the poor labourers working next to Todd's hotel invites Todd for a meal into his humble shanty home, where the American is accepted with great hospitality. It is the new environment that plays an essential part in opening the protagonist's eyes.

**Offshoring and outsourcing:** These business methods were developed in the 1980s as a **result of globalisation**. Whereas offshoring means moving work and jobs outside the country a company has its headquarters in, outsourcing implies sending work to outside contractors – either in the home country or abroad. Due to the increasing influence of the Internet and a widely spread use of computers, our world has become smaller. Sometimes the term "**global village**" is used to describe the phenomenon of being closely connected all over the world. Firms take advantage of this development by **exporting jobs to countries where labour is cheaper**. Dave, Todd's boss, claims the Indian call centre will cost eight times less than Todd's staff in Seattle. For the same reasons most fabrics are produced in China or Bangladesh nowadays. Due to offshoring and outsourcing many workers in **industrialised countries** lose their jobs. Especially unskilled workers are affected by **unemployment**. Meanwhile companies reconsider their business strategies as workers in China and India have begun to earn more, which renders outsourcing and offshoring less lucrative.

**Arranged marriage:** Todd Anderson is confronted with an Indian custom he finds hard to understand. Asha tells him that her parents chose a husband for her when she was only four years old. Todd cannot believe that a young woman as intelligent and strong as Asha would settle for an arranged marriage. Traditionally, the parents also decide when the wedding is to take place. **Candidates** are **chosen according to social and economic aspects**. The wedding partners must belong to the **same caste (class)** and the marriage must provide **social security** for the bride. Love does not play an important role. Today, arranged marriages are still popular, but most young people feel that they can reject candidates only their parents consider suitable. Many **marriages of convenience** work and Asha reminds Todd that in the US half of the "love marriages" end in divorce.

## Hanif Kureishi, "My Son the Fanatic" (1994)

### Author

Hanif Kureishi, born in 1954 in London, is the son of a Pakistani and an English woman. During his youth in South East London he experienced racist attacks by white youths against Pakistanis (so-called "Paki-bashing"), a common phenomenon in the 1960s. After studying philosophy at King's College London he began writing scripts and TV screenplays. His breakthrough came in 1985 with his screenplay *My Beautiful Laundrette* on the relationship of a homosexual Pakistani and a white punk. Other works of Hanif Kureishi include his semi-biographical novel *The Buddha of Suburbia* (1990), the novels *The Black Album* (1995) and *Intimacy* (1998) as well as the non-fiction work *My Ear at His Heart* (2004) and several short stories. The short story "My Son the Fanatic" was first published in the magazine *The New Yorker* in 1994.

### Contents

Parvez, an immigrant from Lahore, Pakistan, has been working as a taxi driver in London for twenty years. He prefers working at night because then he can earn more money which he needs to pay for the expensive education of his son Ali, who is studying accounting. One day Parvez notices significant changes in Ali's behaviour: He is clearing his room of all electronic gadgets and fashionable clothes. What worries Parvez even more is the fact that Ali also breaks up with his English girlfriend. Parvez is afraid that Ali might be taking drugs and confides in Bettina, a prostitute, who he has known for three years. She advises him to watch out carefully for any changes in Ali's appearance, but the drug theory cannot be proved. Parvez' confusion and worries increase when he discovers that Ali is praying five times a day and has given up sports.

In order to find out what is happening Parvez decides to have a talk with his son in a restaurant. Ali only reluctantly agrees to the meeting. But the get-together becomes the worst experience of Parvez' life: Instead of finding out why Ali has changed so dramatically, Parvez is confronted with harsh accusations by his son. Ali criticises his father of having adopted the decadent Western lifestyle – in Ali's opinion the lifestyle of the oppressors. Parvez tries hard to suppress his anger in view of the insolence and ingratitude of his son, for whom he has been working hard all his life. To make things worse for Parvez, Ali starts preaching about the law of Islam, the necessity of jihad (= the struggle of religious Muslims against the infidels or holy war) and the merciless punishment of anybody who does not live a life in accordance with the Koran. Parvez is at a loss and wants Ali to give a reason for his drastic change: Ali blames living in England. He wants to give up his studies to work in prisons supporting incarcerated Muslims.

After this experience, Parvez fears that he will be constantly criticised by his fundamentalist son. He thinks about making Ali leave the house, but Bettina encourages him to stick to Ali, as he might just be going through a phase. During the following two weeks Parvez' attempts to persuade his son to accept his philosophy of life are met with contempt.

A few evenings later Parvez, who is accompanied by Bettina, offers Ali a lift in his taxi when he sees his son coming out of a mosque. As they are driving along, Bettina tries to mediate between father and son by starting a friendly conversation with Ali. But when Ali insults her, she jumps out of the car and runs away. Parvez just about manages to suppress his fury. When they get home, however, he cannot hold his anger back any longer: He enters Ali's room, drags the praying boy up by his shirt and hits him. Ali does not retaliate, but asks Parvez calmly which of them is a fanatic.

## Characters

**Parvez** grew up in Lahore (Pakistan) and immigrated to England where he has been working as a taxi driver for twenty years. He is a **typical first-generation immigrant, who works hard to succeed**. In contrast to his son Ali, Parvez does not feel an outsider as he **has assimilated to the British lifestyle** and adopted its values. He likes English breakfast, pork pies and drinking whisky. **His main aim** in life **is to help his son** get a good education and **climb the social ladder**. Out of frustration, Parvez turns to violence when he realises that Ali rejects everything he has worked for.

Parvez' pride in life is his son **Ali**, a good student and sportsman, who goes to college to study accountancy. Ali, however, changes his life drastically **under the influence of fundamentalist Muslim leaders**, goes to the mosque regularly and prays five times a day. He gets rid of everything that symbolizes the decadent Western lifestyle and materialism to him. He **criticises his father for adhering to Western principles** and lectures him on immoral behaviour. Ali, a **second-generation immigrant**, has turned into a **fanatic**: He is ready for the jihad, thus prepared to fight the unbelievers, in his native country England and abroad.

**Bettina** is a **prostitute** Parvez has known for three years. While Parvez treats his wife in a rather harsh and unfriendly way, he turns to Bettina to talk about his problems. **She tries to help Parvez cope with the increasingly difficult relationship with his son**. To Ali, Bettina symbolises the immorality of Western lifestyle, which is why he despises her openly.

## Themes and Interpretation

**Father-son conflict:** The central theme of Hanif Kureishi's short story is the conflict between Parvez and his son Ali. However, the confrontation **differs from traditional father-son conflicts** in which the father plays the dominant role and criticises the son's behaviour (cf. p. I 4). In "My Son the Fanatic" **the traditional roles are reversed**: Ali gradually develops contempt and hostility against his father because he hates Parvez' adherence to Western lifestyle. Whereas **Parvez' aim in life is to integrate into the society of his new homeland, Ali is no longer interested in following the path** his father has laid out for him. Climbing socially and achieving success has become irrelevant to him. Ali has begun to deliberately reject the opportunities life offers in Britain since he believes in the teachings of fundamentalist Muslims.

**Fundamentalism:** Hanif Kureishi was among the first who observed the emergence of young radical Muslims in Britain's Asian community **following the publication of Salman Rushdie's** allegedly blasphemous **book *The Satanic Verses* in 1988**. The worldwide protests of the followers of Islam eventually led to a *fatwa* imposed by Iran's spiritual and political leader Ayatollah Khomeini. The fatwa means that it was a devout Muslim's duty to kill the infidel author on sight. In Kureishi's story, Ali is the representative of this new generation of young Muslims. **Many children of first-generation immigrants**, born and bred in Britain, lacked the cultural heritage of their parents and felt they were not really wanted in the country their parents had brought them to. In contrast to their parents they **were no longer willing to adapt and put up with humiliation and discrimination**. To Ali and many young Muslims of his generation, the uncompromising adherence to the Koran is a way of establishing an identity. Influenced and led by extremely conservative Muslim leaders, **they repudiate capitalist ideals as well as the striving for material success, and condemn Western immoral and decadent behaviour**. Thus, they distance themselves from the rest of society.
Kureishi wrote his story as early as 1994, and a couple of years later Britain and the world experienced the eruption of Islamic extremism into violence. The most horrific of these attacks against Western capitalism carried out in the name of religion occurred on September 11, 2001 (referred to as 9/11) with the destruction of the World Trade Centre in New York which caused the death of 3,000 people. **London became a target on July 7, 2005**, when fundamentalist young men with an Islamic background carried out suicide bombings in London's Underground, killing 52 people and mutilating dozens. In videotaped statements they explained their religious motivation, saying their action was a protest against military intervention of the West in Afghanistan. **The actions** of "home-grown terrorists" shocked people in England, and **led to second thoughts about the blessings of a multicultural society**. Extremists like the "7/7" bombers represent only a tiny fraction of Britain's Muslim community, but in his story **Kureishi issued a warning of the consequences of failed integration** in an increasingly ethnically and racially diverse society.

## Ben Mezrich, *The Accidental Billionaires* (2009)

### Author

Ben Mezrich was born in 1969 and studied Social Studies at Harvard University until 1991. His first non-fiction work, *Bringing Down the House*, was published in 2003. Other works include *Ugly Americans* (2004) and *Busting Vegas* (2005). *The Accidental Billionaires*, Mezrich's account of the rise of Mark Zuckerberg, came out in 2009 and was used as the basis for the film *The Social Network* (2010). Ben Mezrich lives in Boston, Massachusetts, and works as a columnist for *Boston Common Magazine*.

**Contents**

The book comprises thirty-four short chapters and records the spectacular rise of the social networking site Thefacebook. It is also the story of friendships getting lost, when fame beckons and big money is involved.

**October 2003:** Eduardo Saverin and Mark Zuckerberg, both sophomores (= students in their second year) at Harvard University, meet at a fraternity party. Eduardo, the son of a successful Jewish businessman, who escaped the Holocaust, grew up in Brazil and Miami. He has made some money speculating on oil prices, which had earned him a reputation as a budding businessman among the students at Harvard. Mark Zuckerberg, the son of a dentist and a psychiatrist, came from New York and was already known as a computer science freak who could hack into any computer system. Rumours had it that he had ended up on an FBI list and that Microsoft had offered him between one and two million dollars if he worked for them. Mark, who was still in high school then, turned the offer down.

The identical twins Tyler and Cameron Winklevoss are also at Harvard. They come from a rich family and are members of the highly respected Porcellian Club. They are excellent rowing athletes and have won several national competitions. Together with their mate Divya they are looking for someone to write a computer code for a programme they have developed. As a lot of their time is taken up by training on the River Charles, they have little opportunity to meet girls. A website they want to call "Harvard Connection" would make it easier to increase their contacts with the opposite sex on campus.

Eduardo tries very hard to become a member of the respected Phoenix Club. One of his initiation tasks is to look after a live chicken for a couple of days. Mark, with whom Eduardo has become close friends, hacks into Harvard's computer system and downloads thousands of photos from the facebooks (= name for the databases of student photos) of the different student houses. He writes a programme and publishes the student photos on a website called "Facemash", where students can compare two pictures of undergraduate girls and vote on which one is "hotter". Many people have access to the site and because of a lot of protests, Mark gets in trouble. The case is reported in the university magazine *Crimson*, where Tyler reads about Mark, who is described as socially autistic. Tyler decides on asking Mark to write the code for Harvard Connection.

Mark has to appear in front of the Harvard University Administrative Board. He apologises and is let off with a serious warning. The twins explain to Mark that Harvard Connection is meant to share information and get in touch with fellow students. At a meeting they try to convince Mark to work for them arguing that this might lead to improving his bad reputation. But instead of working for the twins, Mark starts creating an interactive social network to upload pictures and profiles of users. He wants to call it Thefacebook. Mark is not interested in programming the website for the Winklevoss twins because he considers it a boring dating site. He asks Eduardo to put up some money to pay for the servers and other costs. Mark agrees to share the profits and makes Eduardo CFO (= Chief Financial Officer). The Winklevoss twins are frustrated because they might need a new programmer.

**February 2004:** Mark has been working extremely hard to register the domain, rent servers in New York and send out emails to members of the Phoenix Club with Eduardo's help to start the site which is accessible for Harvard students only. Tyler suspects Mark to have stolen their idea and contacts his father to get a lawyer (cf. p. 106)[4]. In the meantime, Mark's site is extremely successful because it is different from other friendship sites: Whereas users search for new people on Friendster or Myspace, they already know the people they want to be friends with on Thefacebook (e. g. classmates or friends of friends). Students on the campus become addicted to Thefacebook and Eduardo and Mark are getting more popular with girls. A letter by Cameron Winklevoss warns Mark of legal action should he further expand and update his site. The twins are also prepared "to petition the Harvard University Administrative Board regarding your breach of ethical standards of conduct, as stated in the Student Handbook." (pp. 113/114). Mark considers their claims an annoyance and believes the Winklevoss twins want to claim a share in his successful production. Meanwhile, two room-mates of Mark, computer geeks Dustin and Chris, join the team to make Thefacebook accessible for students from other schools and consequently be able to earn more money to pay for the bigger amount of servers. Tyler complains to the university that Mark has broken the code of honour, but President Summers refuses to interfere, suggesting they should make it up between themselves.

**March 2004:** At Stanford in California Sean Parker, a computer expert who has already undertaken two major internet ventures, Napster and Plaxo, stumbles upon Thefacebook. Mark and Eduardo, who are looking for advertisers for their website, meet Parker in New York. While Eduardo is not too keen on Parker, Mark adores him like a god. As their website is growing fast, they need more money to pay for both more employees and servers. As Mark has no funds, Eduardo helps out, putting in $ 10,000 of his own money. On April 13 they register Thefacebook as a company in Florida, where Eduardo's family lives. Eduardo spends the summer in New York, whereas Mark has decided to go to California and work from there. After their defeat the Winklevoss twins are bitterly disappointed and launch their own site ConnectU.
In Silicon Valley, Sean Parker meets Mark and his room-mates. He considers Eduardo only as a start-up investor. In his view, the businessman Eduardo is not needed anymore. In New York Eduardo is getting worried about Parker's influence and flies to San Francisco. He notices that Mark and his mates are invited to expensive clubs and restaurants to meet venture capital investors and attractive girls. Eduardo is not inclined to sell Thefacebook yet as he hopes that its value might increase further. The Winklevoss' website is not doing well, whereas Thefacebook is still growing. They realise they have been beat, and the only thing to do is to file a lawsuit against Mark Zuckerberg.

**July 28, 2004:** Back in New York, Eduardo is working hard to acquire advertisements for Thefacebook. He thinks Mark does not actually appreciate his work. Even worse, Mark has begun to make decisions without involving Eduardo. To put things

4 Page numbers refer to: Ben Mezrich, *The Accidental Billionaires: The Founding of Facebook.* Anchor Books 2010.

straight, he writes a letter reminding Mark of their initial agreement: Eduardo as CFO and Mark out in California working on the computer code. Furthermore, Eduardo freezes the bank account for Thefacebook to cut off funds for Mark and cancels "all existing checks and lines of credit" (p. 195). To boot, Mark gets informed about the upcoming lawsuit filed by the Winklevoss twins.
Mark has the company reincorporated to protect it from Eduardo's whims and invests his own money to pay for the servers and keep the website running. In San Francisco, Sean introduces Mark to the investor Peter Thiel, the founding force behind PayPal. Thiel invests $ 500,000 in the site which puts Thefacebook on a new level. The firm is now simply called Facebook and has to be restructured. Mark and his team move to a new place in Silicon Valley and Eduardo returns to Harvard to finish his studies. After two months without almost any contact to California Eduardo is invited back by Mark. When he arrives, he is presented a few legal papers and learns that millions of new shares have been issued, which reduces the value of his own shares to almost nothing. Eduardo realises that he is slowly kicked out of the company and feels betrayed by Mark. More companies invest millions of dollars in Facebook and after 14 months the site is worth $ 100,000,000 but Sean thinks Facebook will triple this sum within six months.

**June 2005:** Eduardo has finished his studies in Harvard and hires lawyers to take legal action against Mark as he would like to be rewarded for making Facebook the successful company it is now. In the meantime, the site has grown immensely and new features such as picture sharing have been added. Following Sean Parker's arrest at a party Mark decides that Sean has to go as he has become a danger to Facebook.

**May 2008:** In a club Eduardo, who is drunk, meets the Winklevoss twins by chance. He apologises to them claiming that he was betrayed by Mark Zuckerberg just as they had been before.

**Epilogue:** Both lawsuits against Mark Zuckerberg have ended by now. Whereas the Winklevoss twins are said to have received $ 65,000,000 compensation, Eduardo Saverin is again mentioned as a cofounder in the Facebook manifest. Despite those lawsuits, Mark Zuckerberg remains a billionaire.

## Characters

**Mark Zuckerberg:** The Harvard undergraduate looks a bit **awkward** and **out of place** among his fellow students. He has a mop of curly hair, blue eyes and always wears a hoodie, cargo shorts instead of slacks and flip-flop sandals. Even later, at business meetings he **does not pay much attention to his appearance**. He is **shy**, keeps to himself, has no girlfriend, and is described as **socially autistic**. Nevertheless, he already has a reputation as a **computer genius**. He is obsessed with computers and spends hours on end writing codes. Aged 17 his talent is spotted by software giant Microsoft, but Mark turns down an enormous offer, which shows that he is not so much interested in making money, but rather in creating something revolutionary. He is very **ambitious** and devotes all his time to making the Facebook website a worldwide success. With the increasing popularity of his invention Mark also shows the **ruthless** and **unscrupulous** side of his character. His old friend Eduardo becomes a victim of Mark's determination to succeed.

**Eduardo Saverin:** Mark Zuckerberg's friend comes from a Jewish family and has made some money by successfully speculating with oil shares at the stock exchange. Eduardo is a **shy outsider** like Mark, but does not know much about computers and consequently concentrates on the management tasks. Whereas Mark fully concentrates all his energy on Facebook, Eduardo tries to succeed at Harvard, not only in his studies, but also in climbing up the social ladder. He **trusts** Mark but underestimates his determination to advance Facebook. In the end, he is bitterly **disappointed** and **feels betrayed** by his former best friend, who used foul tricks to remove him from the firm.

**Sean Parker:** When Mark Zuckerberg and Eduardo Saverin first meet Sean Parker, he is already a **well-known** figure in Silicon Valley because he has been involved more or less successfully with internet enterprises such as Napster, a file-sharing site. Zuckerberg admires Parker, whereas Eduardo regards him with suspicion. On the other hand, Parker plays an important role in removing Eduardo from Facebook. Sean Parker is the person who helps to turn a student invention into a real business thanks to his **manifold contacts** to venture capitalists ready to take risks and invest large sums to get a young start-up company off the ground. He **recognises the enormous potential** of Facebook. Like Eduardo Saverin, he is thrown out of the company as Mark Zuckerberg considers Parker's drinking habits and lack of discipline a danger to the company.

## Themes

**The founding of Facebook:** Ben Mezrich's book is about the development of the most successful networking site today. The author hints at some of the weighty topics of his account in the subtitle to his report: "A Tale of **Sex**, **Money**, **Genius** and **Betrayal**". Mezrich maintains that the driving force for the creators of social networking sites, such as the Winklevoss twins or Zuckerberg, was making **contacts with girls**. In contrast, Mark Zuckerberg, speaking to an audience at Stanford University in California in 2010, claimed he only wanted to create something[5]. In this respect he must be regarded as a **genius**, who first came up with a revolutionary idea and mustered enough energy and stamina to turn his vision into reality.

**Unethical behaviour:** Mark Zuckerberg's product only really took off when big **money** was invested in his enterprise. The funds were necessary to employ more staff, add more features to the site and rent more servers in order to make the service available for an increasing number of users. But money also seems to have brought about a **change in** Mark Zuckerberg's **character**. As a high school student he was primarily interested in writing computer codes, with the arrival of investors he became more

**5** cf. http://www.guardian.co.uk/film/2010/oct/20/mark-zuckerberg-the-social-network

**business-oriented** and **ruthless**, resorting to tricks and doubtful strategies. But even in his Harvard days, Mark has been accused of **cheating** by Cameron and Tyler Winklevoss, who argued he had deliberately delayed working on their programme in order to develop his own concept further and be the first on the net. The Winklevoss' complaint concerning Mark's violation of ethical standards was dismissed by the university.

**Personal betrayal:** Striving for success in the world of big business and the desire to stay competitive and increase growth caused the **end of a long-standing friendship** and resulted in a lawsuit. Eduardo Saverin was led to believe that his share in the company was safe, until he eventually found out that he had been removed from the company and his shares were not worth much anymore. Mark Zuckerberg **sacrificed personal relations** and friendships **for the sake of commercial success**. In this sense, Mezrich's account can be read as an example of how money can spoil a person's character.

## Arthur Miller, *Death of a Salesman* (1949)[6]

### Author

Arthur Miller is one of the most important American dramatists of the 20th century. He was born in New York in 1915 as the son of a wealthy Jewish textile factory owner, Isidore Miller, who had emigrated from Poland to the United States. Due to the Wall Street Crash in 1929 his father ran into great financial difficulties and the family lost its wealth. Young Arthur did several menial jobs to contribute to the family income and pay for his tuition. He had his first important success as a writer with his drama *All My Sons* in 1946. *Death of a Salesman*, which was first produced on Broadway in 1949, became his commercially most successful play. From 1956 to 1961 Miller was married to actress Marilyn Monroe for whom he wrote the script for her film *The Misfits* (1961). Further works include *The Crucible* (1953), *After the Fall* (1964), *Incident at Vichy* (1964), *The American Clock* (1980) and his autobiography *Timebends* (1987). Arthur Miller died in 2005.

### Contents

Arthur Miller's play comprises two acts and shows the last two days in the life of 63-year-old salesman Willy Loman.

**Act One:** Willy returns home unexpectedly late at night from a business trip. He is exhausted and tells his wife Linda that he has had difficulties concentrating on the road while driving because his thoughts went back to the past. His wife Linda advises him to give up his job as a travelling salesman and apply for a position in his firm's head office in New York. Willy is dissatisfied because he thinks all his life he has worked for nothing, as his two grown-up sons, Biff (34) and Happy (32), have not

**6** *Dieses Werk ist nur relevant für Schüler an Beruflichen Gymnasien.*

become as successful as Willy had wanted them to be. Biff has come home for a visit and together with his brother listens to their parents' conversation from their old bedroom. Afterwards, the two start talking about the past and their plans for the future. Sitting in the kitchen Willy dreams about the past, when his two boys were still at school and he had put all his hopes on them, especially on Biff, who was good at sports and very popular. However, it is already indicated that Biff steals things and neglects his studies.
In front of his sons, Willy brags about his popularity with customers and his successes as a salesman, however, in reality his financial situation is desolate. In another flashback he remembers his affair with a woman in Boston. Back in the present, Willy plays cards with his neighbour Charley late at night. Charley knows about Willy's financial problems and offers help. Willy refuses and starts dreaming again, this time about his older brother Ben, who has made a fortune in Africa and initially asked Willy to come with him – as Ben found diamond mines there, Willy has regretted turning the offer down ever since. Willy then finishes daydreaming and leaves the house to work in the garden. Linda has a serious talk with Biff, informing him that his father is thinking about committing suicide. Biff is horrified and promises that he would try to make a new start. Happy tells Willy about Biff's plan to ask an old acquaintance to support his latest business idea financially. Willy is pleased to hear the news.

**Act Two:** The following morning Willy is full of optimism. He promises Linda to apply for a job in the head office and is delighted when she tells him that the boys have invited him to join them for dinner at a restaurant. However, Willy's mood changes dramatically, when his young boss, Howard Wagner, does not only turn down his plea for an office job, but also asks him to take his leave. Willy, who has been working for the firm for 34 years, is completely devastated. He goes to see Charley from whom he has been borrowing money for some time. At Charley's office he meets Charley's son Bernard, who went to school with Biff. They talk about Biff's failed graduation from high school: As Biff did not make his math degree, all he needed to do was go to summer school. Willy has never understood why Biff refused to do that. Bernard supposes that this has something to do with Biff's trip to Boston.
Meanwhile, the two brothers have met at the restaurant. Biff tells Happy that he applied unsuccessfully for a new job and asks his brother to confront their father with reality, to make him give up his exaggerated expectations concerning his sons. Willy joins them and, feeling that Biff has bad news, he remembers how Biff went to Boston to make his father talk to the teacher about the missing credits for his graduation. Biff had turned up unexpectedly and discovered his father's adultery, thus his image of the idolised father disintegrated. Willy seems disturbed, and Biff and Happy leave him in the restaurant and spend the rest of the evening with two girls they have met shortly before. Back at home Linda criticises her sons for not taking better care of Willy. Nevertheless, Biff is still determined to tell Willy the truth about his sons being losers. The heated confrontation ends with Biff starting to cry, which Willy takes as a sign of love. When everything is quiet in the house, Willy drives away at high speed. He wants to end his life so his family can make a new start with the insurance money.

**Requiem:** The final scene shows only the family and a few neighbours attending Willy's funeral. Biff blames Willy's misguided expectations for his suicide. However, Charley claims that those dreams are part of a salesman's profession. Linda cannot understand Willy's decision and feels left alone, now that the house is finally paid up for and all responsibilities are taken care of.

## Characters

**Willy Loman**, aged 63, is the main character of Arthur Miller's play – a **telling name for "low man"**, meaning the average, ordinary man in the street. For 34 years he has been travelling around the country as a salesman for the Wagner Company. Willy has a lot of problems with his job and at home with his family. His wife Linda supports him, but his two grown-up sons, Biff (34) and Happy (32), have not become as successful as Willy had wanted them to be. Willy **refuses to face reality and loses himself in daydreams**. He seems to find it increasingly hard to tell reality and flashbacks apart. But after a heated confrontation with Biff, **it dawns on Willy that his son is a born loser**. Willy suffers another hard blow, when his young boss, Howard Wagner, fires him. He has to face the fact that **he is not the successful salesman he wants the entire world to believe**. For years Willy has been lying to himself and to others, fantasizing and fooling himself into a false vision of his own popularity. Out of pride, he refuses to accept his friend Charley's help who frequently offers him a job. As it is clear to everybody that Willy has been a failure like Biff, he kills himself, so that his family can at least claim the money from his life insurance. It is ironic that **Willy believes his family to benefit more from him being dead than being alive**.

**Linda** is Willy's **loving and devoted wife**, who supports her husband in every way, although – or even because – she knows very well about his shortcomings and problems. Sometimes Willy treats her rough and unfriendly, but Linda puts it down to the pressure and frustration which Willy has experienced. Linda **realises Willy's life is in danger and wants to prevent the worst**. She admonishes her sons to show respect for their father and appeals to Biff to help him.

**Biff and Happy**
When they were kids, **Willy was very proud of his sons and put all his hopes in them**, especially in Biff, who was very good at sports. However, **Biff starts stealing things as a teenager and neglects his studies**. When he discovers that his father has an affair with a woman in Boston, he is completely thrown off his feet: He does not go to summer school and leaves high school without a diploma. Biff takes on several jobs in seven different states, but fails each time and is even sent to prison because of theft. His younger brother **Happy** has never applied himself and did not achieve anything in life, he **is stuck in a meaningless job without any prospects of getting promoted** and still lives at home with his parents. Both sons feel **under pressure due to the exaggerated expectations their father puts on them**.

**Howard Wagner**, Willy's employer, is a **representative of the modern young business generation, profit-oriented and ruthless** if it is in the interest of the firm. In contrast to his father, the founder of the company, he does not care about Willy's personal situation and life-long loyalty. He argues the old salesman might harm the firm's reputation because he cannot adapt to the modern ways of selling and therefore fires Willy, who feels he has been abandoned like a useless thing instead of being treated like a human being.

## Themes and Interpretation

**The American Dream:** Arthur Miller's play **shows the darker side** of the American Dream. Willy Loman still firmly believes in the American **concept of personal success based on discipline, initiative and hard work**. He clings on to the values of old pioneering days and refuses to accept that the extraordinary opportunities once open to the pioneers no longer exist. In our modern world it has become much harder to achieve success. **Arthur Miller criticizes the fact that people think the most important aim in life is to be liked and to make a lot of money**. If we make personal success the guiding principle in our society, Willy and Biff Loman's fate shows what will become of people who are unable to achieve this aim.

**Consumerism:** Miller also denounces the materialistic attitude of our society. Smart **marketing and advertising strategies create needs and desires**. Many people fall victim to the temptations of attractive advertising and sign hire-purchase contracts or overdraw their bank accounts to pay for **expensive must-have goods**, such as cars or clothes. Willy suspects that the industry produces goods to last only for a short time so that they have to be **replaced again just after the last rate is paid**. He recognises the eternal rat race and feels trapped. Aldous Huxley expresses a similar criticism in his dystopian novel *Brave New World* (1932). Idealistic values, such as freedom and creativity have been discredited and replaced by constant consumption. The fact that **people's minds are preoccupied with constantly buying new things** keeps the industry running and, at the same time, enables a small group of powerful leaders to keep the unsuspecting masses under control.

**Contrast town – nature:** Love for nature has always been deeply rooted in Willy's family. His father travelled the open country selling flutes, his brother Ben went into the wilderness of Africa and his sons dream of a ranch in the far West. On his first trips as a salesman Willy enjoyed the fresh air, and he bought a house in an untilled area of New York. However, in the course of time more and more apartment blocks and high-rise buildings sprung up, killing grass and trees and dwarfing his little house. **Willy feels boxed in and suffocated by what many people regard as progress**. Having been left at the restaurant by his sons has disappointed him deeply, which is why he tries to find peace and quiet in his garden by planting seeds. However, his efforts to recreate this small piece of nature in the garden – and literally go back to the roots – seem rather ineffective.

## Arthur Miller, *The Crucible* (1954)

### Author

see *Death of a Salesman*

### Contents

Arthur Miller's drama comprises four acts. The story is set in the town of Salem, Massachusetts, in the late 17th century, where a hysterical witch-hunt took place among the Puritan community.

**Act One:** After discovering his daughter Betty dancing in the woods together with a couple of her friends, Reverend Samuel Parris suspects the group has practised witchcraft and has made a pact with the devil. Since the event Betty has gone into a stupor and is lying motionless in her bed. Concerned about the future of his ministry as well as his daughter's health, Parris asks the ringleader, his niece Abigail Williams, about what happened. Abigail maintains that the girls were merely having fun. In addition, she insists that her dismissal as a servant from the household of John and Elizabeth Proctor had nothing to do with her being "soiled" (p. 23)[7] and that she still has a good reputation in the village. She just did not want to work under Mrs Proctor like a slave. Mrs Putnam enters and confesses to Parris that she asked Tituba, Parris' Negro slave, to practise witchcraft in the woods in order to conjure up the spirits of her seven dead children so as to find out who was to blame for their deaths. Abigail has to admit that witchcraft was practised, but insists that only Tituba and Ruth, Mrs Putnam's daughter, took part. Mr Putnam, whose daughter is in a similarly bad condition as Betty, urges Parris to announce the discovery of witchcraft, but the Reverend refuses, at least until Reverend Hale, a famous exorcist he sent for, arrives to investigate the case.
Abigail and the other girls discuss the situation. Mary Warren, who now works as a servant of the Proctors, fears that they will be accused of witchcraft and encourages the others to tell the truth and get away with a whipping. Abigail does not want to hear any of it and threatens she would kill them should they dare to speak about the events in the woods. John Proctor enters and all the girls apart from Abigail leave the room. Alone with Proctor, Abigail tries to seduce her former employer and resume the affair both had when she worked in the Proctors' household. However, Proctor resists her attempts. As a psalm is heard being sung below, Betty wakes from her stupor, and her hysterical screams make the townspeople rush to the scene. In heated discussions they argue about Parris' preaching, his salary, property and power, which are the real causes of unrest in Salem. The argument stops with the arrival of the exorcist Hale, who Parris had sent for in the hope of proving that Betty is not possessed by the devil. Hale cross-examines Abigail, Tituba and the girls with the result that they hysterically start crying out the names of several women in Salem, claiming to have seen them with the devil.

**7** Page numbers refer to: Arthur Miller, *The Crucible*. Reclam 1990.

**Act Two:** Eight days later in the Proctors' house, Elizabeth Proctor urges her husband to inform the court which has initiated witchcraft trials that the accusations brought forward by Abigail and the girls are a fraud. When Proctor hesitates, Elizabeth suspects that he is still having an affair with Abigail. Mary Warren enters and presents Elizabeth with a small rag doll she made while waiting to serve as a witness in court. She also informs the Proctors about the current state of affairs in Salem and reveals that Elizabeth has been accused of witchcraft. Elizabeth suspects that Abigail is to blame for the charge against her because she wants to replace her. She tells John to go to Abigail, rather than to the court, to stop the accusation.
Hale arrives to investigate the Proctors. He finds that John cannot recite all Ten Commandments (he forgets adultery), which is regarded as proof of witchcraft. Two neighbours, Giles Corey and Francis Nurse, break in with the news that their wives have been arrested. Officers of the court enter, among them Ezekiel Cheever, now clerk of the court, who presents a warrant for Elizabeth and the instruction to search the Proctors' house for dolls. Elizabeth hands over the one that Mary Warren has just given to her. A needle is found in the puppet. It turns out that Abigail accused Elizabeth Proctor of being a witch and that a needle has been found in Abigail's belly this night. Elizabeth Proctor is arrested. The outraged Proctor insists on Mary Warren telling the truth about the doll in court. Mary is afraid of revealing Abigail's pretence and supposes her friend might charge Proctor with lechery to destroy his credibility. Despite these warnings, he is determined to tell the truth about his relationship with Abigail to save the life of his wife.

**Act Three:** In the meeting house of Salem, which serves as a courtroom, Martha Corey is on trial. Deputy Governor Danforth, who has already condemned seventy-two people to be hanged, refuses to hear Giles Corey, who claims he can prove his wife's innocence. Elizabeth Proctor is spared for the moment because she says that she is pregnant. John presents a petition in which many respectable townspeople affirm that the accused women are innocent. However, Mr Danforth does not want to drop charges and, instead, sends for the people who signed the paper to be arrested and questioned. Proctor then hands over Mary Warren's testimony in which she admits that she neither saw Satan nor any spirit. To prove her assertion the girls are led into the courtroom, but Abigail pretends to be bewitched by Mary. As the court is about to believe her, Proctor wants to expose Abigail as a liar and confesses his lechery with her. Mr Danforth sends for Elizabeth Proctor to prove her husband's statement. Elizabeth, who has never lied in her life and does not know about Proctor's confession, wants to protect her husband's name and claims he has always been faithful to her. As a result, Mr Danforth is convinced that Proctor is a liar and merely wants to undermine the court. Mary breaks down and accuses Proctor of being the devil's man. Proctor and Giles Corey are led off to jail, and Hale quits the court.

**Act Four:** Three months later, in the autumn of 1692, the executions continue despite the fact that the main witness Abigail has disappeared taking with her Parris' money. Hale urges Deputy Governor Danforth to pardon the accused and stop the hangings to prevent a rebellion. However, the judge is unrelenting. When the day of John Proctor's hanging has arrived, Danforth asks the pregnant Elizabeth to persuade her husband to save his life by falsely confessing that he is a witch. Elizabeth leaves the decision in Proctor's hands. She feels that she is partly responsible for his affair with Abigail because of her coldness towards her husband. For the sake of his family, Proctor signs the false confession, but tears it up as he learns that it will be made public because he does not want to lose his good name. Together with Rebecca Nurse, he is led to his execution. Both convicts accept their fate as they believe that only God can do them justice in the end.

### Characters

**Reverend Parris** is the minister of the Puritan community Salem in Massachusetts, Betty's father and Abigail's uncle. As Parris is **a very strict minister preaching hell and brimstone**, many townspeople dislike him. He accuses John Proctor of leading a faction against him and **wants to use the witch trials to consolidate his position in the community**.

**Reverend John Hale** is an **expert on witchery**. Reverend Parris asks him to come and examine his daughter Betty, who is lying in bed with unexplainable symptoms. Although Hale **views the trials with a critical mind**, he tries to get the convicted to confess. In the end, he **becomes aware of his destructive role in enforcing an unjust law**. He then has the courage to admit his mistake and regret his actions. The realisation that he failed in his duty leaves Hale dejected because he could not save the lives of the accused. In this respect he can be seen as a **tragic character**.

The farmer **John Proctor**, who is married to Elizabeth, is another **tragic figure** in the play. He **hates hypocrisy** and **tries in vain to stop the hysteria**. The fact that he has not been coming to church regularly makes him suspicious in the eyes of Parris. Proctor stopped going because he disliked listening to Parris's sermons and, in addition, wanted to avoid Abigail with whom he had an affair. However, he knows the girls are telling lies and **publicly admits to adultery to save his wife's life**. When he is finally accused of witchery, he first signs a confession, but then tears it up to preserve his good name. John Proctor dies at the gallows because he **places principle over life**.

**Elizabeth Proctor** is John Proctor's **virtuous wife**, who **dismissed Abigail**, when she discovered that she was having an affair with her husband. She becomes the **victim of Abigail's revenge**, but is spared by the court because of her pregnancy. Later, Elizabeth admits that she **feels partly responsible for her husband's sin because of her coldness**. For the very first time in her life, she tells a lie to protect her husband. Elizabeth accepts John's decision not to falsely confess to witchery and save his life, but instead, to accept death in order to "have his goodness" (p. 185).

**Abigail Williams** is the **cunning and deceitful** niece of Parris and the ringleader of the girls who dabble with witchcraft. When she worked for the Proctor family she **had an affair with John Proctor** and later tries in vain to seduce him and resume the relationship. Out of spite she **accuses** Elizabeth Proctor and **various townspeople of working with the devil**. Having started the hysteria in Salem, she disappears.

**Judge Danforth** is the **Deputy Governor of Massachusetts** and the presiding judge at the witch trials. His mind is firmly set on rooting out witchcraft and he **continues pressing the accused to confess, although he seems to have doubts about their guilt**. Danforth is unrelenting and objects to Hale's pleads of pardon or postponement to fulfil the expectations of the villagers who want to see the accused hanged.

## Themes and Interpretation

**Historical background:** *The Crucible* is Arthur Miller's recreation of the **witch trials in Salem**, Massachusetts, **in 1692**. A group of women, who had been dabbling with the occult, began acting in a strange manner. A local doctor claimed they were afflicted by the "evil hand", setting the stage for **hundreds of people being accused of witchcraft**. Some were enemies of the accusing women's families, others were too outspoken or envied for their property. **The witch hysteria** not only **haunted** Salem, but all **34 towns and villages** in the area. Hundreds of accused witches filled the jails awaiting trial. Some died in prison, 19 people were hanged and an old man was crushed to death. The trials ended after 15 months largely because "spectral evidence", i. e. **claims of attacks by invisible witches, was declared inadmissible**.

**Warning of tyranny and intolerance:** Arthur Miller's most frequently performed play is generally understood as either a warning of future acts of tyranny or a reminder of past examples. In the introduction to his drama, Miller characterises the nature of the society which the Puritans had established in Salem on the edge of the wilderness in their new-found homeland. **To protect themselves against a hostile environment** (in the play Abigail remembers her parents being killed by Indians) **the Puritans created a theocratic society** – "a combine of state and religious power whose function was to keep the community together." (pp. 14/15). This close-knit community was ruled in the name of God **with strict norms to uphold moral values and discipline**. People's lives were devoted to work and prayer. Any refusal to accept the doctrines was regarded as a threat to safety and therefore prosecuted with utter determination. **Dissenters were seen as servants of the devil** and had to be eliminated to keep society intact.
A similar situation manifested itself in the US in the 1950s during the so-called "McCarthy era". Republican **Senator Joseph McCarthy** (1908–1957) **initiated a crusade against alleged Communist infiltration of the US administration, public life and the film industry**. During this campaign, which lasted about six years and became known as "McCarthyism", **many of those accused** of Communist activities **were blacklisted and lost their jobs** (e. g. Charlie Chaplin). McCarthy's hunt for Communists and the methods of interrogation, which he and his committee used, resembled the witch trials conducted in Salem: more than 300 people were accused without any valid evidence. Most of the accusations of subversion brought forward against artists and intellectuals in the House Un-American Activities Committee (HUAC) were unfounded. **Miller used the Salem events** as the backdrop **for his protest against political repression, censorship and thought-control**. Because of his

critical portrait of the McCarthy era in the *The Crucible*, Miller was called before the HUAC and convicted of contempt of Congress for not cooperating. A court of appeal sustained his objection to the verdict in 1958.

**Hysteria and vengeance:** In the introduction to his play Miller points out that the witch-hunt was not only about repression (p. 15). The general hysteria, which developed during the hunt, offered people an opportunity to openly express long-held hatred of neighbours and settle old scores. Quarrels over land, which had been boiling under the surface for years, erupted and suspicions against outsiders were brought forward. People began to accuse others of crimes that were never committed. **The reasons for the accusations were no longer connected with religion or piety, but based on private over-due grudges**. The play mirrors this reality: Abigail wants to take revenge on Elizabeth because John Proctor's wife dismissed her after discovering Abigail's affair with her husband. Therefore she accuses Elizabeth of witchcraft and wants her in prison. Another example is the behaviour of Thomas Putnam, a wealthy and influential citizen of Salem. Putnam seeks revenge on Francis Nurse, who prevented Putnam's brother-in-law from being elected minister. This is why he accuses Rebecca, Francis's sensible and virtuous wife, of witchcraft and the supernatural murders of Ann Putnam's babies. Unfortunately, **history offers numerous examples** of how a hysterical atmosphere can develop (or is created) to find scapegoats for one's own failures, be it **the persecution of the Jews in the Middle Ages**, who were then blamed for poisoning the drinking water in the wells, **as well as during the Nazi regime**. Another example is the xenophobia in many societies which is often based on prejudice or even envy.

## William Shakespeare, *The Merchant of Venice* (about 1596)

### Author

William Shakespeare was baptised on April 26, 1564, in Stratford-upon-Avon. He went to the local grammar school and probably became a teacher himself. In 1582 he married Anne Hathaway (1556–1623), and about three years later the couple moved to London. There he worked as both an actor and a playwright. His first plays, probably the comedies *Love's Labour's Lost* and *The Comedy of Errors*, were produced around 1590. There is no certainty about the date of any of his plays, but for the next 20 years they appeared in a steady stream, 37 altogether. Shakespeare died in Stratford in 1616.

### Contents

Shakespeare's play *The Merchant of Venice*, which was probably written between 1596 and 1598, consists of five acts in verse and prose. The settings are Venice (the world of merchants) and Belmont (the country home of Portia, one of the main characters). The story is set in the time of the Renaissance (15th/16th century).

**Act I:** Bassanio, a young noble Venetian, wants to gain the love of Portia, the rich heiress of Belmont. Portia's late father laid down in his will that Portia cannot freely choose her future husband: the future husband has to solve a riddle first. To woo Portia, Bassanio needs 3,000 ducats, too. His friend Antonio cannot lend him the sum because all his funds are tied up in investment, mostly ships. In order to help Bassanio, Antonio turns to the Jewish moneylender Shylock, who agrees to grant the credit for three months under one condition: If the sum is not paid back at the appointed day, Antonio shall forfeit a pound of flesh. Antonio accepts the unusual terms as he is sure his ships will arrive in time and he will be able to pay Shylock back.

**Act II:** Back in Venice, Bassanio is planning a celebration before leaving for Belmont. As stated in her father's will, Portia may only marry the suitor who chooses the right casket out of three (made of gold, silver and lead): the one which contains her portrait. At Belmont, two suitors fail the test for Portia's hand because both choose the wrong caskets. The Prince of Morocco picks the gold casket, which contains a skull and a piece of paper which warns him "all that glisters is not gold" (II, 7)[8]. The haughty Prince of Arragon chooses the silver box that contains only "the portrait of a blinking idiot" inside (II, 9).
Shylock's daughter Jessica, who is ashamed of her father, runs away from home with Bassanio's friend Lorenzo, taking with her much of her father's gold.

**Act III:** Shylock is shocked, when he learns that his rebellious daughter Jessica has eloped (cf. III, 1), stolen his jewels, converted and is now married to a Christian. His hate of Christians increases and he directs it towards Antonio, whose flesh, should he fail to repay the debt, he would use "to bait fish withal" (III, 1). Bassanio arrives in Belmont. He knows that outer appearance can be deceiving and picks the lead casket with the inscription "Who chooseth me must give and hazard all he hath" (III, 2). It is the right one and contains Portia's portrait. Bassanio marries Portia and his friend Gratiano marries Portia's maid Nerissa. But the lovers have no time for celebrations because news arrive from Venice that all of Antonio's merchant ships have been lost at sea. Portia sends Bassanio and Gratiano off to help Antonio. She develops a secret plan to disguise herself as a lawyer and make her way to Venice accompanied by Nerissa disguised as her page boy.

**Act IV:** Shylock is unrelenting, rejects any financial compensation and insists on his contract with Antonio, which means having a pound of flesh from Antonio's body. Bellario, a doctor of laws, is asked to decide the case. Portia dressed "like a doctor of laws" (IV, 1) arrives in Venice accompanied by Nerissa. Portia pretends to have come in representation of the sick Bellario and urges Shylock to have mercy on Antonio. But Shylock rejects this plea and repeats his demand that the contract must be fulfilled because this is his revenge on Antonio and all Christians. Portia decides in Shylocks favour: "A pound of that same merchant's flesh is thine" (IV, 1). Shylock seems to have won his case, but Portia rules that Shylock is not entitled to spill any blood. Moreover, Portia prosecutes him for having tried to take the life of a Venetian

**8** Die römischen Zahlen beziehen sich auf den Akt, die arabischen Ziffern auf die Szene, auf die hier verwiesen wird.

citizen, sentences him to death and confiscates all his possessions. The Duke of Venice spares Shylock's life. Antonio offers half of the borrowed money to Shylock, if he converts to Christianity and leaves the money to Jessica. Shylock has no choice and agrees. Bassanio, who still does not recognise the disguised Portia, offers to pay for the lawyer's services. Portia asks for the ring which Bassanio wears, but Bassanio hesitates because it is the ring which Portia gave him earlier and he had promised never to part with it. But eventually he hands it over.

**Act V:** Portia and Nerissa return to Belmont just before Bassanio, Antonio and Gratiano arrive. They pretend to be very jealous, accusing their husbands of having given the gold rings to other women. Bassanio assures Portia, "No woman had it, but a civil doctor" (V, 1). Portia produces a ring and hands it to Antonio, who passes it on to Bassanio. Bassanio recognizes it as the same ring he gave the young lawyer in Venice. Portia and Nerissa finally admit their roles as lawyer and lawyer's clerk. To make the happy ending perfect, the good news arrives that Antonio's ships were not lost at sea, but have returned home safely.

### Characters

**Antonio:** He is a **successful merchant** in Venice and a good friend of Bassanio. To help Bassanio gain Portia he is **prepared to risk his life** by accepting Shylock's strange conditions for the credit contract. Antonio is often **melancholic** for no obvious reasons. He **dislikes Jews**, but has mercy on Shylock within certain limits.

**Bassanio:** He is a **poor** noble Venetian gentleman, who is not very successful in business matters. Bassanio loves the rich heiress Portia, whose virtues and beauty he praises, but just as openly her wealth – which makes him look a bit like a **fortune hunter**. In order to win her love he borrows money from his good friend Antonio. He successfully passes the suitors' test by choosing the lead casket that contains Portia's portrait, as he does **not** let himself be **deceived by outer appearance**.

**Portia:** She is the **beautiful** and **intelligent** heiress from Belmont. According to her father's will she cannot choose her husband freely, but is only allowed to marry the suitor who picks the right casket. Portia loves Bassanio and helps him to identify the box with her portrait. Disguised as the young lawyer Balthazar she appears at the Venetian Court of Justice to save Antonio from honouring the contract with Shylock. She **plays tricks** on Bassanio to assure herself of his fidelity.

**Shylock:** He is the **Jewish moneylender** in Venice, who supplies the funds for Bassanio's voyage to Belmont. Shylock **hates Christians**, in particular the merchant Antonio, because they despise him for being an inhuman monster obsessed with money ("call me usurer" = *Wucherer*, III, 1). To take revenge Shylock demands a pound of flesh, should Antonio fail to repay his debt in time. His anger increases when he learns that his daughter has eloped with a Christian and stolen his gold and jewellery. He shows **no mercy** with Antonio and can only be stopped by Portia. In the end, he gives in and complies with the conditions stipulated by Antonio.

## Themes and Interpretation

**Elizabethan views:** In Shakespeare's times **Jews** were regarded as **outsiders** and often **discriminated against**. On the Elizabethan stage they appeared as **caricatures, evil-looking and driven by greed**. So Shakespeare follows a dramatic tradition when he makes Shylock the villain of the play: The revengeful Jewish moneylender is the counterpart of the Christian characters. Portia and Antonio show mercy, whereas Shylock is unrelenting. Although his demands are legally justified, he is expected to forgive, which he refuses. Showing **mercy** is an essential element in the teachings of the **New Testament** and is therefore considered a **Christian rather than a Jewish quality**. Consequently, some viewers and critics consider Shylock a very unpleasant person and argue Shakespeare wanted to express **anti-Semitic feelings** of his time. Others maintain that Shakespeare merely created a **colourful and interesting character** for the stage whose rage was, to some extent, well-founded. Furthermore, Antonio's behaviour towards Shylock does not make him an ideal representative of Christian brotherly love. He spat on Shylock, insulted him and spurred his friends to turn against the Jew.

Shakespeare's play also reflects the Elizabethan attitude toward **charging interest** in the business world. The clash between Antonio and Shylock can be seen as a confrontation of two different work ethics. Antonio represents the traditional method: he lends money without asking for interest. Shylock is the ruthless businessman of the emerging **mercantilism** and charges interest. Antonio, the Christian, who gives his money interest-free to Bassanio is seen as a generous friend. Shylock, the Jew, is despised as a "usurer" (III, 1), who applies unethical business methods. On the other hand, Shakespeare makes fun of the Elizabethan values by contrasting the two places associated with the two men's ways: While Shylock's Venice is the modern world of trade and business, Antonio's beautiful Belmont is portrayed as a fairytale land.

**Elizabethan symbolism:**

- **The three caskets:** To win Portia's hand the suitors have to choose from three caskets – gold, silver and lead – which symbolise moral and ethic values. The golden and the silver casket illustrate that **outer appearances are often deceiving**. Bassanio is not distracted by shining glitter; he knows that being humble and modest is the right attitude. By choosing the inconspicuous lead box he wins the competition and passes the test.
- **The pound of flesh:** The symbolic meaning of the pound of flesh which Shylock demands of Antonio should he be unable to pay back his debt can be interpreted in several ways. On the one hand, it is a **metaphor for the close relationship** between Bassanio and his friend Antonio as the fates of debtor (Bassanio) and creditor (Antonio) are inextricably connected. On the other hand, it could also be seen as a **symbol of revenge**. Shylock wants to make up for the loss of his daughter Jessica – his own flesh and blood – who ran away with a Christian. Demanding a pound of flesh from his debtor Antonio could also show Shylock's cruel and inflexible attitude and point out his urge to take revenge for the long-lasting oppression of the Jewish population by the Christian congregation.

- **The two rings:** Jewellery plays a symbolic role in the comedy. As a bachelor Shylock received a ring from Leah, perhaps his wife and Jessica's mother. The loss of the ring – Jessica takes it with her when she elopes – saddens him. Perhaps Shylock is not only mourning over the material, but also over the sentimental value he has lost. The jewel **adds human qualities** to the unemotional Shylock and shows him capable of deep feelings.
  The other ring symbolises **Portia's love** and dedication to her future husband Bassanio, whose equal commitment to Portia can be doubted as he gives her ring away to pay the lawyer for his services. Portia is the more honest of the two, whereas Bassanio might be at least as interested in his wife as in her fortune.

## William Shakespeare, *Romeo and Juliet* (about 1591)

### Author

see *The Merchant of Venice*

### Contents

Shakespeare's tragedy was probably written between 1591 and 1596. It consists of five acts and is set in the Italian cities of Verona and Mantua at the beginning of the 15th century.
Before the first act begins, the chorus enters, pronouncing in the form of a sonnet the sad ending of the play about the "star-crossed lovers" Romeo and Juliet (Prologue).

**Act I:** A fight breaks out in the streets of Verona between the servants of two noble families, the Capulets and Montagues, who are bitter enemies. Prince Escalus, the ruler of Verona, declares he will not tolerate any more disturbances and decrees death for any individual that disturbs the peace in the future. Lord and Lady Montague are pleased that their son Romeo does not participate in the quarrels but are worried about his behaviour. The reason for Romeo's sadness is his unrequited love for Rosaline, who does not return his affection. His cousin Benvolio suggests to Romeo to look at other girls. He plans to accompany Romeo in disguise to a party of the Capulets. Romeo hopes to meet Rosaline at the ball.
At the Capulets' house, Count Paris, related to the Prince of Verona, tells Lord Capulet about his plan to marry Capulet's fourteen-year-old daughter Juliet. Although Capulet thinks Juliet is too young to marry, he agrees to let the two meet at a masked ball which is to take place in his house that night. At the party Romeo and Juliet meet and instantly fall in love. They kiss, not even knowing the other's name. It is only later that Romeo learns from the Nurse, Juliet's maid, that Juliet is a Capulet and Juliet is informed that Romeo belongs to the Montague family.

**Act II:** The chorus enters again, hinting at the difficulties facing the two lovers but at the same time assuring that "passion lends them power" (II, Prologue) to overcome them.
After the party Romeo climbs the wall into the orchard garden of the Capulets' house and finds Juliet alone at her window. He overhears her professing her love to him, de-

ploring the fact that they belong to feuding families. He calls out to her and both promise eternal love. To arrange the wedding Romeo approaches Friar Laurence, who agrees to marry the two lovers in secret because he hopes the bond will end the hostilities between their families. The next day, the wedding ceremony takes place in Friar Laurence's cell. The Nurse, who knows about the secret, fetches the ladder Romeo will use to climb into Juliet's room on their wedding night.

**Act III:** Tybalt, Lady Capulet's nephew, insults Romeo in the market place to challenge him to a duel. However, as Romeo, now related to the Capulets, does not want to fight, his friend Mercutio takes up the challenge. Romeo cannot prevent the clash: Mercutio is stabbed by Tybalt and to take revenge for his friend's death Romeo kills Tybalt. Escalus, the Prince of Verona, arrives at the scene and banishes Romeo from the city. Romeo hides in Friar Laurence's cell and is about to kill himself because he fears he will never see Juliet again. Friar Laurence can prevent the suicide and advises Romeo to go into exile for the time being, until the crisis has blown over. He and the Nurse arrange for Romeo and Juliet to spend their wedding night in Julia's bedroom. The next morning Romeo has to leave for Mantua, the lovers bid farewell, not knowing when they will be united again. Lady Capulet tells Juliet that she is to marry Count Paris in three days' time. Juliet cannot reveal that she is already married to Romeo. Disgusted by the Nurse's advice to comply with her parents' wishes and forget Romeo, Juliet hurries to Friar Laurence for help.

**Act IV:** Friar Laurence thinks up a drastic plan to reunite Juliet with Romeo in Mantua. He tells Juliet she is to drink a potion the night before her wedding to Count Paris. This drink ought to make her appear dead for 42 hours. Her parents, believing that their daughter is dead, will lay her to rest in the family's vault. In the meantime Romeo will be informed of the trick and will come to secretly rescue her and take her away to Mantua. At first, everything goes according to plan. Juliet drinks the potion and is found dead in her bedroom.

**Act V:** Juliet is buried in the Capulets' crypt. The rest of Friar Laurence's scheme fails because his messenger is detained and cannot inform Romeo of the manoeuvre in time. Romeo only gets the false news of Juliet's death. He is devastated and buys a vial of poison to kill himself. He hurries back to see Juliet for the last time. In front of the crypt he meets Count Paris, who is putting flowers on Juliet's grave. After a short fight Romeo kills Paris. He then kisses the "dead" Juliet and drinks the poison. Friar Laurence is informed that his messenger did not meet Romeo and hurries to the crypt. He finds Paris and Romeo dead and has to tell the waking Juliet about what has happened. She kisses him and wants to kill herself with the poison in Romeo's vial. As it is empty, she stabs herself with Romeo's dagger. The Capulets and Montagues arrive and Friar Laurence explains why the tragedy happened. In view of the dead bodies of their children the two families promise to end their feud.

**Characters**

**Juliet:** The daughter of Lord and Lady Capulet is very **young** (not even fourteen) and **beautiful**. In the course of events Juliet undergoes a remarkable change. When the play begins she is still an innocent child, cared for by her nurse and mother and **obediently complies with wishes of her parents**. The profound change comes when she meets Romeo. From then on she **takes her life in her own hands**, thinking seriously about her own and Romeo's future. She is prepared to take risks (she lets Romeo into her room) and refuses to accept her parents' proposal of marrying Paris. Although she is madly in love, she **keeps a cool head**, knowing very well that her relationship to Romeo is fragile because he is a Montague. She is also well aware that Father Laurence's plan could fail but drinks the friar's potion because she firmly believes that her love for Romeo is strong enough to withstand death.

**Romeo:** The son and heir of the Montague family is about sixteen years old. In the beginning he is a **romantic dreamer** but is transformed into a **passionate**, **resolute** and **daring lover** by his deep affection for Juliet. Juliet tries to restrain his **impetuous actions**.

**Friar Laurence:** The Franciscan monk is a friend both to Romeo and Juliet and tries to help them. He secretly marries the two lovers and develops a **cunning** plan, which unfortunately fails. His activities do not save Romeo's and Juliet's love, but eventually **bring about peace** between the Capulets and Montagues.

**Lord and Lady Capulet:** Juliet's father, an **important and respected citizen** of Verona, is head of the Capulets, who are embittered enemies of the Montague family. He is rather **jovial**, jokes with guests and likes to play the role of the gracious **patriarch**. However, he is also **concerned with maintaining order in his own house**. Juliet's refusal to marry Paris enrages him and he threatens to throw her out on the street to starve. He grieves over Juliet's death, but he is just as **worried that he will** now **die without heirs**. He has an unhappy relationship with his wife. Lady Capulet married her husband when she was very young (about the same age as Juliet) and likes to make life difficult for him. She **does not have a very close relationship to Juliet**, who prefers to confide her problems to her Nurse. Lady Capulet **urges her daughter to marry Paris** and becomes very angry when she refuses. She is genuinely **saddened by Juliet's death**.

**Lord and Lady Montague:** Romeo's parents have a **closer and happier relationship** than Juliet's. They **love their son** and are **worried about his depressive mood**. Lady Montague cannot get over Romeo's banishment from the city and dies of grief. As head of the House of Montague **Romeo's father** takes an **active role in the feud** between the two families and thus has to take some of the blame for his son's death.

**Juliet's Nurse:** The servant is very close to Juliet who shares her secrets with her. Apart from being **Juliet's confidant** she also takes the role of the **messenger between the two lovers** and tries to make sure that Romeo's intentions are sincere. Her concepts of marriage and love are much more **down-to-earth** and provide a contrast to Juliet's idealistic ideas.

**Escalus, Prince of Verona:** He is the **strict ruler of Verona** and tries to stop the feud between the Capulets and the Montagues by laying down a law that anyone involved in senseless fighting will face death. He **gives in to Lord Montague's pleading** and banishes Romeo instead of executing him. After Romeo's and Juliet's death he regrets that he has not been strict enough to prevent the catastrophe.

## Themes and Interpretation

**The power of love:** Shakespeare's play is the perfect example of genuine and passionate love. Romeo's and Juliet's love is not a romantic and enraptured feeling, it is an **absolute force** and passion that hits the two young people like a stroke of lightning and takes complete possession of them as soon as they meet at the masked ball. Romeo's feeling for Juliet is much deeper than his affection for Rosaline. Thinking about his unrequited love for Rosaline makes him feel sorry for himself but for Juliet he is prepared to give up his family connections and social contacts. The same is true for Juliet. She pleads with Romeo: "Deny thy father and refuse thy name" (II, 2) and is also willing to sacrifice her former life for Romeo, "And I'll no longer be a Capulet" (II, 2). Their **unconditional love** is frustrated by the hate and hostility of their families who finally realise their responsibility for the tragic outcome.

**Hatred:** The bitter hostility and hate between the Capulets and Montagues provides a **stark contrast to the love Romeo and Juliet feel**. The feud is the cause for the killings of Mercutio, Tybalt and Paris, the separation of the two lovers and their suicide. In the Prologue, the audience learns that the **strife and rage** will end with the death of the two lovers. Both families finally conclude peace when it is too late – over the graves of their children.

**Guilt:** The play is one of Shakespeare's early tragedies. Romeo and Juliet are displayed as **innocent victims of an inescapable fate**, the stars are against them. In Shakespeare's time, astrology was a highly respected science, and even the King studied the constellation of the stars and tried to interpret their influence on people's lives. Romeo calls himself a "fortune's fool" (III, 1) to express his **helplessness against a superior force**. In Shakespeare's later tragedies the main character is himself responsible for his doom because of a flaw (= a defect) in his personality. By contrast, Romeo and Juliet are only to a certain extent responsible for their tragic end, as they acted hastily and irresponsibly due to their **lack of experience and their youth**. The **real culprits** in the play are **Lord Montague** and **Lord Capulet** who allowed the feud to go on. They pay for their guilt with the deaths of their children.

## Gymnasium Niedersachsen – Englisch
## Abiturähnliche Übungsaufgabe 1

### Leseverstehen

**Paul Kingsnorth, *Business as usual***

Thomas Friedman is a big man in more ways than one. This moustachioed bear of a journalist counts many of America's top CEOs and politicians among his friends. He has won the Pulitzer Prize three times. *The New York Times* calls him "the most important columnist in America today". *Vanity Fair* describes him as "the country's best newspaper columnist, period". How does he do it? Reading this book, the answer becomes clear – Friedman is an expert at telling the powerful what they want to hear.

The thesis of *The World is Flat* is that neoliberal globalisation is "flattening" the world, breaking down commercial, cultural and even geographical barriers at ever-increasing speed. The result, if we are lucky, will be a super-efficient, hyper-productive world in which we all have wireless-enabled laptops, and everyone from Delhi to Darwin thinks and talks like a Harvard MBA graduate.

The book starts with Friedman going to India to play golf, where he sees many giant billboards for American products. He then visits the CEO of a fast-growing information technology company, who tells him how quickly barriers to trade are coming down. "The playing field is being levelled," he tells Friedman.

What to anyone else would be a throwaway cliche is, to this author, a eureka moment. "What Nandan is saying, I thought, is that the playing field is being flattened … Flattened? Flattened? My God, he's telling me the world is flat!" Never mind that this isn't what Nandan is actually saying; Friedman has found himself a great book title and he's not about to let it go. He repeats it eight times in the next two paragraphs, and then phones his wife. "Honey," he says, "I think the world is flat." He does not record her response.

Friedman whizzes around India, visiting call-centres where workers stay up late talking on the phone to Americans whose computers have broken. They give themselves names such as "Jerry" and "Sonia", and speak in American accents so as not to cause offence. Roughly 245,000 Indians work in call-centres, servicing the needs of rich people elsewhere. American CEOs can now hire a PA in India who will do everything a PA in America could do, for a fraction of the cost. In other words, Friedman's new hyper-globalisation means that all the shitty jobs get done by poor people in the developing world. So much for progress.

Friedman is an optimist, excited by possibilities. This ought to be an appealing trait but it can actually get depressing. He talks about the vast array of choices, technologies and opportunities that globalisation presents, yet each of them, after a while, seems curiously similar. It feels like walking through a huge Tesco marvelling at the range of bread: choice, yes, but within a very limiting framework. In Friedman's bright future, all choices lead to the same ultimate destination – a world of urban consumers, living in a market economy, working in offices, getting excited by software.

There is something else, too. After a few hundred pages, you realise that what Friedman is actually doing is scooping up truisms and disguising them as profundities. The internet and email have changed the world! China and India are growing really fast! Computer software is getting cleverer all the time! How does he get such praise for such basic observations? Simple: by thinking up slogans. Friedman is less a journalist than an advertising copywriter, and his real talent is for giving catchy names to obvious phenomena.

In 1989, "the walls came down and the windows went up" (that's the Berlin Wall and Microsoft Windows). File-sharing and video-conferencing are "steroids" that allow the computer industry to take off at light-speed. What this has led to is a "triple convergence" of computing factors, creating a historical era called "Globalisation 3.0". There are still some annoyingly "unflat" parts of the world – the Middle East, for example – but more consumer opportunities will sort them out. After all, the "Dell theory of conflict prevention" states that "no two countries that are part of a major supply chain, like Dell's, will ever fight a war against each other".

No wonder the establishment likes Friedman. He tells us that there's gold at the end of the rainbow, and that all we need to do to get it is keep walking in the same direction, only faster. The world will be made safe for Harvard MBA graduates and smarty-pants journalists with slogans coming out of their Palm Pilots. Thank God for the future. […] *747 words*

*From:* New Statesman, *30 May 2005. By Paul Kingsnorth.*
*Review of* The World Is Flat: A brief history of the globalised world in the 21st century
*by Thomas Friedman*

**Annotations:**
11 MBA: Master of Business Administration; Harvard is a very prestigious American university
27 PA: Personal Assistant
34 Tesco: a big British supermarket chain

**Aufgabenstellung**

1. Read the text and decide whether the following statements are true or false. Support your decision by giving evidence from the text (5 to 25 words). There is an example at the beginning (a).

| Statement | True | False | Evidence |
|---|---|---|---|
| a) Kingsnorth thinks Friedman is a "big man", by which he is referring to his career. | ☐ | ☑ | "big man in more ways than one" (l. 1); "bear of a journalist" (ll. 1/2); "won the Pulitzer Prize three times" (l. 3)/"the most important columnist in America" (ll. 3/4)/"the country's best newspaper columnist" (ll. 4/5) |
| b) According to the text Friedman's success is based on him appealing to elites. | ☐ | ☐ | |
| c) According to the text Friedman states that the disadvantage of the flattening process is that boundaries have to be overcome in different areas, e. g. in commerce or culture. | ☐ | ☐ | |
| d) In his book Friedman explains that about 245,000 Asian Americans are working in call centres or as PAs. | ☐ | ☐ | |
| e) Friedman thinks that a globalised world looks like a bread display in a supermarket: lots of choice, but hardly any difference between the products. | ☐ | ☐ | |
| f) Friedman is sure that soon the whole world will be flat. | ☐ | ☐ | |

2. Based on the text, tick the correct box.

a) Kingsnorth thinks that what Friedman considers …

- ☐ major ideas are just banalities.
- ☐ negligible factors are in fact scandalous discoveries.
- ☐ spectacular new insights are in reality ideas that have been well known for centuries.
- ☐ philosophical discoveries are in fact blatant lies.

b) According to Kingsnorth Friedman might also be good as …

- ☐ a journalist.
- ☐ an ad writer.
- ☐ an IT specialist.
- ☐ a film scriptwriter.

c) According to the text Globalisation 3.0 …

- ☐ triggered the widespread use of file-sharing and video-conferencing.
- ☐ is the name of the historical era in which three new computing factors were developed.
- ☐ means that the worldwide use of IT has increased threefold.
- ☐ is the result of new inventions in information technology.

3. Complete the sentence in your own words.

According to the Dell Theory of conflict prevention, there will be …

____________________________________________

____________________________________________

____________________________________________

4. Choose the best overall description of the text.

Paul Kingsnorth …

- ☐ sees Friedman's work critically and uses irony to make his readers aware of weak spots in Friedman's theory.
- ☐ shares the opinion expressed in most of the reviews of Friedman's work.
- ☐ does not wholly share Friedman's view but acknowledges Friedman's talent for asking catchy questions.

## Textaufgabe

**Excerpt from: N. H. Kleinbaum, *Dead Poets Society***

"Hey," Cameron shouted as the boys started into Mr. Keating's room the next afternoon. "There's a note on the board to meet in the courtyard."

"I wonder what Mr. Keating is up to today." Pitts grinned expectantly.

The boys raced down the hall and out the door into the chilly courtyard. Mr. McAllister peered out from his classroom door, shaking his head in annoyance.

"People," Keating said as the boys gathered around him. "A dangerous element of conformity has been seeping into your work. Mister Pitts, Cameron, Overstreet, and Chapman, line up over here please." He pointed to the four boys to stand near him. "On the count of four, I want you to begin walking together around the courtyard. Nothing to think about. No grade here. One, two, three, go!"

The boys began walking. They walked down one side of the courtyard, across the back, up the other side, and across the front, completing the square.

"That's the way," Keating said. "Please continue."

The boys walked around the courtyard again as the rest of the class and the teacher watched. Soon they began to walk in step, a march-like cadence emanating from the pavement. They continued in a one-two-three-four pattern as Keating began to clap to the rhythm.

"There it is … Hear it?" he called, clapping louder in time. "One two, one two, one two, one two … we're all having fun, in Mr. Keating's class …"

Sitting in his empty classroom grading papers, McAllister observed the commotion through the window. The four marchers picked up on their cadence. They lifted their legs high and swung their arms back and forth, keeping the rhythm alive. The class joined in clapping out the beat.

Distracted by the clapping and cheering, Dean Nolan put down his work and peered through the window at the drill-team activity below. Nolan's eyebrows furrowed as he frowned at Keating clapping and shouting to the English class. *What in the world are they doing?* he wondered.

"All right, stop," Mr. Keating called to the marchers. "You may have noticed how at the beginning Misters Overstreet and Pitts seemed to have a different stride than the others – Pitts with his long lurches, Knox with that light little bounce – but soon all were walking in the same cadence. Our encouragement made it even more marked," he pointed out.

"Now, this experiment was not to single out Pitts or Overstreet. What it demonstrates is how difficult it is for any of us to listen to our own voice or maintain our own beliefs in the presence of others. If any of you think you would have marched differently, then ask yourself why you were clapping. Lads, there is a great need in all of us to be accepted, but you must trust what is unique or different about yourself, even if it is odd or unpopular. As Frost said, "'Two roads diverged in a wood, and I – I took the one less traveled by, / And that has made all the difference.'"

The bell rang, but the boys remained rooted in their spots, watching Keating and absorbing his message. Then Keating saluted the class and walked off. *531 words*



**Cartoon**

© *Paul Fell/cartoonstock.com*

**Aufgabenstellung**

You are spending an ERASMUS year at Cambridge University. You have applied for a job as language assistant in the German department where you would like to help teaching German to British students.
In order to find out whether you are qualified for the job the German department has set you the following tasks based on the excerpt from *Dead Poets Society* and the cartoon.

1. First of all, you should outline the scene and explain Mr Keating's teaching philosophy.
2. Secondly, you should compare Mr Keating's teaching philosophy with that of a teacher you have had in school.
3. Further, you should analyse the cartoon.
4. In your final presentation you have to submit a paper entitled "Teaching and education in the globalised world". In this paper, it is your job to assess which teaching philosophy prepares students best for life in a globalised world. You are required to use your background knowledge as well as the material at hand.

# Lösungsvorschläge

## Leseverstehen

1. *Read the statements first and then scan the text for key words (or synonyms for the key words) from these statements. The order of the statements follows the chronological order of the text. When you have found the relevant passage, compare text and statement carefully before you make your decision. Keep in mind that you are not supposed to use your background knowledge here.*
   *Possible key words:*
   *a) big man, career*
   *b) elites (important/powerful people), to appeal (to do or say sth. s.o. wants you to do or say)*
   *c) disadvantage, to overcome boundaries*
   *d) 245,000, Asian Americans, call centre*
   *e) supermarket, choice*
   *f) whole world, flat*
   *Support your decision by quoting or paraphrasing the relevant passages from the text. Write down the lines where you can find these passages as well.*

| Statement | True | False | Evidence |
|---|---|---|---|
| a) Kingsnorth thinks Friedman is a "big man", by which he is referring to his career. | ☐ | ☑ | "big man in more ways than one" (l. 1); "bear of a journalist" (ll. 1/2); "won the Pulitzer Prize three times" (l. 3) / "the most important columnist in America" (ll. 3/4) / "the country's best newspaper columnist" (ll. 4/5) |
| b) According to the text Friedman's success is based on him appealing to elites. | ☑ | ☐ | "Friedman is an expert at telling the powerful what they want to hear." (l. 6) |
| c) According to the text Friedman states that the disadvantage of the flattening process is that boundaries have to be overcome in different areas, e. g. in commerce or culture. | ☐ | ☑ | "The thesis of *The World is Flat* is that neoliberal globalisation is 'flattening' the world, breaking down commercial, cultural […] barriers." (ll. 7/8) |

| | | | |
|---|---|---|---|
| d) In his book Friedman explains that about 245,000 Asian Americans are working in call centres or as PAs. | ☐ | ☑ | "Roughly 245,000 Indians work in call-centres, servicing the needs of rich people elsewhere." (ll. 26/27) "American CEOs can now hire a PA in India who will do everything a PA in America could do" (ll. 27/28) |
| e) Friedman thinks that a globalised world looks like a bread display in a super-market: lots of choice, but hardly any difference between the products. | ☑ | ☐ | "It feels like walking through a huge Tesco marvelling at the range of bread: choice, yes, but within a very limiting framework." (ll. 34/35) |
| f) Friedman is sure that soon the whole world will be flat. | ☑ | ☐ | "There are still some annoyingly 'unflat' parts of the world […] but more consumer opportunities will sort them out." (ll. 49/50) |

2. *Read the statements and the possible options and look for the relevant passages in the text. Then compare each option to the text and decide.*
*The relevant passages from the text are:*
*a) lines 38–42*
*b) lines 41–44*
*c) lines 45–49*

a) Kingsnorth thinks that what Friedman considers …
- ☑ major ideas are just banalities.
- ☐ negligible factors are in fact scandalous discoveries.
- ☐ spectacular new insights are in reality ideas that have been well known for centuries.
- ☐ philosophical discoveries are in fact blatant lies.

b) According to Kingsnorth Friedman might also be good as …
- ☐ a journalist.
- ☑ an ad writer.
- ☐ an IT specialist.
- ☐ a film scriptwriter.

c) According to the text Globalisation 3.0 …

- ☐ triggered the widespread use of file-sharing and video-conferencing.
- ☐ is the name of the historical era in which three new computing factors were developed.
- ☐ means that the worldwide use of IT has increased threefold.
- ☑ is the result of new inventions in information technology.

3. *First, scan the text for the term "Dell theory of conflict prevention" and read the relevant passage (ll. 50/51). Then complete the sentence by giving a brief explanation of this theory. If possible, do not quote from the text. Use your own words.*

According to the Dell theory of conflict prevention, there will be …
**no wars between countries that are involved in making the same product.**

4. *To be able to solve this task you must have read and understood the whole text. Compare each option to the text. Be careful, sometimes only one or two words in one option do not match the text.*
   - *Option 1: Look for other opinions of* The World is Flat *that are expressed in Kingsnorth's article. Does the author share these opinions?*
   - *Option 2: Does Kingsnorth say something about "catchy questions"?*
   - *Option 3: Can you spot irony in the text? Does Kingsnorth criticize Friedman?*

Paul Kingsnorth …

- ☑ sees Friedman's work critically and uses irony to make his readers aware of weak spots in Friedman's theory.
- ☐ shares the opinion expressed in most of the reviews of Friedman's work.
- ☐ does not wholly share Friedman's view but acknowledges Friedman's talent for asking catchy questions.

## Textaufgabe

1. *The first task involves reproducing certain aspects of a text. Here you are asked to sum up the main aspects of Mr Keating's educational philosophy. Stick to the relevant aspects and ignore aspects that are less significant.*
   *The key points are:*
   - *Mr Keating's teaching aims: pupils should become independent thinkers, should make decisions themselves*
   - *He has them experience things themselves instead of telling them what to think.*

   In the excerpt from the novel *Dead Poets Society* by N. H. Kleinbaum, Mr Keating, the protagonist of the novel, is shown teaching one of his classes. He tells four pupils to walk around the courtyard and soon they fall into step accompanied by Mr Keating's and their classmates' clapping. After this experiment Keating points their attention to the fact that they followed the masses without thinking and abandoned their individual beliefs.
   From this scene, you can deduce what Mr Keating's teaching philosophy appears to be. In terms of his aims, Mr Keating wants his pupils to become critical thinkers who make decisions independently of other people, regardless of whether or not their answers fit in with the mainstream. He does so by having his pupils experience for themselves how they automatically try to fit in when told just to walk. His way of teaching, or his methodology, is very important for him to reach this aim. It might be described as unorthodox, which becomes clear when looking at the reaction of Mr Keating's colleagues. Mr Keating's approach is based on experience; instead of telling his pupils to think independently, he puts theory into practice and has the pupils experience things for themselves. Instead of teaching by the book or having them learn things by heart, he stresses the importance of their own individual approach.
   All in all, Mr Keating's teaching philosophy is more about enabling the students to think for themselves rather them telling them what they should be thinking.

2. *In this task you are asked to make connections between the 'new' material you are presented with in the exam and your own experiences from the perspective of a pupil. In this case, you are asked to compare Mr Keating and his teaching philosophy with the methods of a teacher you have had in class. This sample solution refers to a fictitious teacher. Before you start writing, make a list of similarities and differences between the teachers you are comparing:*
   - *Similarities:*
     - *way of teaching differs from the norm, unusual for the time they live in*
     - *act independently of textbooks or syllabus*
     - *special relationship between teacher and students*

- *Differences:*
  - *different aims: Keating wants his students to think independently – my own teacher wanted everyone to share her own views*
  - *Keating focuses on the individual, enables his students to find their own way – my own teacher tried to push each of her students into a direction that seemed suitable to her*

*In your answer you can include an introductory sentence that links your text to the answer of task 1. Make sure to give your text a good structure: present your argument, give evidence from the novels, explain this evidence and then link this idea to the next paragraph.*

Mr Keating's teaching philosophy seems to focus on enabling the students to truly exercise self-determination. In my last two years at school, I have had a History teacher who managed to influence her pupils to a great extent as well. In the following those two teaching personalities should be compared.

In terms of method, it seems noteworthy that both Mr Keating and my teacher use rather atypical teaching methods. They both act independently of their school and its textbooks, and follow a rather unique approach that is distinctly different from the norm.

Like Mr Keating, my History teacher did not follow the standard approach to teaching. She deviated from the school's set syllabus because she thought that it did not provide the students with enough background knowledge to fully understand the historical facts that they were taught. Another similarity can be observed when it comes to the relationship between teacher and students.

Both Mr Keating and my teacher seem to have a special bond with students that goes beyond the normal relationship between teacher and student, which can be observed in the excerpt through the way the students react to what Mr Keating is doing. Both address them as individuals. Like Mr Keating, who has a tongue-in-cheek way of speaking to his students and thus signals to them that he takes them seriously and views them as grown-ups, my teacher frequently told us about the time when she was a teenager herself. Sharing her memories and experiences with us, she included us in her life.

As closely related as Keating and my History teacher may be in this respect, they do differ in their philosophy as far as their aims are concerned. Keating encourages his students to follow their own instincts and talents and leaves it open as to what he thinks their talents might be. On the contrary: By telling them that each and every one of them should follow their own individual pace, he stresses the importance of every individual in the group.

This runs counter to my teacher's approach. All her teaching was rather teacher-centred in so far as she did not see the students for what they were, but rather emphasised her spiritual leadership over them. Unlike Keating, she told her pupils exactly what to think and do and tried to impose her own view on them. She even told us which subjects to study at university and wanted us to share her adoration for communism, for example.

3. *Cartoons are media that – generally speaking – comment on people, events or current developments in society. By means of exaggeration, the use of irony and pointing you at something, they often criticize these people, events or developments humorously. The message very often is given away in the text elements.*
*The key points in this cartoon are:*
   - *Exaggeration: The overweight child from the US (note pizza, hamburger and soft drink) has collapsed because the coursework from China is too demanding.*
   - *Humour: Contrary to the expectations, the American boy has been knocked down not because of a physical fight, but due to his ignorance.*
   - *Criticism conveyed: The US educational system is lagging behind the Chinese system.*

The cartoon criticizes the educational system in the US by ridiculing it and comparing it with the Chinese system.
In the cartoon, you can see a lady who looks like a teacher or tutor and who seems to be telling off a small boy. The boy, who seems to be Asian, is wearing a T-shirt with a star on the front – obviously an allusion to the Chinese flag.
On the ground in front of the little boy you can see another, rather overweight boy wearing a shirt with the imprint "USA" on the back, who seems to have suddenly fainted, as a piece of pizza, a hamburger and a bottle of coke seem to have just dropped to the ground in front of him. An obvious interpretation could be that the boy has lost consciousness because he has had too much to eat, or because the other boy has slapped him. Yet whereas you would expect the explanation in the speech bubble to be just that, the actual explanation gives away the cartoon's message: Having been shown what children in China are doing at school, the American student has had a breakdown because he could not digest all the information the Chinese boy presented to him.
Summing up, the cartoon suggests that the US and its schools and students are lagging behind Chinese schools in terms of academic achievement by exaggerating the ignorance and sluggishness of American students.

4. *Here the operator requires you to "assess" different teaching philosophies, which means to investigate or examine by argument, by giving reasons for and against. The reference to the text and the cartoon clearly asks you to come back to points you have discussed at an earlier point in the exam. The reference to the knowledge from your coursework requires you to use arguments from texts or books you have discussed in class.*
*A possible structure for your answer could be: introduction, description of the situation in the globalised world (e. g. with reference to the film* Outsourced*), consequences for students, and characteristics of different teaching philosophies (Mr Keating, Chinese approach) that could be useful for students in a globalised world.*

*Aspects of recent developments within the globalised world you could focus on:*
- *Characteristics of the globalised world:*
  - *IT has changed the way people communicate around the world*
  - *parts of the production process are outsourced (cf. the film* Outsourced*)*
- *Consequences for students:*
  - *need to get qualifications that cannot be outsourced*
  - *possibility of finding a job worldwide*

*Possible teaching goals in a globalised world:*
- *IT skills, foreign language skills, intercultural skills, ability to carry out research*
- *ability to identify problems, explore solutions and reflect on them*
- *attitude towards education/performance (Chinese approach)*
- *need to think critically, to be able to reflect on one's weaknesses and strengths, to be able to be an independent solution finder (Mr Keating)*

As could be observed in both the text and the cartoon, teaching philosophies have differed over time and between cultures, and they have all pursued different objectives. Yet which teaching philosophy prepares students best for a globalised world? In order to answer this question, we first have to define what exactly makes the globalised world different from other times in history.

In the last decades, technological inventions have had a huge impact on the way people work. Whereas in the old days, unskilled jobs such as work on a production line or at a call centre were done in the country a company was based in, many jobs are nowadays outsourced to countries where the production costs are significantly lower than in the so-called "Western world". The film *Outsourced* gives a vivid example of how quickly a company is willing to move to another country just to reduce the employment costs any further: in the film, a call centre is moved from the US to India and finally to China at the very moment the protagonist finally got it to work perfectly well. In this respect, the world has become a smaller place, as goods and services can easily be sold and shipped around the world. This has positive and negative effects for students like me in the Western world.

On the one hand, there is a need for me to get qualifications which cannot be easily outsourced. On the other hand, there are vast opportunities at hand as outsourcing does not only go from west to east, but also the other way round. So, in other words, my job opportunities increase as I am no longer limited to applying for jobs in companies that are based in my home country, but I can work for companies all over the world. Yet what are the things young people need to learn in order to be able to be well-prepared for this globalised world?

In my opinion, schools should put a special emphasis on IT and foreign language skills as well as intercultural learning. Mastering IT is crucial to participate in international projects; and if you do not know how to use web 2.0.-based tools, for example, you simply cannot succeed on the international job market. The same is true for foreign language skills and intercultural understanding. You may be very skilled in a special field, but this knowledge does not get you anywhere if you do not know how to put your thoughts into words, or if you do not know how to avoid certain

social gaffes. Being aware of people's values or of the way they interact socially could pave the way for successful international cooperation.
Yet the most important skill in a globalised world for me is to know how to research information. As work crosses boundaries, and as IT develops faster and faster, schools can no longer provide you with a toolkit that, once learned and revised, will always help you to perform well. In a globalised world, you have to be able to be good at identifying problems, exploring solutions, and reflecting on them. Things work differently in different countries. So whereas plagiarism in the Western world may be a well-known offence, other countries simply have a different perspective on it. Whereas sustainability is a key issue from the Western perspective, other countries may not find this aspect important at all.
So which teaching philosophy would be able to prepare students best for this?
The Chinese education system, as positively as it may have been portrayed in the cartoon, has its drawbacks. The drill-based pedagogical approach which is often applied in Chinese schools, and the high pressure which is put on Chinese pupils in their schools may be beneficial in some ways. However, it also leads to workers who might not be able to appreciate the joy of work, and who might not be able to think critically for themselves. Nevertheless, it should also be noted that German schools and families could follow Chinese society, where education and performance in general is held in high regard.
As far as the teaching philosophies of Mr Keating is concerned, I think it might help young people to develop the skills needed in a globalised world: The need to think critically, to be able to reflect on one's weaknesses and strengths, and to be able to be an independent solution finder – just like Mr Keating's students in the excerpt.

## Gymnasium Niedersachsen – Englisch
## Abiturähnliche Übungsaufgabe 2

### Leseverstehen

**Text 1: "The Chinese Mother"** by Amy Chua

A lot of people wonder how Chinese parents raise such stereotypically successful kids. They wonder what these parents do to produce so many math whizzes and music prodigies, what it's like inside the family, and whether they could do it too. Well, I can tell them, because I've done it. Here are some things my daughters, Sophia and Louisa, were never allowed to do:

- attend a sleepover
- have a playdate
- be in a school play
- complain about not being in a school play
- watch TV or play computer games
- choose their own extracurricular activities
- get any grade less than an A
- not be the #1 student in every subject except gym and drama
- play any instrument other than the piano or violin
- not play the piano or violin.

I'm using the term "Chinese mother" loosely. I recently met a supersuccessful white guy from South Dakota (you've seen him on television), and after comparing notes we decided that his working-class father had definitely been a Chinese mother. I know some Korean, Indian, Jamaican, Irish, and Ghanaian parents who qualify too. Conversely, I know some mothers of Chinese heritage, almost always born in the West, who are not Chinese mothers, by choice or otherwise. [...]

Despite our squeamishness about cultural stereotypes, there are tons of studies out there showing marked and quantifiable differences between Chinese and Westerners when it comes to parenting. In one study of 50 Western American mothers and 48 Chinese immigrant mothers, almost 70 % of the Western mothers said either that "stressing academic success is not good for children" or that "parents need to foster the idea that learning is fun." By contrast, roughly 0 % of the Chinese mothers felt the same way. Instead, the vast majority of the Chinese mothers said that they believe their children can be "the best" students, that "academic achievement reflects successful parenting," and that if children did not excel at school then there was "a problem" and parents "were not doing their job." Other studies indicate that compared to Western parents, Chinese parents spend approximately ten times as long every day drilling academic activities with their children. By contrast, Western kids are more likely to participate in sports teams. [...]

What Chinese parents understand is that nothing is fun until you're good at it. To get good at anything you have to work, and children on their own never want to work, which is why it is crucial to override their preferences. This often requires fortitude on the part of the parents because the child will resist: things are always hardest at the beginning, which is where Western parents tend to give up. But if done properly, the Chinese strategy produces a virtuous circle. Tenacious practice, practice, practice is crucial for excellence; rote repetition is underrated in America. Once a child starts to excel at something – whether it's math, piano, pitching or ballet – he or she gets praise, admiration and satisfaction. This builds confidence and makes the once not-fun activity fun. This in turn makes it easier for the parent to get the child to work even more.

*517 words*

*From: Amy Chua,* Battle Hymn of the Tiger Mother. *© 2011 Bloomsbury Publishing Plc.*

**Aufgabenstellung Text 1**

1. Read text 1 and decide whether the following statements are true or false. Quote or paraphrase from the text to support your decision (5 to 20 words). There is an example at the beginning (a).

| Statement | True | False | Evidence |
|---|---|---|---|
| a) A lot of Chinese children are good at maths or music. | ☑ | ☐ | "Chinese parents […] produce so many math whizzes and music prodigies" (ll. 1–3) |
| b) The author's daughters are successful. | ☐ | ☐ | |
| c) The author's children had to be the best at every subject. | ☐ | ☐ | |

| | | | |
|---|---|---|---|
| d) The white man from South Dakota is half Chinese. | ☐ | ☐ | |
| e) Not all Chinese mothers follow the same principles. | ☐ | ☐ | |
| f) The differences between the Chinese and Western way of parenting are not real. | ☐ | ☐ | |
| g) You can't enjoy an activity if you are not good at it. | ☐ | ☐ | |
| h) When a Western child shows resistance, it is allowed to do something else. | ☐ | ☐ | |

2. The studies mentioned in the text show Western and Chinese attitudes towards parenting. Match the attitudes that were proved by the studies.

| Attitudes | Western parents | Chinese parents | Neither |
|---|---|---|---|
| a) Parents are responsible for teaching their children to enjoy learning. | ☐ | ☐ | ☐ |
| b) Academic success is the result of talent. | ☐ | ☐ | ☐ |
| c) All children can be successful. | ☐ | ☐ | ☐ |
| d) Everyone works for the honour of the family. | ☐ | ☐ | ☐ |
| e) It is the parents' fault if their children are not good at school. | ☐ | ☐ | ☐ |
| f) Sport is important. | ☐ | ☐ | ☐ |

**Text 2: *Battle Hymn of the Tiger Mother* by Amy Chua – Review**

[…] Amy Chua's book has hit a nerve. Her daughters are straight-A students and music prodigies, with the older daughter playing at Carnegie Hall at 14. Anything less would be a disgrace to the Tiger Mother.

__________ **[Gap 0]** __________ Chinese students do better in school than other nationalities, just about everywhere. This is not, of course, because we are innately cleverer than other people; we just work much, much harder. This is clear from the oppressively strict regime that Chua describes. She finds it strange that western parents cannot comprehend why her daughters should be required to devote every single afternoon, 365 days a year, to homework and music practice, with no sleep-overs, no playdates, no TV or computer games. __________ **[Gap 1]** __________ […]

But Chua's Chinese parenting backfired when her younger daughter Lulu cracked under her mother's non-stop pressure. She simply refused to obey, a huge crime for Chinese kids. Worse, she openly challenged her mother in public, screaming: "I don't want to be Chinese. Why can't you get that through your head? I hate the violin. I hate my life. I hate you, and I hate this family!" Chua did not mind her daughters hating her; as she constantly reminds them, her job is "to prepare you for the future – not to make you like me". __________ **[Gap 2]** __________

__________ **[Gap 3]** __________ She admits that she had moments of self-doubt, as when she suddenly felt a pang for Sophia, running home from school with an armful of books to have time for piano practice. __________ **[Gap 4]** __________ That was how Chua was brought up, and she was a great success – getting into Yale Law School and becoming a professor there, with a clever and loving husband and two equally clever children. She simply cannot understand what was wrong. __________ **[Gap 5]** __________ She sets the goals and goes for them: she even believed Coco, the family dog, had hidden talents and should be pushed to excel as a show dog – even if she eventually concluded that it was "perfectly fine for most dogs not to have a profession".

Chua's book would have benefited from more reflection. She says she does not know why she adopted the approach she did – it is just what Chinese families do. In fact, it goes back to the 2,500-year-old Confucian belief that education is superior and all else is inferior. For over a millennium, Chinese emperors chose officials to run China, from the county clerk to prime minister, out of the successful candidates in the imperial exam. __________ **[Gap 6]** __________

Chua is tough with her children because, like many Chinese people, she thinks of childhood as an investment – the most crucial one. […]

In helping to start a debate about what is good and what is missing in both Chinese and western parenting, this book has already served a purpose its author probably did not intend. Chua hammers western parenting, but she could learn from it too. And if she knew her Confucius, she would know that moderation in all things is the essence of Chinese culture. *496 words*

*From:* The Observer, *30 January 2011. By Sun Shuyun.*
*http://www.guardian.co.uk/books/2011/jan/30/battle-hymn-tiger-mother-review?INTCMP=SRCH*

### Aufgabenstellung Text 2

1. Read the text and choose from the sentences A–H the one which fits each gap. There is an example (Gap 0). Write the correct letters in the grid. There is one extra sentence that you do not need to use.

**A** Doing well would change your life and that of your family.

**B** But then, as Chua admits herself, she rarely reflects.

**C** Does she have regrets?

**D** And when they refuse to obey her, she makes them stand in the freezing cold, or threatens to give their toys to the Salvation Army.

**E** What inspires awe, however, is not the sheer force of maternal control.

**F** It's a familiar story.

**G** But they were rare, and only moments.

**H** Still, her defeat made her pause and take a step back.

| Gap 0 | Gap 1 | Gap 2 | Gap 3 | Gap 4 | Gap 5 | Gap 6 |
|---|---|---|---|---|---|---|
| F | | | | | | |

2. Multiple choice: Based on the text, tick the correct statements. Only one statement is correct in each item.

   a) Chinese people …
      - [ ] are not as intelligent as other people.
      - [ ] are more intelligent than other people.
      - [ ] achieve better results at school.
      - [ ] are better university students.

   b) When the author of the review says "we" (l. 5) she means …
      - [ ] we – the Chinese.
      - [ ] we – the British.
      - [ ] we – the Western parents.
      - [ ] we – the readers.

   c) "[…] she suddenly felt a pang for Sophia" (l. 19) means …
      - [ ] Sophia hurt herself when she ran home.
      - [ ] she didn't like her own methods.
      - [ ] she didn't think Sophia worked hard enough.
      - [ ] she was sorry for Sophia.

   d) Coco, the family dog …
      - [ ] is better than other dogs.
      - [ ] can do something that other dogs cannot.
      - [ ] is a normal dog.
      - [ ] is not liked by the author of the book.

3. Read the text and pay attention to the author's attitude towards Chua's parenting.

   a) Look for three passages in the text that show Sun Shuyun's attitude towards Amy Chua's parenting.
      (You do not have to copy the text, just note down the lines where you find the relevant quotes.)

      ______________________________________________

      ______________________________________________

      ______________________________________________

   b) Characterize her attitude in one sentence.

      ______________________________________________

      ______________________________________________

      ______________________________________________

## Textaufgabe

**Margaret Atwood, *The Handmaid's Tale***

*The novel "The Handmaid's Tale" is set in the north of the United States in the not too distant future. A fundamentalist regime has taken over; the official state doctrine is based on a literal understanding of the Old Testament. The new state is called the "Republic of Gilead".*

*Women have no rights and have to dress in a way that shows as little of their bodies as possible. People are strictly controlled by a secret police force called "the Eyes" (cf. l. 28). "Aunts" (cf. l. 30) are women who teach others the new doctrine.*

*The story is told by a woman named Offred, who in the following extract from the book is out shopping with her friend Ofglen. They meet a group of Japanese tourists and their guide.*

A group of people is coming towards us. They're tourists, from Japan it looks like, a trade delegation perhaps, on a tour of the historic landmarks or out for local color. They're diminutive and neatly turned out; each has his or her camera, his or her smile. They look around, bright-eyed, cocking their heads to one side like robins, their very cheerfulness aggressive, and I can't help staring. It's been a long time since I've seen skirts that short on women. The skirts reach just below the knee and the legs come out from beneath them, nearly naked in their thin stockings, blatant, the high-heeled shoes with their straps attached to the feet like delicate instruments of torture. The women teeter on their spiked feet as if on stilts, but off balance; their backs arch at the waist, thrusting the buttocks out. Their heads are uncovered and their hair too is exposed, in all its darkness and sexuality. They wear lipstick, red, outlining the damp cavities of their mouths, like scrawls on a washroom wall, of the time before.

I stop walking. Ofglen stops beside me and I know that she too cannot take her eyes off these women. We are fascinated, but also repelled. They seem undressed. It has taken so little time to change our minds, about things like this.

Then I think; I used to dress like that. That was freedom.

*Westernized*, they used to call it.

The Japanese tourists come towards us, twittering, and we turn our heads away too late: our faces have been seen.

There's an interpreter, in the standard blue suit and red-patterned tie, with the winged-eye tie pin. He's the one who steps forward, out of the group, in front of us, blocking our way. The tourists bunch behind him; one of them raises a camera.

"Excuse me," he says to both of us, politely enough. "They're asking if they can take your picture."

I look down at the sidewalk, shake my head for no. What they must see is the white wings only, a scrap of face, my chin and part of my mouth. Not the eyes. I know better than to look the interpreter in the face. Most of the interpreters are Eyes, or so it's said.

I also know better than to say yes. Modesty is invisibility, said Aunt Lydia. Never forget it. To be seen – to be seen – is to be – her voice trembled – penetrated. What you must be, girls, is impenetrable. She called us girls.

Beside me, Ofglen is also silent. She's tucked her red-gloved hands up into her sleeves, to hide them.

The interpreter turns back to the group, chatters at them in staccato. I know what he'll be saying, I know the line. He'll be telling them that the women here have different customs, that to stare at them through the lens of a camera is, for them, an experience of violation.

I'm looking down, at the sidewalk, mesmerized by the women's feet. One of them is wearing open-toed sandals, the toenails painted pink. I remember the smell of nail polish, the way it wrinkled if you put the second coat on too soon, the satiny brushing of sheer pantyhose against the skin, the way the toes felt, pushed towards the opening in the shoe by the whole weight of the body. The woman with painted toes shifts from one foot to the other. I can feel her shoes, on my own feet. The smell of nail polish has made me hungry.

"Excuse me," says the interpreter again, to catch our attention. I nod, to show I've heard him.

"He asks, are you happy," says the interpreter. I can imagine it, their curiosity: *Are they happy? How can they be happy?* I can feel their bright black eyes on us, the way they lean a little forward to catch our answers, the women especially but the men too: we are secret, forbidden, we excite them.

Ofglen says nothing. There is a silence. But sometimes it's as dangerous not to speak.

"Yes, we are very happy", I murmur. I have to say something. What else can I say?

*692 words*



**Aufgabenstellung**

1. Summarize the text.
2. Analyse the narrator's feelings.
3. Re-tell the passage from a tourist's point of view.
4. Explain the effect of the last line.

## Lösungsvorschläge

### Leseverstehen

#### Aufgabenstellung Text 1

1. *Scan the text for key words (or synonyms for key words) from the given statements. When you have found the relevant passage in the text, compare text and statement carefully before you make your decision.*
   *Possible key words:*
   *a) maths, music (example)*
   *b) successful, daughters*
   *c) best (synonym: #1), subject*
   *d) South Dakota, Chinese*
   *e) Chinese, mothers, same principles (synonym: "be a Chinese mother")*
   *f) differences, parenting*
   *g) enjoy (synonym: be fun), be good at sth.*
   *h) resistance, Western, child*

| Statement | True | False | Evidence |
|---|---|---|---|
| a) A lot of Chinese children are good at maths or music. | ☑ | ☐ | "Chinese parents […] produce so many math whizzes and music prodigies" (ll. 1–3) |
| b) The author's daughters are successful. | ☑ | ☐ | "people wonder how Chinese parents raise […] successful kids" (l. 1); "I've done it" (l. 4) |
| c) The author's children had to be the best at every subject. | ☐ | ☑ | "be the #1 student in every subject except gym and drama" (l. 13) |
| d) The white man from South Dakota is half Chinese. | ☐ | ☑ | "I'm using the term 'Chinese mother' loosely" (l. 16); "his working-class father had definitely been a Chinese mother" (l. 18) |
| e) Not all Chinese mothers follow the same principles. | ☑ | ☐ | "I know some mothers of Chinese heritage, […], who are not Chinese mothers" (ll. 20/21) |
| f) The differences between the Chinese and Western way of parenting are not real. | ☐ | ☑ | "there are […] studies […] showing marked and quantifiable differences between Chinese and Westerners when it comes to parenting" (ll. 22–24) |

| | | | |
|---|---|---|---|
| g) You can't enjoy an activity if you are not good at it. | ☑ | ☐ | "nothing is fun until you're good at it" (l. 35) |
| h) When a Western child shows resistance, it is allowed to do something else. | ☑ | ☐ | "because the child will resist [...] which is where Western parents tend to give up" (ll. 38/39) |

2. *Scan the text for key words from the given statements. There are two statements that you can attribute neither to Western nor to Chinese parents. You might not find these statements in the text at all.*
*If you have difficulty in finding the relevant passages, use the following hints:*
- *a): ll. 26/27*
- *b): –*
- *c): ll. 28/29*
- *d): –*
- *e): ll. 29–31*
- *f): ll. 33/34*

*Check whose opinion is expressed in these passages and tick the appropriate box.*

| **Attitudes** | **Western parents** | **Chinese parents** | **Neither** |
|---|---|---|---|
| a) Parents are responsible for teaching their children to enjoy learning. | ☑ | ☐ | ☐ |
| b) Academic success is the result of talent. | ☐ | ☐ | ☑ |
| c) All children can be successful. | ☐ | ☑ | ☐ |
| d) Everyone works for the honour of the family. | ☐ | ☐ | ☑ |
| e) It is the parents' fault if their children are not good at school. | ☐ | ☑ | ☐ |
| f) Sport is important. | ☑ | ☐ | ☐ |

## Aufgabenstellung Text 2

1. *Read the whole text first and try to understand the gist. To decide which sentence fits into which gap, pay attention to the paragraphs preceding and following the gap. Look for words and phrases from the sentences that are referred to in the passages surrounding the gap. Start with the sentence you feel most sure about.*
   - *Gap 0: The preceding paragraph sums up the "story" of Amy Chua's family.*
   - *Gap 1: The sentence before the gap outlines the children's duty. The reader might expect to find out what will happen in case the children do not fulfill these duties.*
   - *Gap 2: Look for the content that Chua refers to when she talks about 'defeat'.*
   - *Gap 3: Look for a sentence that goes with "self-doubt" (l. 18).*
   - *Gap 4: The "moments of self-doubt" (l. 18) are referred to again.*
   - *Gap 5: Look for expressions that match "understand what was wrong" (l. 23).*
   - *Gap 6: Look for a neutral statement, i. e. a sentence that does not refer to Amy Chua and her family.*

   *The sentence you do not need is E.*

| Gap 0 | Gap 1 | Gap 2 | Gap 3 | Gap 4 | Gap 5 | Gap 6 |
|---|---|---|---|---|---|---|
| F | D | H | C | G | B | A |

2. *Look for relevant passages in the text. If you have problems, use these hints:*
   *a) lines 4–6*
   *b) lines 4/5*
   *c) "pang"(l. 19) means 'feeling of pain'*
   *d) lines 24–27*

   a) Chinese people …
   - ☐ are not as intelligent as other people.
   - ☐ are more intelligent than other people.
   - ☑ achieve better results at school.
   - ☐ are better university students.

   b) When the author of the review says "we" (l. 5) she means …
   - ☑ we – the Chinese.
   - ☐ we – the British.
   - ☐ we – the Western parents.
   - ☐ we – the readers.

c) "[…] she suddenly felt a pang for Sophia" (l. 19) means …

- [ ] Sophia hurt herself when she ran home.
- [ ] she didn't like her own methods.
- [ ] she didn't think Sophia worked hard enough.
- [x] she was sorry for Sophia.

d) Coco, the family dog, …

- [ ] is better than other dogs.
- [ ] can do something that other dogs cannot.
- [x] is a normal dog.
- [ ] is not liked by the author of the book.

3. *In this task you do not only have to show that you understand the text, but you also have to interpret and explain the author's attitude.*
   *The following passages show the author's opinion about Amy Chua's parenting:*
   - *"Chua's book would have benefited from more reflection" (l. 28)*
   - *"Chua hammers western parenting, but she could learn from it too" (ll. 38/39)*
   - *"And if she knew her Confucius, she would know that moderation in all things is the essence of Chinese culture." (ll. 39/40)*

   a) l. 28, ll. 38/39, ll. 39/40

   b) In contrast to Amy Chua, the author of the review, Sun Shuyun, thinks that you should not see Chinese parenting as the only possibility, but some aspects of Western parenting are also worth considering.

## Textaufgabe

1. *In task 1 follow the rules for writing a summary. Make sure you bring out the characteristic element of the text: It is told by a first-person narrator, who shows her true thoughts and feelings only to the reader but not to the people around her. Your summary might read like this:*

The text is an extract from Margaret Atwood's novel, *The Handmaid's Tale*. It is set in the future and plays in the north of the USA, which is now ruled by a fundamentalist regime and has been renamed the "Republic of Gilead".
The story is told by a first-person narrator, a woman called Offred. She is out shopping with another woman when they meet a group of Japanese tourists. The way those tourists dress and use make-up reminds Offred of her own life before Gilead. When the tourists ask questions through their interpreter, Offred responds as a woman in Gilead is supposed to: she refuses to have her photo taken, does not show her face, but declares that she is happy. Her thoughts, however, which she communicates only to the reader, make it clear that she does not mean what she says but is acting out of fear of the "Eyes", the secret police of that state.

2. *Task 2 asks you to take a detailed look at the text and find what is said "between the lines". It is always a good idea to look out for relevant quotations first. You will find:*
   - *"fascinated, but also repelled" (l. 15)*
   - *"I know better than ..." (ll. 27/28 and 30)*
   - *"... has made me hungry" (l. 45)*
   - *"dangerous" (l. 52)*

   *Your answer might read like this:*

The narrator describes her feelings with the words "fascinated, but also repelled" (l. 15). Seeing the tourist women move around and talk freely, wearing what they like makes her jealous and long for a past in which she might have been one of them.
At the same time, however, she feels "repelled" (l. 15). Although she used to dress just like those tourists before the Gilead regime took over, she is shocked by what looks now almost like nakedness to her. With some surprise she realizes that it "has taken so little time to change our minds" (l. 16).
Besides, Offred seems to live in fear of the secret police. Twice she says "I know better than ..." (ll. 27/28 and 30). She has been trained to follow the rules. The text does not explain what might happen to her otherwise, but the word "dangerous" (l. 52) implies that any unorthodoxy is likely to get her in serious trouble.

3. *Task 3 requires you to assume a role. Do not just start writing. First read the text carefully to find clues which help you to form an idea of the person whose perspective you are supposed to take. You will find:*
   - *"They're asking ..." (l. 24); women in the street must be a rare sight in Gilead, otherwise Offred and her friend would not receive so much attention. The visitors act politely – they do not just take out their cameras and start clicking away.*
   - *"He asks, are you happy" (l. 48); this is a very personal question – the visitors seem to doubt whether women in Gilead can really be happy*
   - *"... secret, forbidden, we excite them" (l. 51); to foreign visitors life in Gilead seems to have an exotic fascination*

   *Your answer might read like this:*

   During our stay in Gilead we went on a guided tour around one of their cities one morning. We had a local guide who was fairly fluent in our language. It was fascinating to see how different life in that country has become. We had heard that women rarely leave their houses, and if they do, they are dressed so that one can hardly see their faces.
   Suddenly we saw two women walking along the street. Most of our group just could not help staring at such a rare sight. They seemed to notice and looked shy and embarrassed. When one of our group asked them whether he could take a photo, one of them shook her head. Our guide explained that to be photographed means an experience of violation for those women – in a sense they feel raped by being stared at through the lens of a camera.
   Somehow we were all strangely fascinated by those women, who were so very different from us. One of our group just could not help asking them very directly if they were happy. Our interpreter translated and one of the women answered, barely audibly, but I could make out a clear "yes".
   The experience has left a lasting impression on me. It has taught me not to judge too quickly and to respect other cultures – however different they may be from ours.

4. *Task 4 takes you back to the main character again. You will have realized by now the strong contrast between her feelings and the impression she creates to observers from the outside. The last line mainly indicates her resignation to a fate which she could not avoid and which she has no hope of changing.*
   *Your answer might read like this:*

   The last line, especially Offred's final question, "What else can I say?" (l. 54) are a strong expression of the utter hopelessness of the narrator's situation. She used to live in a "westernized" (l. 18) culture similar to that of the Japanese tourists, and her memories make her "hungry" (l. 45), but now she is caught up in a situation and kept there obviously by force.
   This arouses the reader's pity and sympathy and makes us critical towards simple explanations of "cultural differences".

## Gymnasium Niedersachsen – Englisch
## Abiturähnliche Übungsaufgabe 3

### Leseverstehen

#### Text 1: Multiculturalism: not a minority problem

*Multiculturalism has made progress in Britain – but white reticence is still the stumbling block*

Notices of the death of multiculturalism began in Britain as far back as 1989, with the Salman Rushdie/*Satanic Verses* affair. It became clear that the minority-majority faultline was not going to be simply about colour racism, and that the definition of multiculturalism could not be confined to "steelbands, saris and samosas". For some liberals that meant an end to their support for the concept, as angry Muslims muscled in on something that was intended only for the likes of gay people or black youth. Their protests were supported as "right on", but a passionate religious identity was too multicultural for many.

And yet, a decade on political multiculturalism flourished as Labour came to accept ethno-religious communitarianism as it had previously accepted other assertive identity movements. The sanctioning of faith schools, religious discrimination legislation, bringing Muslims into the networks of governance – all these happened well after the original "death of multiculturalism". Indeed, some occurred after 9/11 and 7/7, events that were also meant to have killed it. [...]

After all, many worry about residential segregation and inward-looking communities. But population distribution could only be achieved by, to coin a phrase, muscular illiberalism. Residential concentrations result more from fear of racism and "white flight" than self-ghettoisation. Research shows that all minorities – including Muslims – want to live in mixed neighbourhoods, and ghettos are created by those who move out.

It is individual or institutional choices, then, that create outcomes – multiculturalist or otherwise. Schools that choose their pupils, like faith schools, are less ethnically mixed than where pupils are allocated places by local authorities. The expansion of faith schools and indeed the "big society" concept in general – in so far as it hands over resources and decision-making to neighbourhoods, communities, charities and organised religion – should see the development, not the decline, of ethno-religious communitarianism.

Unlike Cameron I call that "multiculturalism" and I am in favour of it, with certain conditions. One is that it must be within a context of robust individual rights. Society cannot be reduced to individuals, and so integration must be about bringing new communities, and not just new individuals, into relations of equal respect. This means challenging racism and Islamophobia and so on, not by denying that there are groups in society but by developing positive group identities and adapting customs and institutions that enable that.

[…] Multiculturalism is incomplete and one-sided without a continual remaking of national identity.

This aspect has been understated, and so the inattentive assume that multiculturalism is all about emphasising difference and separatism. In fact it's about creating a new, ongoing "We" out of all the little, medium-sized and large platoons that make up the country.

In Britain we have made some progress. […] Even today ethnic minorities are more likely than white people to say they are British. It is white reticence, not minority separatism, that is an obstacle to an inclusive national identity; without overcoming this, multicultural nation-building is difficult. *488 words*

*From:* The Guardian, *7 February 2011. By Tariq Modood.*
*http://www.guardian.co.uk/commentisfree/2011/feb/07/multiculturalism-not-minority-problem*

**Annotation:**
2 Salman Rushdie's fourth novel, *The Satanic Verses* (1988), caused massive protests from Muslims in several countries as especially conservative Muslims felt that certain passages in the book ridiculed their religion.

## Aufgabenstellung Text 1

1. Read the statements below (a–e) and the text. Decide whether the statements are true or false. Then give evidence from the text to confirm or disprove the ideas given in the statements.

| Statement | True | False | Evidence |
|---|---|---|---|
| a) At the end of the 1980s the concept of multiculturalism was abandoned by some liberals. | ☐ | ☐ | |
| b) In the 1980s most liberals thought Muslims should have the same basic rights as gay people. | ☐ | ☐ | |
| c) The event of 9/11 caused the death of multiculturalism in Britain. | ☐ | ☐ | |

| | | | |
|---|---|---|---|
| d) Residential segregation is the result of minorities not wanting to live in mixed neighbourhoods. | ☐ | ☐ | |
| e) Schools are more ethnically mixed when they do not choose their pupils. | ☐ | ☐ | |

2. Answer the following questions in no more than ten words per aspect. Use your own words.

| **Question** | **Answer** |
|---|---|
| a) What are the conditions that would bring about multiculturalism in a positive sense according to the author? Name three of them. | •<br>•<br>• |
| b) Which group makes it the most difficult to create a feeling of national identity? | |
| c) What reason is given for this behaviour? | |

## Text 2: What Britons really think about immigration

*New study shows that economic pessimism has led many to feel negative about immigrants – but findings are not all bad news.*

**0** "Fear and Hope", the report Searchlight Educational Trust is publishing on attitudes to immigration, identity and multiculturalism, gives those of us committed to the fight against extremism nowhere to hide. The survey of 5,000 people, the largest of its kind ever conducted, is stark, brutal and unequivocal.
Some 39 % of Asian Britons, 34 % of white Britons and 21 % of black Britons now believe all immigration into the UK should be stopped permanently, or at least until the UK's economic situation improves. Meanwhile, 52 % of Britons agree with the proposition "Muslims create problems in the UK", and 43 % of Asian Britons, 63 % of white Britons and 17 % of black Britons agree with the proposition that "on the whole, immigration into Britain has been a bad thing for the country". In addition, 48 % of Britons say they would consider supporting a new far right-wing party, if it shunned violence and fascist imagery.

**1** These findings will be shocking to many. They shatter many of our liberal preconceptions. And they demonstrate conclusively that when it comes to the narrative of migration and race, our politicians and our community leaders are now running far behind those they seek to represent.

**2** A new politics of identity, culture, and nation has grown out of the politics of race and immigration, and is increasingly the opinion driver in modern British politics. There are now in effect six "identity tribes" in our society. These are: confident multiculturalists (8 % of the population); mainstream liberals (16 %); identity ambivalents (28 %); cultural integrationists (24 %); latent hostiles (10 %); and active enmity (13 %).
The cherished "middle ground" of British politics is occupied by two of these groups; the cultural integrationists, motivated by authority and order; and identity ambivalents, who are concerned about their economic security and social change. Together they make up 52 % of the population.

**3** The current failure of the political mainstream risks pushing the identity ambivalents to the right, unless they tackle the social and economic insecurity which dominates their attitudes. This is a challenge for the current government – which is implementing deep spending cuts – and for the Labour Party, which is the traditional home of many of these voters. Almost half of all voters who do not identify with a party are identity ambivalents.

**4** Our report reveals a clear correlation between economic pessimism and negative attitudes towards immigration. The more pessimistic people are about their own economic situation and their prospects for the future, the more hostile their attitudes are to new and old immigrants. [...] Despite the challenging nature of the report, there is much which is positive. Political violence is strongly opposed. Over two-thirds of people view "English nationalist extremists" and "Muslim extremists" as bad as each other. There is a real appetite for a positive campaigning organisation that opposes political extremism through bringing communities together.

**5** But at its heart, "Fear and Hope" exposes the dangers that lie ahead if the issues highlighted in the research are not addressed. It throws down a challenge to the political parties to really understand what is happening in the body politic and then do something about it.

The future is unwritten and it is all to play for. If we can understand the new politics of identity, then we can win them over. If we fail to do so then we risk their fear turning to hate. It is the challenge we all face, and one we can no longer afford to ignore.

*585 words*

*From:* The Guardian, *26 February 2011. By Nick Lowles.*
*http://www.guardian.co.uk/uk/2011/feb/26/britons-immigration-multiculturalism-study*

## Aufgabenstellung Text 2

Read the text and choose from the headlines A–H the one which fits each paragraph (0–5). Have a look at the example (paragraph 0) first.
Write the correct letter in the grid.
There are two extra headlines that you do not need.

**A** Authorities and representatives out of touch with voters

**B** Multiculturalism has huge impact on public opinion

**C** Immigrants facing tough times in the UK

**D** British nation's hard luck attributed to immigrants' presence

**E** Radical attitudes widely rejected

**F** Politicians need to take action to prevent swing to the right

**G** Recent study asks political parties for immediate action

**H** The richer, the more racist

| Paragraph | 0 | 1 | 2 | 3 | 4 | 5 |
|---|---|---|---|---|---|---|
| Headline | D | | | | | |

## Textaufgabe

**Ban Ki-moon, "Clean Industrial Revolution"**
(Durban, South Africa, 6 December 2011)

I am pleased to see such a diverse group here today.

One of the main lessons I have learned during my five years as Secretary-General is that broad partnerships are the key to solving broad challenges.

When governments, the United Nations, businesses, philanthropies and civil society work hand-in-hand, we can achieve great things.

We have seen it in the field of women's and children's health and in scaling up food nutrition.

And we are applying the same proven approach to energy.

Energy is central to everything we do.

It cuts across all sectors of government and lies at the heart of a country's core interests.

Energy also lies at the heart of our efforts to avoid dangerous climate change.

It is central to achieving the Millennium Development Goals.

It is key to sustainable development.

The world population now stands at 7 billion people – and rising.

Forty per cent of these people still lack access to modern forms of energy.

They are the energy poor.

Energy poverty means children cannot study at night.

Clinics and hospitals cannot offer quality healthcare.

Businesses and economies cannot grow in the dark.

We need to tackle energy poverty.

Yet the clear and present danger of climate change means we cannot burn our way to prosperity.

We already rely too heavily on fossil fuels.

We need to find a new, sustainable path to the future we want.

We need a clean industrial revolution.

Last year, the United Nations General Assembly passed a resolution declaring 2012 the International Year of Sustainable Energy for All.

I was 'energized' by that resolution.

This September, I launched my Sustainable Energy for All Initiative.

It is gathering the broad-based support we need from emerging economies, developing countries, developed countries, the private sector and civil society.

To help to develop an Action Agenda and catalyze action on the ground, I have appointed a High Level Group on Sustainable Energy for All.

The Group includes global leaders from business, finance, governments and civil society around the world.

I am calling for action around three objectives, all to be achieved by 2030.

First: to ensure universal access to modern energy services.

Second: to double the rate of improvement of energy efficiency.

Third: to double the share of renewable energy in the global energy mix.

Taken together, these sustainable development goals will enhance equity, revitalise the global economy, and help protect our ecosystems.

Next month marks the launch of the International Year of Sustainable Energy for All.

I will be at the World Future Energy Summit in Abu Dhabi where we will preview a framework of our global Action Agenda.

Six months later, at Rio + 20 UN Conference on Sustainable Development, we will announce commitments from the private sector, governments and civil society that will drive our agenda forward.

Many of you in this room today are from the private sector. You are here because you realise that business as usual is no longer viable.

You can contribute to Sustainable Energy for All by making your companies, practices and supply chains more efficient.

And you can put the weight of your investment behind innovation.

Many are already doing so.

A newly released study found that, last year, for the first time, renewable energy surpassed fossil fuels in new power-plant investments.

Investments in electricity from wind, sun, waves and biomass outpaced natural gas, oil and coal by almost 20 per cent.

This is encouraging news.

Despite a difficult economic climate, companies and investors are seeing the long-term benefits in the renewable energy sector.

Here at Durban, we are asking governments to take the same long view – to invest in our common future by making progress towards a comprehensive binding climate agreement that is fair to all.

Fair to business, that needs a solid market framework.

Fair to developed and developing economies alike.

And fair to the poorest and most vulnerable people of our planet who stand to be hit first and worst by the increasing impacts of climate change.

Here in Durban, I urge all to take the long view, for the sake of the future we want.

Thank you.

*685 words*

*From: http://www.un.org/apps/news/infocus/sgspeeches/search_full.asp?statID=1407*

**Aufgabenstellung**

Imagine you have been invited to take part in a panel discussion at an international summer school on the issue "How can we save the world?" As Ban Ki-moon's speech is the latest contribution to this issue, you use this text to prepare yourself for the debate. You need to work with the text to be able to use certain aspects for your own arguments.

1. Explain the author's attitude towards sustainable sources of energy.
2. Analyse the way Ban Ki-moon structures his speech in order to convince the audience of his point of view.
   You should also keep an eye on the language he uses.
3. Comment on Ban Ki-moon's point of view.

## Lösungsvorschläge

## Leseverstehen

### Aufgabenstellung Text 1

1. *Read the statements first and then scan the text for key words. The statements are in chronological order. When you have found the relevant passage, compare text and statement carefully. Do not quote the whole statement. You should use only a limited amount of words per point of evidence and indicate where you have got the information from by giving lines. Possible key words:*
   *a) multiculturalism, concept*
   *b) Muslims, gay people*
   *c) 9/11, multiculturalism*
   *d) residential segregation, minorities*
   *e) schools, ethnically mixed*

| Statement | True | False | Evidence |
|---|---|---|---|
| a) At the end of the 1980s the concept of multiculturalism was abandoned by some liberals. | ☑ | ☐ | "[The] death of multiculturalism began in Britain as far back as 1989" (l. 1);<br>"For some liberals that meant an end to their support for the concept [i. e. multiculturalism]" (ll. 4/5) |
| b) In the 1980s most liberals thought Muslims should have the same basic rights as gay people. | ☐ | ☑ | "Muslims muscled in on something […] intended only for the likes of gay people or black youth. Their protests were supported as 'right on' but a passionate religious identity was too multicultural for many." (ll. 5–8) |
| c) The event of 9/11 caused the death of multiculturalism in Britain. | ☐ | ☑ | "The sanctioning of faith schools, religious discrimination legislation […] occurred after 9/11" (ll. 11–13) |
| d) Residential segregation is the result of minorities not wanting to live in mixed neighbourhoods. | ☐ | ☑ | "Residential concentrations result more from fear of racism and 'white flight' than self-ghetto-isation" (ll. 17/18) |
| e) Schools are more ethnically mixed when they do not choose their pupils. | ☑ | ☐ | "Schools that choose their pupils […] are less ethnically mixed than where pupils are allocated places by local authorities." (ll. 21/22) |

2. *In this case, you need to make sure you have found the right passage in the text. You can answer the questions one after the other as they are in chronological order. Again, key words might prove helpful. Answering the questions in complete sentences is not required; bullet points would be sufficient.*
*Useful key words:*
*a) conditions, positive attitude towards multiculturalism (ll. 28–33)*
*b) sense of national identity (cf. ll. 41–43)*
*c) national identity (l. 42)*

| Question | Answer |
|---|---|
| a) What are the conditions that would bring about multiculturalism in a positive sense according to the author? Name three of them. | • individual rights should be guaranteed to everyone (cf. l. 28)<br>• different groups should respect each other (cf. ll. 29/30)<br>• individual groups should develop their own identity (by cherishing their traditions and establishing their authorities) (cf. ll. 32/33) |
| b) Which group makes it the most difficult to create a feeling of national identity? | white British people (cf. ll. 41/42) |
| c) What reason is given for this behaviour? | white British people's reluctance to identify with a multicultural society (cf. ll. 41–43) |

## Aufgabenstellung Text 2

*For this task, you first need to read the headlines carefully. Then go through the text paragraph by paragraph. Sum up each paragraph in your own words. Then go through the headlines and pick the one that matches your own suggestion. Make sure to read the two statements that are still left when you have completed the task and check whether you have made the right choices. Watch out: Sometimes it is one word that makes the headline inapplicable to a paragraph.*

| Paragraph | 0 | 1 | 2 | 3 | 4 | 5 |
|---|---|---|---|---|---|---|
| Headline | D | A | B | F | E | G |

## Textaufgabe

1. *Explaining the author's attitude requires that you focus on the main aspects of the text and give a brief explanation of the facts.*
*Your answer should contain the following ideas:*
- *climate change the more dangerous as world population on the rise*
- *caution required concerning use of energy resources*
- *investment in renewable energy necessary*
- *climate agreement to join forces with all businesses and governments involved*

In Ban Ki-moon's view, using sustainable sources of energy ought to be a matter of common interest as further climate change will only aggravate the problem of world population growth.
According to him the world needs to take care of the energy resources which are still left. Meanwhile, businesses focus too much on fossil fuels (cf. l. 24). Ban urges them to start "a clean industrial revolution" (l. 26) instead. This means that companies should increase their efforts to invest in renewable sources of energy such as wind, sun, water power or biomass (cf. l. 58) and rely less on traditional sources of energy such as fossil fuels. In his opinion, all parties concerned – businesses, society and the environment (cf. ll. 41/42 and 66–69) – could only benefit from such a development. Ban feels that a climate agreement is necessary to make governments and businesses keep their promise to support his mission. For this reason, he has already announced new summit meetings (cf. ll. 45–49), set an agenda (cf. ll. 37–40) and appointed a group of experts to coordinate the measures taken and work on realising his goals (cf. l. 34).
Finally, he stresses the fact that focusing on traditional energy resources might prove to be short-sighted and dangerous. Therefore, people need to increase their efforts to invest in renewable sources of energy such as wind, sun and water power.

2. *This task aims at analysing how Ban Ki-moon delivers his speech by structuring his text meaningfully. You should pay attention to the language used as well. As his speech is mainly designed to be listened to and not to be read, he puts emphasis on repeating words and phrases in order to make sure that his audience remembers his central ideas afterwards. The key points are:*
- *reminding the audience of successful projects in the past: future projects likely to have the same success*
- *need of support and cooperation concerning sustainable sources of energy: repetition of issue throughout the speech*
- *mentioning of a to-do list, announcement of summit meetings: seriousness of issue requires immediate action*
- *urging of governments to invest in renewable energy*
- *use of "fair": repetition, emphasis*

At the beginning of his speech he wants to show the audience that there have been several common projects – such as women's and children's health and improved nutrition (cf. ll. 6/7) – which have been quite successful due to joint efforts of various bodies. These examples are intended to encourage the audience to take joint action again in order to tackle the problem of a deteriorating climate threatening the life of mankind.

This is when the concept of sustainable sources of energy becomes his central issue. It is his constant fear that global warming might aggravate the already tense situation due to overpopulation on earth: energy poverty seems to be the crucial point when it comes to solving health problems, poor business development and low living standards in developing countries (cf. ll. 10–21). He makes it clear to his audience that energy is a key source to which all humans should have access – preferably in an environmentally friendly way, too. To stress the urgency of the matter, he gives proof of his being "energized" (l. 29) by the issue: he provides an outlook on future summit meetings that will be held on this topic, presents a to-do list (cf. ll. 37–40) and has already named an expert group to "catalyze action on the ground" (l. 33).

Furthermore, he keeps repeating certain phrases over and over again, such as "energy poor" (l. 17)/"energy poverty" (ll. 18, 21); "Sustainable Energy for All" (ll. 28, 30, 34, 43/44, 52), "fair" (ll. 65–68) and "climate change" (ll. 12, 22, 69). This serves diverse purposes: by mentioning climate change again and again he wants to make people focus on a common aim, to cooperate in order to overcome the danger of climate change.

Furthermore, he would like his audience to understand that without tackling the issue of energy poverty, a lot of other problems (such as health issues) in developing countries cannot be solved either because they, too, depend on energy. To be able to join forces, a common goal is needed, which he refers to as "Sustainable Energy for All". To make the audience remember that term, it is repeated constantly throughout the speech.

As it is Ban's aim to increase investment in renewable sources of energy, he stresses that businesses will not regret contributing to the common aim as all parties concerned can only benefit from the arrangement (cf. ll. 66–69). For the same reason he urges governments to make long-term investments as he needs all the money and support he can get for his project (cf. ll. 63–65).

3. *Have a look at task 1 again. It sums up briefly Ban Ki-moon's opinion and explains the most important points of his speech. You are expected to give convincing reasons for your own opinion in reaction to Ban's point of view. Refer to the statements given in the text and then present your own ideas. The arguments given below could be part of an exemplary answer supporting Ban's view:*
   - *avoiding further global warming and its dangerous consequences (e. g. flooding, hurricanes)*
   - *facing our responsibility towards future generations*
   - *global players joining individual efforts*

In Ban Ki-moon's view, using renewable sources of energy is essential so that global warming does not further increase. For my part I can only say that I share his opinion completely. In the long run this is the only answer to tackling the problem of global warming with all its devastating consequences such as flooding or hurricanes. That we will have to deal with natural hazards as a consequence of global warming is quite evident, as it has been proved by several scientific long-term studies already.

Additionally we carry responsibility for future generations. Luckily, there is still time to take countermeasures that will help us live in a clean and healthy environment. The first steps in the right direction have already been made, for example, the creation of hybrid cars, the increasing support for the sorting of waste and the collecting of used batteries in supermarket chains, not to mention the ban on styrofoam dishes at McDonald's in Europe in the nineties. All this should encourage us to continue to follow the path taken. Nevertheless, we should not get tired of making more and more people aware of the current situation and demanding their willingness to take action immediately.

Still, all individual efforts are bound to come to nothing if the big companies and national governments do not contribute to the common goal. This is why the commitment of influential people like Ban is essential to achieve the promised "clean industrial revolution". It is all the more encouraging knowing that global players are going to join in the effort of making our world a better place to live in. Then we will have a good chance to look optimistically into the future.

## Sprachmittlung

### Text 1: Kulturschock in Indien […]

*Das Neugeborene darf nicht ausreisen, weil es keinen Einreisestempel hat – Gerd Höfner überraschen solche bürokratischen Hürden nicht mehr. Seit zehn Jahren leitet er das IT-Büro von Siemens in Bangalore, 4500 Inder arbeiten dort. Seine erste Frage an neue Mitarbeiter würde er in Deutschland nicht stellen.*

„Als ich vor zehn Jahren das Angebot bekam, für Siemens in Bangalore die Software-Entwicklung zu übernehmen, war mir schnell klar: Das mache ich, aber nur mit einem interkulturellen Training als Vorbereitung auf die indischen Gepflogenheiten. Ich hatte vorher nämlich eineinhalb Jahre für Siemens in Italien gearbeitet und war damals ins kalte Wasser gesprungen, ohne große Vorbereitung. Dieses Mal wollte ich es besser machen und schon vorher wissen, wie die indischen Mitarbeiter ticken, in welchem kulturellen Umfeld sie leben und welche Umgangsformen wichtig sind.

Das einwöchige Training hat mir viel gebracht. Was zum Beispiel sehr gut angekommen ist: Ich habe mich in Bangalore als Erstes mit allen Abteilungsleitern ausführlich über persönliche Dinge unterhalten. Bist du verheiratet? Wie viele Kinder hast du? Bei deutschen Mitarbeitern stehen beim ersten Kontakt ja rein berufliche Dinge im Vordergrund, bei indischen Mitarbeitern kommt die Familie für viele an erster Stelle und spielt auch für den Berufsalltag eine wichtige Rolle.

Es ist zum Beispiel ganz üblich, dass man sich eine berufliche Auszeit von mehreren Monaten nimmt, um sein Kind etwa beim Abitur zu unterstützen. Einer meiner Mitarbeiter arbeitet aus diesem Grund jetzt vier Wochen von zu Hause aus. Ich habe damit gute Erfahrungen gemacht. Die Arbeit wird genauso gut erledigt wie sonst auch.

[…] Im Alltag gibt es viele Kleinigkeiten, die anders laufen als in Deutschland. Ich fand zum Beispiel das Essen mit den Fingern am Anfang gewöhnungsbedürftig, aber es hat auch seine Vorteile: Man verbrennt sich nie die Zunge und durch das Anfassen erlebt man das Essen auf einer weiteren sinnlichen Ebene. […] Kultur ist eben nie gut oder schlecht, sondern nur anders.

Ebenfalls gewöhnungsbedürftig ist der Verkehr in Bangalore. Es gibt viele Staus, und rote Ampeln werden oft eher als Empfehlung gesehen. Für die 20 Kilometer von zu Hause ins Büro brauche ich mindestens eine Dreiviertelstunde, was mich aber nicht stört. Ich nutze die Zeit für E-Mails und zum Telefonieren.

Was ich in meinem Umfeld sehr schätze, ist die positive Grundhaltung. In der Regel gehen die Menschen sehr pragmatisch an Aufgaben heran und packen zu. Es herrscht eine regelrechte Aufbruchsstimmung. […]

Ich habe in Indien sehr viel gelernt, unter anderem, den Dingen gelassener entgegenzutreten. Zum Beispiel durfte meine Tochter nach der Geburt nicht aus Indien ausreisen, weil sie keinen Einreisestempel in ihrem Pass hatte. Wo sollte sie den auch her haben? Sie ist ja schließlich hier geboren. Es hat lange gedauert, die nötigen Papiere zu beschaffen, aber letztendlich hat es doch rechtzeitig funktioniert. So ist es mit den meisten Dingen: Irgendwann klappt es doch." *419 Wörter*

*Quelle:* Spiegel Online. *31. Juli 2012. Von Verena Töpper.*
*http://www.spiegel.de/karriere/ausland/arbeiten-in-indien-ein-siemens-manager-erzaehlt-vom-leben-in-bangalore-a-847231.html*

## Text 2: Unterrichten in Indien

*Englisch unterrichten im Ausland als Freiwilligendienst oder Praktikum an der Schule*

Du möchtest nach dem Abi einen Freiwilligendienst im Ausland machen? Oder du bist berufstätig und planst ein Sabbatjahr? Vielleicht studierst du auch auf Lehramt und suchst ein Praktikum an einer Schule im Ausland? Dann auf nach Indien! Im südlichen Bundesstaat Tamil Nadu kannst du an einer Schule ehrenamtlich Englisch unterrichten. Für das Unterrichts-Projekt benötigst du keine pädagogischen Vorkenntnisse, du solltest allerdings über gute Englisch-Kenntnisse verfügen und Einsatzbereitschaft mitbringen. […]

Die Schulen, an denen du in Indien unterrichten kannst, befinden sich in und um Madurai. Madurai ist die zweitgrößte Stadt in Tamil Nadu. […] Dort kannst du Schüler unterschiedlichen Alters unterrichten: Von den ganz Kleinen, die etwa drei Jahre alt sind, bis hin zu jungen Erwachsenen, die sich auf ihre Abschlussarbeit vorbereiten.

Die Unterrichtsmethoden an vielen Schulen in Indien sind recht starr, oft wird der Stoff abgeschrieben und auswendig gelernt. Vielleicht hast du ja kreative und innovative Ideen, die das Lernen leichter und den Unterricht angenehmer gestalten? Das Unterrichten beschränkt sich nicht nur auf Englisch. Auch Musik- und Sport-Unterricht sind als Ergänzung willkommen. Gerne kannst du […] auch Aktivitäten außerhalb des Lehrplans organisieren – beispielsweise ein Theater-Projekt.

Die Arbeitszeit an der Schule beläuft sich auf etwa 18 Stunden die Woche. Dazu kommt noch die Vorbereitungszeit für deinen Englisch-Unterricht. Die einzelnen Klassen sind unterschiedlich groß, im Durchschnitt unterrichtest du etwa 30 Schüler. […] *219 Wörter*

*Quelle: Projects Abroad, http://www.projects-abroad.de/ziellander/indien/unterrichten-in-indien/*

## Aufgabenstellung

Sie arbeiten in den Ferien bei einer Agentur, die die englischsprachige Website around-the-world.com unterhält. Diese Seite dient Arbeitgebern und Arbeitssuchenden als Kontaktplattform, u. a. für kurzfristige Jobangebote im Bereich „Work and Travel". Sie werden gebeten, einen Artikel über die Möglichkeiten zu schreiben, die Deutschen offenstehen, welche zeitweise in Indien arbeiten möchten. Geben Sie zusätzlich Ratschläge zum Umgang mit kulturellen Besonderheiten.
Exemplarisch sollten Sie sich dabei auf die Informationen der beiden obigen Texte stützen. Ihr Text sollte etwa 250 Wörter umfassen.

## Textaufgabe

**Text: The truth about Twitter, Facebook and the uprisings in the Arab world**
By Peter Beaumont

*Recent events in Libya, Tunisia and Egypt have been called 'Twitter revolutions' – but can social networking overthrow a government? […]*

Think of the defining image of the uprisings in the Middle East and North Africa. […] Instead, that defining image is this: a young woman or a young man with a smartphone. She's in the Medina in Tunis with a BlackBerry held aloft, taking a picture of a demonstration outside the prime minister's house. He is an angry Egyptian doctor in an aid station stooping to capture the image of a man with a head injury from missiles. […]

All of them are images that have found their way on to the internet through social media sites. […] Most often, though, [commentators] have tried to conceive [the images] through the media that informed them – as the result of WikiLeaks, as "Twitter revolutions" or inspired by Facebook. All of which, as American media commentator Jay Rosen has written, has generated an equally controversialist class of article in reply, most often written far from the revolutions. These stories are not simply sceptical about the contribution of social media, but determined to deny it has played any part. Those at the vanguard of this argument include Malcolm Gladwell in the New Yorker […] and even David Kravets of Wired.co.uk. […] All have argued one way or another that since there were revolutions before social media, and it is people who make revolutions, how could it be important?

Except social media has played a role. For those of us who have covered these events, it has been unavoidable.

Precisely how we communicate in these moments of historic crisis and transformation is important. The medium that carries the message shapes and defines as well as the message itself. The instantaneous nature of how social media communicate self-broadcast ideas, unlimited by publication deadlines and broadcast news slots, explains in part the speed at which these revolutions have unravelled, their almost viral spread across a region. It explains, too, the often loose and non-hierarchical organisation of the protest movements unconsciously modelled on the networks of the web.

Speaking recently to the Huffington Post, Rosen argued that those taking positions at either extreme of the debate were being lazy and inaccurate. "Wildly overdrawn claims about social media, often made with weaselly question marks (like: 'Tunisia's Twitter revolution?') and the derisive debunking that follows from those claims ('It's not that simple!') only appear to be opposite perspectives. […]

Rosen is right. […] For neither the notion of the "Twitter Revolutions" or their un-Twitterness, accurately reflects the reality. Often, the contribution of social networks to the Arab uprisings has been as important as it also has been complex, contradictory and misunderstood. […] In Egypt, details of demonstrations were circulated by both Facebook and Twitter. […] Then, the Mubarak regime […] pulled the plug on the country's internet services and 3 G network. What social media was replaced by then – oddly enough – was the analogue equivalent of Twitter: handheld signs held aloft at demonstrations saying where and when people should gather the next day.

Sultan Al Qassemi, a columnist based in the United Arab Emirates who has tweeted non-stop on the uprisings, passing on information and English translations of key speeches, believes that some claims about the impact of social media need to be taken with a pinch of salt.

"Social media has certainly played a part in the Arab Spring Revolutions but its impact is often exaggerated on the inside. Egypt was disconnected from the outside world for days and yet the movement never stopped. [...]

Where social media had a major impact was conveying the news to the outside world, bloggers and Twitter users were able to transmit news bites that would otherwise never make it to mainstream news media. This information has been instrumental in garnering the attention of the citizens of the world who expressed solidarity with those suppressed individuals and may even put pressure on their own governments to react." [...]

The unedited and unmediated nature of the stories that have been told have led to inaccuracies, which have sometimes proven beneficial to those opposing the regime. [...] And while it is unclear how the story came to be so widely believed, what is certain is that some people have planted material they believe is helpful, even if it is not true. Video of a demonstration – claimed to be a recent gathering in Iran – and placed on social media sites was actually a protest that occurred in 2009. The footage was unmasked as a fraud by Twitter users, ironically enough. [...]

For me it is a phenomena best summed up by an encounter I had with a group of young Tunisians I met during a demonstration on the day after my arrival in Tunis. I asked them what they were photographing with their phones. "Ourselves. Our revolution. We put it on Facebook," one replied laughing, as if it were a stupid question. "It's how we tell the world what's happening." *814 words*

*From:* The Guardian, *25 February 2011. By Peter Beaumont.*

**Annotations:**

5 to stoop: to bend down
24 to unravel: here: develop at high speed
30 weaselly: here: synonym for dishonest and hypocritical behaviour
31 derisive: making it clear through your behaviour that sb. or sth. is stupid, unimportant or useless
31 to debunk: to provide proof that sth., e. g. an information, is false or unreliable
37/38 to pull the plug: to stop an activity by not allowing it to continue
45 to take sth. with a pinch of salt: not believe sth. to be true without further proof
52 to garner: to collect a huge amount of sth. important

**Cartoon**

"...and do you solemnly swear to update your facebook status to 'married'?"

*© Huw Aaron/cartoonstock.com*

**Aufgabenstellung**

As a regular user of social networks you have been invited to take part in a class debate about social networks and their influence on modern society. With the article printed above in hand, you prepare yourself for the discussion by using the text and cartoon at hand.

1. Analyse the means the author uses to convince the reader of his opinion.
2. You want to find out whether the cartoon is a suitable illustration for the author's view as expressed in the text: Describe and analyse the cartoon.
3. You know that you will be confronted with different opinions about the necessity of using social networks in general. In a newspaper you see the following question: "Social media – A blessing or a curse?" Discuss.

## Sprachmittlung

*How to approach the task: First of all, decide on the target group and the purpose your text will be written for. That makes it easier to select the information that is truly relevant. Be prepared to explain words or ideas that are hard to understand from a different cultural perspective or for this special target group. It might be helpful to collect the most important aspects in German first. Afterwards you can write down your text in English. Keep in mind that you were asked to write an article. Thus, your mediation needs a logical structure, a catchy title and an introductory sentence.*
*Your text should contain the following information:*
- *description of the different possibilities of working abroad*
- *cultural peculiarities that will strike foreigners as different to what they are used to*
- *advice on how to deal with cultural differences and avoid misunderstandings*

**India offers both jobs and challenges**
If you are planning to spend some time working in India, there are of course many different possibilities. Big international companies such as Siemens, for example, have offshoots there and support their employees in gaining experience abroad. For students, teachers and anybody willing to face a challenge, there is another more flexible alternative: teaching pupils in Indian schools. Teachers will be working with up to 30 pupils from a vast range of ages, 3-year-olds to graduates. They are therefore expected to have a proficient command of English and be truly committed to the cause. Neither teaching experience nor pedagogical background knowledge are compulsory. On the contrary, creativity is most welcome to spice up the pupils' daily routine. The workload to be expected is 18 classes a week in addition to preparation time.
Besides the professional challenges, newcomers to India will be faced with a remarkably different culture. Thus, they need to be aware of intercultural differences to avoid offending people by mistake. For instance, in professional Indian life, family comes first. Instead of "talking shop", sharing private stories with colleagues is the done thing. Commuting to and from work can be a real hassle due to the traffic, so a relaxed attitude and open-mindedness are also quite helpful. The same applies to hot food and the humid climate – in general, the experience is best if people adapt and make do with what is already there. The positive Indian way of coping with challenges might set a good example.

## Textaufgabe

1. *Task 1 requires you to analyse the text. Therefore, you need to make sure that you have understood what the article is about. Then find out what the author wants to achieve by publishing his article. In the next step, you need to find out how he manages to achieve this. The following facts might help you:*
   *Position of the author: the impact of social media is highly exaggerated*
   - *Structural means:*
     - *experts are cited: supports the author's point of view*
     - *the author's own experiences in Tunis: makes the text vivid and authentic*
     - *arguments that either support the author's view or contradict it: objectivity*
     - *reader advised to maintain critical distance*
   - *Stylistic means:*
     - *quotes and facts: author seems reliable*
     - *negative adjectives for description of social media ("complex, contradictory and misunderstood" (ll. 35/36), "unedited and unmediated nature of the stories" (l. 55), "unavoidable" (l. 19), unreliable (cf. ll. 44/45)*
     - *personal opinion of the author*

In the author's view the influence of social media during the Arab uprising has been highly exaggerated. To support his opinion, he quotes two experts: an American media commentator, Jay Rosen, and a columnist from the United Arab Emirates (cf. ll. 11, 42). To boot, the author has been to Tunis himself, where he met a group of teenagers (cf. ll. 62–66). Citing experts, giving facts and including personal experience make his story vivid and authentic. The experts' comments show that people who have been working in and with social media share the author's point of view. Thus, he cannot be wrong.
Although the author considers social media unreliable, contradictory and often used to manipulate public opinion (cf. ll. 34–36, 55–61), he tries to be as objective as possible. Therefore, he mentions both arguments that support his view and those that contradict it. For example, the author believes that the whole information process in connection with the Arab uprising is too complex to be reduced to only one cause, i. e. social media (cf. ll. 34–36). To prove this, he quotes an expert who claims that while the access to the internet was blocked by government authorities, the Arab uprising did not dwindle (cf. ll. 46–48).
On the other hand, the author has to admit that social media can put pressure on national governments, which are then pushed by their citizens to take action (cf. ll. 51–54). Presenting all sides of the story, the author wants the reader to believe that the article has been researched properly and thoroughly and that the author is a journalist who can be trusted.
Still, the number of negative adjectives in connection with social media gives us more than just a clue about the tendency of the article: according to the many sources mentioned in the text, social media is "complex, contradictory and misunderstood" (ll. 35/36), the "unedited and unmediated nature of the stories" leads

"to inaccuracies" (ll. 55/56) and working with social media is as "unavoidable" (l. 19) as it is unreliable (cf. ll. 44/45).

Finally, the reader is advised to be careful with the amount of information available on social media. The author achieves this subtly at first by giving negative examples of how images and videos can be misinterpreted or are deliberately uploaded in order to give false evidence (cf. ll. 55–61). Additionally, he tells the reader about a conversation he had with a group of young Tunisians to illustrate that pictures taken of a demonstration could easily be misjudged by people who see them but have not been present at the event themselves.

The message to the reader is simple: It is important not to believe every item of news as there is no control over the internet other than by other users (cf. l. 61). So maintaining a critical distance to the information revealed, as expert Al Qassemi suggests (cf. ll. 42–45), is the right thing to do.

2. *Have a close look at the cartoon and describe what you see.*
   - *Happy couple in front of a man holding a book (the Bible: priest)*
   - *Situation: wedding ceremony*
   - *Special wedding vow: "… and do you solemnly swear to update your Facebook status to 'married'?"*

   *Then analyse the meaning of the cartoon:*
   - *Ironic display of a social development: social media as common phenomenon*
   - *Warning: Do we really want them to influence our lives to such an extent?*

The cartoon illustrates a wedding ceremony in a church. The bride and groom are standing happily in front of a clergyman, who seems to be holding the Bible in his hands. He has obviously asked them the usual questions which form part of the wedding vows. He has just added a new question: "Do you solemnly swear to update your Facebook status to 'married'?"

The couples' body language does not reveal any surprise or confusion. Therefore, the question does not seem to be unusual in modern times. The caption is quite ironic and makes the viewer laugh. The cartoonist wants to point out that social networks seem to have influenced us so much that we cannot do without them anymore. We have even stopped considering surfing social media sites for hours to be a strange way of spending our free time. They have already become part of our daily life. It is this strong dependency on social networks which is typical of our modern generation and which establishes a connection between the article and the cartoon. Although both media deal with completely different issues, it is the influence of social media such as Facebook that is blamed for negative social developments.

All in all, the cartoonist wants to warn us: Do we really want social media to influence our lives to such an extent that we cannot even do without them during our wedding ceremonies?

3. *Task 3 requires you to discuss whether social networks are a blessing or a curse. As you should take both sides into account, it is useful to collect arguments concerning the advantages and disadvantages of social networks.*
   *Your answer may include some of the following aspects:*
   - *Advantages:*
     - *staying in touch with family members and friends over long distances*
     - *informative way to spend one's time*
   - *Disadvantages:*
     - *danger of getting addicted to social networks*
     - *complete waste of time*
     - *danger of data being misused*

Most people around us use social media at least once a day. For many teenagers having to live without an internet connection is a major catastrophe and they do not know how to spend their free time differently – even if it is just for a few hours due to a power cut. Therefore, our society should urgently ask itself whether social media are a blessing or a curse for modern society.

First of all, it should be pointed out that social networks are a good way of staying in contact with friends or family members who live far away or maybe even in a different country. But in my opinion some people exaggerate the usage of social networks. They spend too much time on the web or send hundreds of messages a day. Instead they could meet their friends, talk to them face to face and spend the afternoon or evening in their company. However, more and more teenagers have lost interest in reality and prefer to spend the whole day in the virtual jungle of social networks.

Additionally, teenagers in particular are often not aware of the fact that it can even be dangerous to become too careless about using social networks. Several times, for example, teenagers have invited some friends to their house because their parents have planned to spend the evening somewhere else, but instead of a dozen people, whole crowds have arrived at the house and caused a lot of damage. All this happened because these teenagers completely underestimated Facebook's range and did not think of blocking everyone who did not belong to their closest circle of friends when sending a message of invitation. Just recently, a teenage girl was even murdered in the Netherlands because she had spread rumours on social networks about people she knew.

To boot, employers tend more and more to check on social networks before they offer a contract to a potential employee. They want to find out if the person can be trusted and how he or she behaves in public. If they consider the candidate's behaviour a potential disgrace to the company, this person does not stand a chance of getting the job. These are just some of the reasons why no kind of private data should ever be published on the web.

On the whole, it can be said that if you obey such rules and do not exaggerate social networking it can be amusing and a good pastime to enter a certain chat room and talk to different people or post messages on Facebook to stay in touch with friends and family members.

## Sprachmittlung

### Text 1: Der Tag der Steuersünderinnen

*Saudi-Arabien ist weltweit das einzige Land, in dem Frauen nicht Auto fahren dürfen. Heute wollen sich Aktivistinnen trotzdem ans Steuer setzen. Sie riskieren damit eine Festnahme durch die Religionspolizei – und einem Scheich zufolge Unfruchtbarkeit.*

1 Sie trägt Abaya, das schwarze lange Gewand, das die meisten Frauen in Saudi-Arabien in der Öffentlichkeit tragen, um den streng-religiösen Sitten im Land Genüge zu tun. Sie ist sogar vollverschleiert und beobachtet nur aus schmalen Sehschlitzen heraus den Stadtverkehr. Und dennoch ist Ajroush eine Gesetzesbrecherin, der schlimmstenfalls Gefängnis droht: Denn Ajroush sitzt gerade am Steuer ihres Wagens und kurvt eine Runde durch Riad.

Autofahren ist in Saudi-Arabien aber für Frauen verboten. „Für wie lange sollen wir noch in so einer bedenklichen Gesellschaft leben, die uns nicht unsere vollen Rechte gibt?", fragt Ajroush. „Dabei ist es an der Zeit, dass saudische Frauen Auto fahren. Ich bin bereit. Meine Tochter ist bereit. Und die Gesellschaft auch."

Die vorbeifahrenden Autofahrer scheinen das zu bestätigen. Als sie Ajroush am Lenkrad ihres Autos entdecken, hupen sie begeistert und recken ihr den nach oben gehaltenen Daumen entgegen. Ajroush winkt kurz zurück. Dann hält sie das Lenkrad wieder fest in den Händen, die in feinen, schwarzen Handschuhen stecken: „Ich habe schon beim ersten Aktionstag 1990 mitgemacht", sagt sie. „Und jetzt, 23 Jahre später, dürfen wir Frauen immer noch nicht Auto fahren. Wie lang soll das noch dauern?"

[…]

Immer mehr Frauen in Saudi-Arabien haben keine Geduld mehr. Im Rahmen der Kampagne „Mein Recht, meine Würde" haben sie zum landesweiten Frauenfahrtag aufgerufen. Mitinitiatorin ist die Aktivistin und Bloggerin Eman al Nafdschan, die auch ganz praktische Gründe dafür aufführt, warum sie das gesetzliche Fahrverbot kippen will: „Warum soll ich 1500 Rial, das sind knapp 300 Euro im Monat, für einen Fahrer bezahlen? Das Geld kann ich besser für mich und meine Kinder gebrauchen", sagt sie in einem Interview, ebenfalls am Steuer sitzend. „Ich möchte dadurch, dass ich illegal Auto fahre, die Aufmerksamkeit der Öffentlichkeit wecken."

Gelungen ist es ihr. Seit Beginn der Internet-Kampagne im vergangenen Monat haben die Frauen bereits über 20.000 Unterstützer gewonnen, darunter auch viele Männer. Vor fünf Jahren hatte der saudische König Abdullah noch betont, das Fahrverbot sei „gesellschaftlicher Konsens". Doch die frauenfeindliche Front scheint zu bröckeln. Selbst im Schura-Rat kam die Aufhebung des Fahrverbotes jetzt zur Sprache. In dem parlamentsähnlichen Gremium wurden zwar auch erst Anfang des Jahres Frauen zugelassen. Doch die brachten das heikle Thema gleich auf die Tagesordnung und fanden auch die Unterstützung etlicher männlicher Abgeordneter.

Aber im streng islamischen Königreich – in dem Frauen zwar Professorin werden, aber nicht ohne männlichen Vormund zum Arzt gehen dürfen, gibt es auch noch ganz andere Stimmen. Die der Scheichs. „Frauen sind von Natur aus sanfter geschaffen als Männer“, erläuterte Scheich Saleh bin Saad unlängst im saudi-arabischen Fernsehen. „Wenn eine Frau das Auto fährt, dann beschäftigt sie sich mental damit und das drückt auf das Becken und auf die Eierstöcke. Das sagt eine wissenschaftliche Studie“, so der Bärtige vor laufender Kamera. „Frauen in Frankreich und ganz Europa haben deshalb auch immer nur zwei oder drei Kinder. Das sind Folgen des Autofahrens!“

Noch in der gleichen Fernsehsendung stellte ein saudi-arabischer Frauenarzt klar, dass der Scheich mit Verlaub völligen Blödsinn erzähle. Doch im saudi-arabischen Innenministerium scheint man noch den alten Weltbildern nachzuhängen. Kurz vor dem Frauenfahrtag verschärfte es seinen Strafkatalog: Wer gegen das Frauenfahrverbot demonstriere, gefährde nämlich „den gesellschaftlichen Frieden“, wurde mitgeteilt. Wer die Internet-Seite der Frauenfahr-Kampagne anklicken will, sieht inzwischen nur noch schwarz – die Website wurde von Hackern lahmgelegt. *541 words*

*Quelle: Von Cornelia Wegerhoff. ARD.DE MAINZ.*

**Anmerkung:**

30 Schura-Rat: Der Rat hat lediglich eine beratende Funktion gegenüber dem Saudischen Königshaus. Saudi-Arabien ist eine absolutistische Monarchie, in der die gesetzgebende Gewalt allein dem König vorbehalten ist. Die Mitglieder des Schura-Rats werden vom König ernannt.

### Text 2: Frauen dürfen nicht einmal Auto fahren

[…] “Zivilrechtlich sind Frauen saudischer Staatsangehörigkeit nicht voll geschäftsfähig. Das heißt sie können Rechtsgeschäfte ohne den männlichen Vormund nicht tätigen”, erklärt die deutsche Botschaft in Riad auf ihrer Website.

[…]

Auch die Tatsache, dass Saudi-Arabien das einzige Land der Welt ist, in dem Frauen nicht selber Auto fahren dürfen, steht beispielhaft für die nicht vorhandene Gleichstellung der Geschlechter. […]

Nach und nach soll sich die Situation der saudischen Frau jedoch verbessern. “König Abdallah hat durch zahlreiche Reforminitiativen Frauen die Chance zu stärkerer gesellschaftlicher Teilhabe eröffnet”, schreibt die deutsche Botschaft. So treten immer mehr Frauen ein Studium an und auch bei der Berufswahl öffnen sich nach und nach weitere Optionen. *108 Wörter*

*Quelle:* FOCUS. *Von mde.*
*http://www.focus.de/politik/ausland/rueckschlag-fuer-arabische-frauen-frauen-duerften-nicht-einmal-auto-fahren_id_3623472.html*

## Aufgabenstellung

Im Rahmen eines Betriebspraktikums bei einem namhaften deutschen Automobilkonzern erhalten Sie die Aufgabe, für die internationale Internetpräsenz des Konzerns einen englischsprachigen Artikel über saudi-arabische Frauen als potenzielle Kundinnen zu verfassen.
Stellen Sie die gegenwärtige gesellschaftliche und wirtschaftliche Stellung der Frau in Saudi-Arabien dar und ziehen Sie daraus Rückschlüsse auf zukünftige Entwicklungen und mögliche Auswirkungen auf das Kaufverhalten von Frauen in Saudi-Arabien, die für die westliche Autoindustrie von Bedeutung sein könnten. Als Basis dienen Ihnen die beiden oben stehenden Texte.
Ihr Text sollte etwa 250 Wörter umfassen.

## Textaufgabe

**Is American dream fragile? History says it's strong.**
By Laurent Belsie

The ideological distance between the first Tea Party rally in Seattle and the "Occupy Wall Street" protest that got its start in New York City is about as wide as political chasms get in America.

The Tea Partyers and the Occupiers clash on just about everything: the role of government, the cause of the nation's economic woes, and solutions to them. But they agree on this: They fear that the American dream is vanishing.

For Tea Party activists, the dream seems on the verge of being finished off by higher taxes and bigger government. For the young Occupy Wall Street protesters, the dream seems unlikely to get started.

"You have both the Tea Party element out there – people who are going to have stuff taken away – and you have youth that have got it right: that they're going to live in their parents' broom closets for the next decade," says Lawrence Rosenthal, executive director of the Center for the Comparative Study of Right-Wing Movements at the University of California, Berkeley.

More than 70 percent of Americans rate their standard of living as fair or poor, just the reverse of what they said before the Great Recession, according to an October American Pulse Survey. Nearly half of young adults think their generation will be worse off than their parents', according to a survey by policy center Demos and a youth advocacy organization called Young Invincibles. Just as in the Great Depression, the last time that the United States endured a major financial crisis, the future looks bleak.

But the long-term future is not as nightmarish as it may look. Once the Great Recession is firmly in the rearview mirror, someone with talent and a good work ethic will still be able to move up.

That's been the historical record despite recession, war, stagflation, and other economic problems, according to three economists who analyzed Social Security data going back to 1937. The ability to get ahead during one's career – what economists call long-term mobility – has been increasing for the past 60 years.

The details are a bit less cheery. The driving force behind that improvement is the dramatic rise in long-term mobility for women. In 1980, 2 percent of the top fifth of income earners were women; by 2004, they represented 14 percent and their share was still growing rapidly. In the next fifth of earners, women moved from 8 percent in 1966 to around 34 percent by the early 1990s. That dynamic has overshadowed a slight decrease in men's mobility in recent decades.

What about the kids? Two-thirds of them are doing better than their parents, thanks to economic growth, according to a 2008 study by the Pew Charitable Trusts in Washington.

The Great Recession may stall these trends. What's remarkable, though, is their staying power over the decades, especially in the face of mounting income inequality. Even as the rich have been getting richer, people in the middle class (especially women) have seen their situation improve and their children, on average, earn more than they did at a comparable stage.

Women's long-term standing is likely to keep improving because they are still making strides into most of the top echelons of income earners, says Wojciech Kopczuk, one of the three authors of the mobility study and economics professor at Columbia University in New York.

The American dream looks a little deflated right now. But don't count it out in the long run. *572 words*

**Table 697. Money Income of Families – Median Income by Race and Hispanic Origin in Current and Constant (2009) Dollars: 1990 to 2009**

| Year | Median income in current dollars | | | | | Median income in constant (2009) dollars | | | | |
|---|---|---|---|---|---|---|---|---|---|---|
| | All families[1] | White | Black | Asian, Pacific Islander | Hispanic | All families[1] | White | Black | Asian, Pacific Islander | Hispanic |
| 1990 | 35,353 | 36,915 | 21,423 | 42,246 | 23,431 | 56,243 | 58,728 | 34,082 | 67,210 | 37,277 |
| 1995 | 40,611 | 42,646 | 25,970 | 46,356 | 24,570 | 56,755 | 59,598 | 36,293 | 64,783 | 34,337 |
| 2000 | 50,732 | 53,029 | 33,676 | 62,617 | 34,442 | 63,189 | 66,050 | 41,945 | 77,993 | 42,899 |
| 2004 | 54,061 | 56,723 | 35,148 | 65,420 | 35,440 | 61,389 | 64,411 | 39,912 | 74,287 | 40,244 |
| 2005 | 56,194 | 59,317 | 35,464 | 68,957 | 37,867 | 61,741 | 65,172 | 38,965 | 75,764 | 41,605 |
| 2006 | 58,407 | 61,280 | 38,269 | 74,612 | 40,000 | 62,135 | 65,191 | 40,712 | 79,374 | 42,553 |
| 2007 | 61,335 | 64,427 | 40,143 | 77,133 | 40,566 | 63,471 | 66,649 | 41,527 | 79,793 | 41,965 |
| 2008 | 61,521 | 65,000 | 39,879 | 73,578 | 40,466 | 61,288 | 64,753 | 39,728 | 73,299 | 40,312 |
| 2009 | 60,088 | 62,545 | 38,409 | 75,027 | 39,730 | 60,088 | 62,545 | 38,409 | 75,027 | 39,730 |

1 includes other races not shown separately

*From: The 2012 Statistical Abstract by U.S. Census Bureau, Income, Poverty and Health Insurance Coverage in the United States: 2009. Current Population Reports, P60-238, and Historical Tables – Table F-05, September 2010. See also http://www.census.gov/hhes/www/income/income.html and http://www.census.gov/hhes/www/income/data/historical/families/index.html*

**Annotations:**
Current dollars: amount of money received in a particular year as an income
Constant dollars: inflation rate taken into account, representation of actual purchasing power to compare the rise and fall of income rates over the years

## Aufgabenstellung

Imagine that you are working on a school project on the American dream. It is your task to research interesting material on that topic on the internet. You believe you have found a suitable text and statistics. To present it in class, complete the following tasks:

1. Characterise the type of text.
2. Analyse the statistics printed above and explain to what extent they illustrate the text.
3. Nobody has responded to the article on the website yet. Other people's reactions would be important to you as you need to know how the article is judged by the parties concerned. Therefore, you decide to make the first move and comment on the idea of the American dream yourself.

## Lösungsvorschläge

### Sprachmittlung

*How to approach the task: First make sure you know the context in which your text should be written (e. g. target group, text type, focus). Then go through the two German texts and select the information that is relevant regarding the assignment. Ask yourself if any aspects require further explanation (e. g. due to cultural differences, geographical or regional particularities). As soon as the content is clear, structure your text by arranging the information logically. Connect the single paragraphs idiomatically. Find a suitable heading as you are required to write an article.*
*The following information should be included in your text:*

- *Saudi Arabian women between tradition and change:*
  - *not allowed to drive: male drivers needed*
  - *legally not equal to men: guardian decides for them*
  - *more and more open protests with growing support from men and women*
  - *increasing political and academic influence of women*
- *possibilities for the automobile industry:*
  - *if rights were extended, more women would want a car*
  - *luxury cars as symbols of both status and freedom*

**Saudi Women – A Driving Force?**

When contemplating the potential of increasing car sales in Saudi Arabia by targeting female buyers, one has to keep in mind that Saudi women are torn between tradition and change: On the one hand, a woman's life in Saudi Arabia is very restricted: She has no legal power and cannot make any decision without the consent of a male guardian. Saudi Arabia is the only country in the world where women can own a car, but must hire a driver as they are not allowed to drive themselves. Their role is traditionally that of a housewife and mother; some conservatives even claim that driving is harmful to women's health.

On the other hand, women's influence on Saudi Arabian politics has slowly improved. Lately, they have been allowed seats in the Schura council, a kind of parliament that advises the king on important matters; a fact which led to a new rise in activism against anti-driving legislation for women. Society mainly seems to support the women's cause: The campaign "My Rights, My Dignity" called for a nation-wide illegal women's driving day and, despite being prohibited, gained a lot of supporters, many of whom were men.

Whether women can be reckoned with as future customers depends on how thorough the proposed liberalisation of women's rights in Saudi Arabia is going to be. The automobile industry would largely gain from a more progressive Saudi Arabia. If women needn't hire drivers anymore, they could spend more money on a car. There are already many modern, academically and professionally successful women to whom driving their own high-end car would be an attractive symbol of freedom and status.

## Textaufgabe

1. *To answer this question you need to have a close look at the structure and style of the text. Every text serves a particular purpose that depends on the aim its author wants to achieve. In this case, you should uncover the following clues:*
   - *Type of text: argumentative text*
   - *Style:*
     - *expert opinions, results of certain studies and historical data: the author would like to convince the reader by providing as many sources as possible*
     - *use of technical terms: author seems well-informed about topic*
     - *factual information, matter-of-fact tone*
   - *Structure: author's judgement presented in the end*

   The article "Is American dream fragile? History says it's strong" by Laurent Belsie is an argumentative text, of which both structure and style give sufficient proof. The crucial question is asked by Belsie at the very beginning in the headline: "Is American dream fragile?" Although the headline answers the question immediately in its second part: "History says it's strong", Belsie provides enough evidence in the text to illustrate his point: First he quickly outlines the common fear of the conservative Tea Party movement and the rather left-wing Occupy Wall Street protesters: Both are afraid of awakening from the American dream (cf. ll. 1–9) – although for different reasons: Whereas Tea Party activists feel their freedom restricted by taxes and government regulations (cf. ll. 7/8), the sympathisers of Occupy Wall Street worry about never being given a chance to prove themselves (cf. ll. 8/9). Experts are quoted (cf. ll. 10–14 and ll. 43–46), studies cited (cf. ll. 15–21 and ll. 35–37) and historical evidence is given (cf. ll. 25–34). The author uses a huge quantity of historical terms such as "Great Depression" (ll. 19/20), "Great Recession" (ll. 16, 22/23, 38), "long-term mobility" (ll. 28, 30), "recession, war, stagflation" (l. 25) in order to assure the readers that he knows what he is talking about. Moreover, Belsie does not make any attempt to explain those technical terms as he seems to address his article to an educated readership. All the sources mentioned provide enough facts to prove that the author is a reliable source of information.

   As the author gives both arguments for and against the continuation of the American dream, it is quite obvious that he wants to inform the readers first and then convince them that his position is the right one. Therefore, he avoids commenting on the different points of view until the very end of the article and concentrates on giving factual information first. Merely against the backdrop of historical facts which allay the fears articulated by Occupy Wall Street and the Tea Partyers (cf. ll. 25–34), he ventures a prognosis concerning the future of the American society (cf. ll. 38–42) and finally comes to the conclusion: "The American dream looks a little deflated right now. But don't count it out in the long run." (cf. ll. 47/48).

Given the factual information provided by the author, this is the only answer one could possibly give to the question of whether the American dream has meanwhile turned into a nightmare or not.

2. *You need to consider all information provided by the statistics and make sure that you have read the annotations, which will prove helpful to fully understanding how to interpret the data. First of all, you should concentrate on analysing the numbers cited. Afterwards compare the text to the statistical evidence in relation to the American dream.*
   *You should mention the following aspects:*
   - *Analysis:*
     - *general increase in income in current dollars over the last twenty years (major profiteers: White and Asian population)*
     - *huge increase in current dollars is not reflected in purchasing power (constant dollars); exception to the rule: Asian population*
   - *Comparison:*
     - *plausible author's prognosis concerning the future of the middle class based on historical facts*
     - *American dream difficult to reach according to statistics*

Table 697, taken from "The 2012 Statistical Abstract" by the U.S. Census Bureau, shows the average annual income of US families between 1990 and 2009. The average annual income of all families covered by the statistics is split up further according to race. Three particularities of the respective statistics have to be taken into account: First of all, data was not made available for every single year. Furthermore, not every race was taken into account. Finally, there is a difference between income in current dollars and income in constant dollars. While current dollars refer to the money paid as income in the respective year, constant dollars indicate the value of this money in regard to purchasing power. Nevertheless, the statistics reflect general trends which are analysed below:
Whereas all groups experienced a rise in income in current dollars, it is the White and Asian population that benefited most. White families' average income rose from $ 36,915 in 1990 to $ 62,545 in 2009 and families of Asian origin also managed to almost double their income in those two decades. Black and Hispanic families were not able to increase their income to such a significant extent: the average Black family had $ 21,423 at their disposal in 1990 compared to $ 38,409 in 2009. Hispanic incomes only slightly differ with an average of $ 23,431 in 1990 and $ 39,730 in 2009. Economically speaking, the year 2007 seems to have been the most successful for all parties concerned as incomes reached a peak before the financial crisis arose. But when it comes to constant dollars, the huge difference between the income of the White and Asian population on the one hand and that of the Blacks and Hispanics on the other hand is not reflected that strongly. The purchasing power of Whites and Blacks only increased by about $ 4,000, Hispanics achieved an even smaller rise of approximately $ 2,500; meanwhile, the Asian

population improved their average income in constant dollars immensely by almost $ 8,000.
Compared to the text, the statistics certainly reinforce the argument that "the long-term future is not as nightmarish as it may look" (l. 22). Even the huge impact of the financial crisis did not lessen the average income of all groups in question. In the past, middle-class people tended to improve their financial standing, and children used to earn more money than their parents did, most likely due to better education, job opportunities and social status (cf. ll. 40–42). It should not be forgotten that the numbers given in the statistics reflect average wages and that individual cases cannot influence statistics like this to a great extent. Still, for the majority of the American people, the American dream did not come true in the last two decades. Only the Asian population was able to considerably increase their income. Therefore, instead of what has been pointed out by Belsie, Occupy Wall Street and the Tea Party movement are not entirely mistaken about the state of the nation – although they are about twenty years late.

3. *It is completely up to you whether you want to comment on the article from a protester's point of view or choose to have a rather objective view of the whole issue. Therefore, it is useful to collect arguments first and then decide which position to take. The following points mentioned are just one possible way to write the comment:*
   - *definition of the American dream as an introduction*
   - *American dream out of reach for people of African-American or Hispanic origin; purchasing power not risen considerably for more than a decade: no upward trend anymore, no "from rags to riches"*
   - *real estate bubble and financial crisis as a catalyst for rendering the American dream an illusion*
   - *individual success less likely due to international companies*

The American dream has always been an ideal that countless immigrants and Americans residents have longed to live up to. This concept included both freedom and unlimited opportunities to improve one's income and social status. The importance of the American dream is obvious: by constitutional right, "all men are created equal" and everybody is guaranteed the right to "liberty and happiness". Many US citizens have proved that it is possible to turn "from rags to riches". However, with the financial crisis hitting America hard in 2007, one has to ask the question whether the American dream is still an idea worth believing in. I have just read Laurent Belsie's article "Is American dream fragile? History says it's strong" on this homepage and have to disagree strongly: I believe the American dream is fading.
Firstly, recent statistics on "Money Income of Families" by the US Census Bureau indicate that for the majority of American people, this dream has never become a reality. With constant dollar incomes not having risen significantly in the last two decades as far as purchasing power is concerned, the average American citizen

has not been able to improve his/her situation. The only exception to the rule is members of the Asian-American community, who managed to increase their income (in constant dollars) by an average of almost $ 10,000.
Furthermore, the financial sector contributed its share to the crisis of faith American society is suffering from. Poor people with badly-paid jobs were encouraged to take loans they would never be able to pay back. As a result the real estate bubble was bound to burst sooner or later. The poor might have hoped to be able to realise their American dream, but the reverse was true: Due to the financial crisis, the whole of American society became less likely to reach this goal. It is therefore American society itself that has contributed to the failure of the American dream.
Finally, realising the American dream used to be a lot easier than it is now. With global companies controlling the market, individuals stand a much smaller chance of success. In recent years, many local businesses in my hometown finally had to give in to companies operating on an international level. It is not so much personal abilities as connections that enable people to make a career.
All in all, the American dream seems to be rather a theoretical concept which is quite impossible to put into practice – at least as far as the financial situation is concerned. Of course, each person's version of the American dream – what is defined as freedom and what opportunities are considered worth taking – is entirely subjective.

## Sprachmittlung

### Unsere zweite Haut

*Schön, wenn die Bluse nur zehn Euro kostet. Nicht gut, wenn dafür die Umwelt leidet und Arbeiter ausgebeutet werden. […]*

Beutestück Nummer zwei ist roséfarben und glänzt. Die junge Frau hält das Kleid in die Kamera, dreht und wendet es, Metallic-Optik sei das und habe 5,99 Euro gekostet. Ein Hammerpreis, sagt Funnypilgrim, wie sie sich auf YouTube nennt. Die weiteren Eroberungen der Shoppingtour: noch ein Kleid, ein Pulli, fünf Hosen, ein Oberteil, eine Strickjacke und ein Gürtel. Willkommen im Polyester-Paradies. […]

Die Konsumenten, die Polyesterkleidchen für 5,99 Euro und ebenso billige Baumwoll-T-Shirts kaufen, sind Teil des Systems Fast Fashion. Viele tragen ihre Kleider nur ein paar Mal, dann muss etwas Neues her – weil die Mode sich geändert hat oder die Teile schlicht kaputt sind. Modeketten produzieren Kleidung in immer kürzerer Zeit und bringen ständig neue Stücke in die Läden. Die Billigproduktion und der schnelle Modezyklus gehen zulasten von Arbeitern, Umwelt, Klima und der Gesundheit derjenigen, die die Kleider am Ende tragen. […]

Die Produktionsstrecke vom Entwurf bis zum ausgelieferten Kleidungsstück dauert heute nur noch wenige Wochen. Neue Kollektionen kommen nicht mehr wie früher zweimal pro Jahr in die Läden, es treffen kontinuierlich neue Kleider ein. So signalisieren die Anbieter den Kunden, dass sie ständig ihre Garderobe erneuern sollten – und machen dies möglich, indem ein T-Shirt oft kaum mehr kostet als ein Kaffee. Wer bei Billiganbietern wie H&M, Zara oder der gerade expandierenden irischen Kette Primark kauft, kann bei allen Trends mitmachen, ohne viel Geld auszugeben. Die Kunden spielen da gerne mit. Wegwerfen und Neukaufen wird zum Prinzip.

„Je mehr Kleidung hergestellt wird, desto größer wird auch die Belastung für die Umwelt", sagt Kirsten Brodde, Textilexpertin von Greenpeace. Bei der Produktion werden Hunderte verschiedener Chemikalien eingesetzt – Farbstoffe, Färbebeschleuniger und Bleichmittel, zusätzlich Substanzen, die dafür sorgen, dass Kleider griffiger werden, weniger knittern, mehr glänzen oder dass Leder nicht schimmelt. Gerade in Ländern wie China, Indien und Bangladesch, aus denen ein großer Teil unserer Textilien kommt, sind gefährliche Stoffe verfügbar. Greenpeace analysierte das Abwasser chinesischer Fabriken, die auch deutsche und multinationale Textilunternehmen beliefern, und fand langlebige giftige Chemikalien.

Die Menschen, die in solchen Fabriken unsere Kleidung herstellen, gefährden ihre Gesundheit. Bei der Sandstrahl-Methode etwa – mit der neue Jeans behandelt werden, damit sie abgetragen aussehen – atmen die Arbeiter Quarz ein, das die Lunge angreift. Nach heftiger Kritik verpflichteten sich H&M und das Jeanslabel Levi Strauss dazu, die Technik nicht mehr anzuwenden. Insgesamt haben sich die Sozialstandards jedoch kaum verbessert, obwohl die Zustände in den Fabriken lange bekannt sind. Die Organisation „Kampagne Saubere Kleidung“ kritisiert niedrige Löhne und mangelnde Sicherheit. Bei einem Brand in einer Textilfabrik in Pakistan, die unter anderem für KiK produzierte, starben im September mehr als 250 Arbeiter.

**20 Kilogramm Textilien pro Jahr**

Auch hierzulande sorgt das Prinzip Fast Fashion für Umweltprobleme – in Form von Müll. Der durchschnittliche Europäer verbrauche im Jahr 20 Kilogramm Textilien, der Amerikaner sogar 35, schreibt Textil-Experte Andreas Engelhardt in seinem Buch *Schwarzbuch Baumwolle*. Der weltweite Fasermarkt umfasste nach Angaben der Bremer Baumwollbörse 1990 ein Volumen von 38 Millionen Tonnen, im Jahr 2000 von knapp 50 Millionen und 2012 sogar von 75 Millionen Tonnen. Etwa die Hälfte dieser Fasern wird für Kleidung genutzt, schätzt Engelhardt.

Die vielen chemischen Zusätze in Textilien schaden vor allem den Arbeitern, womöglich aber auch den Käufern. Einige der Textil-Chemikalien können Kontaktallergien auslösen, zum Beispiel Formaldehyd. Damit werden Kleider behandelt, damit sie weniger knittern und ihre Form behalten. Zinnorganische Verbindungen, die Kleidung während des Transports vor Pilzbefall schützen, könnten nach Einschätzung des Bundesinstituts für Risikobewertung (BfR) die Fruchtbarkeit einschränken und das Nervensystem angreifen. Sie sind in der EU verboten. Andere Substanzen stehen im Verdacht, das Krebsrisiko zu erhöhen, zum Beispiel einige Azofarbstoffe. Nach Angaben des BfR verzichtet die deutsche Industrie schon lange auf die gefährlichen Mittel, nur wird ja kaum noch Kleidung in Deutschland hergestellt. „Man muss davon ausgehen, dass in einigen importierten Textilien, insbesondere aus Nicht-EU-Staaten, solche problematischen Farbstoffe enthalten sein können“, schreibt das BfR. […]

*632 Wörter*

*Quelle:* ZEIT Wissen, *Nr. 1/2013. Von Susanne Schäfer.*
*http://www.zeit.de/zeit-wissen/2013/01/Nachhaltige-Kleidung*

**Aufgabenstellung**

Sie machen ein Praktikum im IT- und Marketingbereich bei einem Versandhaus für nachhaltig produzierte Kleidung, das die Internetseite letsgetfair.com betreibt. Bald soll sie auch einem nicht-deutschsprachigen Publikum offen stehen. Eine Internet-Kampagne soll auf die Website aufmerksam machen. Sie werden gebeten, einen englischsprachigen Text zu verfassen, um die Verbraucher über die negativen Konsequenzen der Kleidungsproduktion aufzuklären. Als Grundlage dient Ihnen der ZEIT-Artikel „Unsere zweite Haut“.
Ihr Text sollte ca. 250 Wörter umfassen.

## Textaufgabe

### Life after the end of economic growth

*A continually rising GDP is not necessarily possible – or even desirable. So why do policymakers obsess over it?*

[...] The tide of economic growth that has flowed since the second world war may finally be ebbing. For politicians and most economists, this is like saying the sky is falling. Growth has become guidepost and grail, the *sine qua non* of economic existence. Growth is necessary to job creation and the health of businesses. Without growth the rolls of the homeless and jobless swell, requiring governments to shoulder more responsibility; yet at the same time tax revenues fall, making both new and existing government debt unbearable.

Stimulating growth has become job No 1 for policymakers. David Cameron insists that his nation must deregulate business and reform employment law in order to "go for growth". And at the conclusion of the recent G 20 global economic summit, the US president, Barack Obama, reported that the discussions there had revolved around the question, "How do we achieve greater global growth?" Such statements raise nary an eyebrow; they are entirely expected.

Nonetheless, in recent years a few economists have advanced a contrary view. Tim Jackson in the UK, Herman Daly in the US, and Serge Latouche in France have argued that growth is not always good for the environment or for the real health of communities, and that GDP growth is impossible to sustain over the long run anyway because we live on a planet with limited natural resources. Their position has won few adherents in the mainstream. In the "real" worlds of politics and economics, questioning growth is like arguing against gasoline at a Formula One race.

But doubts about growth are no longer theoretical. We seem to have arrived at a moment when further economic expansion is hemmed in by financial as well as natural limits. [...]

If policymakers fail to recognise this and continue assuming that the current debt crisis is just another turning of the business cycle, then we may lose whatever opportunity still remains to avert a crash that could bring civilisation to its knees. Over the short run, this is scary business. Financial markets have a hair trigger, and fears about flagging growth could bring down governments and banks.

Still, over the longer term there will undoubtedly be life after growth, and it doesn't have to play out under miserable conditions. With less energy to fuel globalisation and mechanisation there should be increasing requirement for local production and manual labour. We could meet everyone's basic needs by prioritising jobs in manufacturing and agriculture while downsizing the financial industry and the military. We will also have to reduce economic inequality and corruption [...].

As we do these things, we must reform economics to reflect ecological reality: nature is not, after all, just a pile of raw materials waiting to be transformed into products and then waste; rather, ecosystem integrity is a precondition for society's survival. Adaptive responses cannot only be left up to government officials and economists;

for their part, households must rein in debt and overconsumption while contributing more to community resilience.

There's light at the end of the tunnel. If we focus on improving quality of life rather than boosting quantity of consumption, we could be happier even as our economy downsizes to fit nature's limits.

But a benign future is unlikely to transpire if we all continue living in a dream world where growth knows no bounds, where debt can be repaid with more debt, and where natural resources are assumed to be endless. [...] *568 words*

*From:* The Guardian, *30 November 2011. By Richard Heinberg.*
*http://www.guardian.co.uk/commentisfree/2011/nov/30/end-of-growth?INTCMP=SRCH*

**Annotations:**
3 grail: sth. that is desired strongly by numerous people because it is special (e. g. the Holy Grail)
5 rolls: official register of names
13 nary: old-fashioned: not a single one
27 hair trigger: only needs a small impulse to react
40 resilience: synonym for recovery

## Cartoon

© *Adrian Teal/cartoonstock.com*

**Aufgabenstellung**

Every year, your school celebrates "Eco Day", which means that each class has to introduce useful concepts to make the world a better, more environmentally friendly place to live in. You have been chosen to present the most essential aspects of the text printed above to an interested audience of parents.
To prepare yourself for the talk, you need to work with the text:

1. Analyse the means the author uses to convince the readers of his opinion.
   Pay attention to both language and structure used.
2. Describe the cartoon and interpret it in the context of the text.
3. According to the author, households also need to contribute their fair share to a world after the end of economic growth (cf. ll. 39/40).
   Comment on this attitude.

## Lösungsvorschläge

### Sprachmittlung

*How to approach the task: Keep in mind that your text should make people aware of the negative consequences of "fast fashion". First of all, you need to gather all facts, e. g. problems in the producing as well as in the consuming countries. As you are writing for a company that also sells clothes, your text cannot be neutral: It is the purpose of your writing to convince consumers that your website is a trustworthy alternative to other brands. You might find it easier to sum up the most important aspects in German first, before you start writing the text in English. Do not forget to provide your text with a catchy title and to structure it logically.*
*Your text should contain the following information:*
- *the consequences of producing cheap clothes in low-wage countries*
- *motivating the readers to buy sustainably produced clothes on letsgetfair.com*

**Bloody clothes – Fashion victims cause victims of fashion**
Have you ever wondered how it is possible to buy a dress for only €5.99? Western consumers are trapped in the vicious circle of "fast fashion" that makes us buy new clothes constantly, only to replace them quickly after some time because they are not up-to-date anymore.
But someone has to pay the price for our craving for the biggest bargain: In this case, it is the workers who produce cheap fashion in India, China, Bangladesh and Pakistan. Due to lack of safety measures, 250 workers died recently when their factory burned to the ground. In China and Bangladesh, toxic substances used in production endanger the workers' health and pollute the underground water. Workers run huge risks in the sweatshops of Western fashion labels, for example, but cannot be paid appropriate wages as the big companies would then not be able to sell their products as cheaply as they do now.
But in the long run, we as consumers have to face the consequences of our greed. More and more waste is produced due to our endless hunger for fashionable clothing. Chemical substances used to prevent clothes from wrinkling or becoming mouldy can damage our health severely, threaten fertility and even enhance the risk of cancer.
The good news is: You can help put an end to all that: Start shopping at letsgetfair.com and feel better instantly.

## Textaufgabe

1. *You are required to analyse the text concerning structural and stylistic means the author uses to convince the reader of his point of view. To be able to do this, you have to make sure that you understand what the article is about. Then find out which aim the author wants to reach by publishing his article. In the next step, you need to find out how he manages to achieve this aim. The following facts might help you:*
   - *Position of the author: Economic growth cannot go on forever*
   - *Structural means:*
     - *listing the benefits of economic growth (cf. ll. 1–7): objectivity*
     - *naming influential politicians on the wrong track (cf. ll. 8–13): reader not the only one in doubt*
     - *citing experts against economic growth (cf. ll. 14–20): convincing, reliable*
     - *advertising a life after economic growth (cf. ll. 21–46): creating a doomsday scenario and offering prospects*
   - *Stylistic means:*
     - *use of facts, names, experts' opinions to make the text convincing*
     - *figurative language: comparison (cf. l. 20), metaphors (cf. ll. 25/26, l. 41), parallelisms (cf. ll. 45/46), irony (cf. ll. 44/45) – easier to imagine the disaster we are in if nothing changes*

The author of "Life after the end of economic growth", published online by the *Guardian* on 30 November 2011, is of the opinion that economic growth is no longer essential for the well-being of a country. In the first part of the text (cf. ll. 1–13) he sums up the traditional stand on economic growth and names the two most influential statesmen in the English-speaking world, the British Prime Minister David Cameron and the US President Barack Obama as the stereotypical politicians who still believe in economic growth overcoming all obstacles (cf. ll. 8–13). He points out that stimulating growth has long been seen as "job No 1 for policymakers" (l. 8) such as Cameron or Obama but that this view is an outdated one. Asking Obama's question ("How do we achieve greater global growth?", l. 12) again in direct speech is intended to involve the readers and make them think about the question themselves. Obviously, this is the crucial question which all politicians think about. Therefore, the doubtful reader is in good company.
The author goes on to quote well-known economists to emphasise that more and more experts claim we are exploiting our natural resources, a development that will ruin both the environment and the mental, physical and emotional state of mankind (cf. ll. 16/17). Readers might find it more convincing to have the author's opinion supported by renowned economists. Presenting first the positive aspects of economic growth and then taking a tough stand against it also shows that the author wishes his readers to be well-informed on the issue and then to make up their minds afterwards, which presents him as quite a reliable source of information.

The figurative language the author uses throughout the text becomes the most impressive when he starts to concentrate on predicting a future with and without economic growth, respectively. Simultaneously, these devices make the text more vivid and interesting. Using a comparison ("questioning growth is like arguing against gasoline at a Formula One race", l. 20) makes it easier for the reader to understand the revolutionary potential of the author's suggestions. Moreover, he uses a metaphor to show what a doomsday scenario we would have to face if we carried on living and working in the traditional way: ("we may lose whatever opportunity still remains to avert a crash that could bring civilisation to its knees", ll. 25/26).
The prospect of changing our ways makes the future look bright in comparison: local production and manual work will help to create jobs in manufacturing and agriculture as far as the author is concerned. Living standards all over the globe will increase as corruption and inequality come to an end; instead of finances and military, nature will be prioritised with households contributing their fair share by consuming little and running into debt even less (cf. ll. 32–43).
These promises make a change of lifestyle most desirable in order to finally see the "light at the end of the tunnel" (l. 41) as the author metaphorically illustrates the prospect. It seems cruel to have to turn to reality again and face a sea of problems, their boundlessness stressed by three parallel structured sub-clauses (cf. ll. 45/46). The term "dream world" (ll. 44/45) has an ironic touch to it in this context – again, the readers are urged to finally face the truth about economic growth.

2. *Describing the cartoon requires you to collect the most essential information you can gain from the picture. It is important to pay attention to every detail as this might prove helpful when interpreting the cartoon afterwards.*
   - *Description:*
     - *a cat with a whip and cigar and an elephant with a blanket in a circus ring*
     - *evil smiles*
     - *animal balancing on a ball that looks like the Earth (looking as if it is in pain)*
   - *Interpretation:*
     - *the elephant: economic growth*
     - *its trainer: the politicians*

The cartoon shows a scene in a circus ring with an elephant trainer making the elephant do a stunt on a ball. A pleased and overweight cat figures as the elephant trainer and has a big cigar in its mouth, a whip in its left hand and is supervising the elephant's performance. The elephant is covered by a blanket on which "economic growth" is written.
The ball the animal is balancing on symbolises the globe. It is humanised as one can see the face of a person distorted with pain. The elephant trainer can be compared to ruthless politicians whose single aim is to stimulate economic growth as they believe it necessary to create jobs and secure both their personal well-being and the health of businesses. The key point of the cartoon is the sharp contrast be-

tween the economic growth that politicians favour and the natural resources that are exploited and have a negative effect upon life on Earth.
However, the more considerable the economic growth, the bigger the amount of natural resources on Earth which are exploited. As the resources are limited, the damage caused can never be repaired. It is not only the natural resources that will suffer from the whole development but human beings will also fall victim to the whole process as their quality of life will be badly affected as well. Against the backdrop of the text, the cartoon intends us to realise that we should deal responsibly with our environment and stop "living in a dream world where growth knows no bounds [...] and where natural resources are assumed to be endless" (ll. 44–46).

3. *For task 3 you need to focus on the position of the author again, who believes that households need to contribute to economic growth. It is not necessary to agree with his view but your personal remarks must be consistent. Take care that you do not contradict yourself and that you link the sentences in a way that makes your comment sound more vivid and demanding. You have to decide on whether you agree or disagree with this position and give reasons for your decision.*
*In favour of the author's opinion:*
- *reduce your litter and separate the waste*
- *reduction of overconsumption through hybrid cars or well-chosen holiday destinations*

In his article "Life after the end of economic growth" the author Richard Heinberg argues that economic growth cannot continue forever and even considers this development a positive one as it could improve life on Earth. Instead of making the economy a priority, we should concentrate on manufacturing, agriculture and nature. He also demands that not only governments, but also each individual household contributes to the common good.
I fully share the author's view. We have to face new challenges and cannot go on wasting our natural sources of energy, believing them to be endless. Changing attitudes and reforming economies does not automatically result in worse living conditions. The reverse is true: those changes could add more quality to life. Another point to consider is that we have to take responsibility for future generations, too. We can easily get started by separating waste and having it recycled, collecting batteries and only buying bottles that can be recycled.
Furthermore, Heinberg mentions overconsumption as a massive problem that households should try to reduce if possible. Again, there are so many ways to reduce consumption: With jobs in the manufacturing and agricultural sectors, there might not be so many commuters on the roads every morning and evening anymore. People who still need to drive long distances every day should reconsider their choice of car. Driving a hybrid car instead of a fast car with high petrol consumption is much more environmentally friendly. In addition, there is no need to spend every holiday abroad.

Finally, Heinberg points out that households should reduce their debts in order to render our communities healthier. Although I believe that this might be difficult to achieve, as a lot of households are deeply in debt, downsizing the financial sector might weaken the position of several credit institutes. Therefore, people might not be granted loans that they cannot repay. To boot, as overconsumption will cease to be a common aim, it might no longer be so essential for people to possess the latest TV set, DVD player or fashionable clothes. Quite often, these items are the reason why many people get into debt. As they lose in value, there may be a decline in the number of people in debt.

All in all, I believe that if we all followed the author's suggestions, we could make the world a much better place to live in and would all be a lot happier.

# Gymnasium Niedersachsen – Englisch
# Erhöhtes Anforderungsniveau 2011 – Abiturprüfungsaufgabe 1

## A. Higgins-Wyndham, Preface to *Re-Imagining Ireland* (2006)

If you ask for directions in Ireland, or the West of Ireland anyway, the person you are addressing may begin by saying, "Well, first you go down to the cross," meaning not a Celtic cross but a crossroads, a place where people and traffic intersect. Not so long ago, I encountered just such a kindly representative of Old Ireland on the Dingle Peninsula near the village of Cloghane. She directed me to "the cross" – and a field there – to park my car, leaving it while I hiked an unnamed mountain on the Connor Pass, across the way from Mount Brandon.

From about age six to thirteen, I grew up in Ireland, mostly outside Dublin, near Stillorgan, then still a distinct village. We had a central "cross" too. My Polish father was a bit of an anomaly there, though an Italian opened up a fish-and-chip shop up the hill around that time also. We had come from England, to which my Dublin-born mother had emigrated to find adventure and work after finishing school. So when I arrived in Ireland, I had an English accent, not the most advantageous of assets among my schoolmates at the time, but mostly they let it go.

We had moved to Dublin at a kind of crossroads for the country, which was just beginning to scope out and implement plans to encourage foreign investment. Within a few years we were living at Shannon, with its then nascent industrial park, where my father, who was an electronics engineer, got a job with a Rhodesian company and where most of my friends had foreign – meaning non-Irish – accents. Their fathers worked for American, South African, German, and Japanese businesses. But I went to school in Limerick, where I continued to learn a very curiously accented Irish, at least compared to the version given me by the priests at my Dublin school in preparation for the national Primary Exam.

My mother, Eileen Higgins, loved her country. But because she also relished the good things that the world had on offer, she spent her life mostly longing for Ireland at a distance, being impelled to seek abroad what the land of the Higginses could not then provide. It was she who encouraged my father to look across the Atlantic, where he found a new position with General Electric. Again she was up and leaving the land of her youth, and now mine. There was no Irish wake – we went down to the Shannon Shamrock Inn at Bunratty for a farewell dinner. And, having sold most all of our things, we headed off for the United States essentially empty-handed, save for our suitcases, taking not an emigrants' "coffin ship" but a gleaming vessel of the developing global transport system – a Pan American DC-8 jet. We arrived at the crossroads of New York but headed down south to Virginia, where I have lived, and from which I have frequently visited Ireland, since that time.

Ireland was at a crossroads then; it was a place of modest intersections, encounters, and change. Today it is at an "interchange" on a freeway, having taken a quantum leap, emerging as the most globalized society in the world. Now Stillorgan is subsumed by Dublin's urban sprawl, the original plan for Shannon has become the road map for the "siliconized" country, individuals with foreign accents and various skin colors are a commonplace, and people who speak different dialects of Irish are at home with each other on the Internet. Dublin airport is again expanding to accommodate the global traffic, and citizens like my mother are coming back to stay, permanently, because Ireland now offers most everything available in the world at large.

We kids used to go into the poorer areas of Dublin to buy illegal British fireworks that were, we were told, smuggled by rail from the distant and uninviting North and thrown off before the train pulled into Dublin – such was the myth. Today, those areas of Dublin are being renovated in concert with the long-time local residents; they are renewing and recovering community. Of greater moment, Northern Ireland and Ireland and the people within their respective polities have taken some giant steps to create genuinely democratic solutions to long-standing civil problems – and people of all allegiances are hopeful that gunrunning is permanently in the past. I knew nothing about such things then, just as I knew nothing about issues of civil rights and violence in the American South, where we were moving from Ireland. Today, the Enterprise Unlimited speeds back and forth about every two hours between Dublin and Belfast. The Belfast waterfront is booming, and people are getting used to a postwar environment, gradually building confidence.

The island of Ireland is in so many ways new to itself. It is also new – if, as Fintan O'Toole says, eerily familiar – to those who are returning. And it is often viewed as alien by those who have read Yeats and Synge and Joyce and who arrive on holiday, filled with visions handed down by literature, or their parents' and grandparents' stories, and recharged with longing by the latest glossy tourist brochures. In truth, there are still great treasures of heritage and landscape and tradition to be found in Ireland, but they can reasonably be seen as under threat. At the same time, while many Irish have assumed a palpable and justifiable sense of pride in the country's astonishing development, others are ambivalent and asking serious questions about the ultimate social and cultural costs and consequences of growth. The Irish, awash in change, globally connected, are asking who they are, what Ireland is, where their country or island is going, how to make sense of what it all means. They are, in short, at an intellectual and psychological – even a spiritual – crossroads. *964 words*

*From: Wyndham, Andrew Higgins, ed. Re-Imaging Ireland*


**Annotations:**

16 to scope out: G.: *Möglichkeiten erweitern*
17 nascent: starting to develop
23 national Primary Exam: a standardized national exam (until 1967) taken after eight years of primary education at age 12
29 Irish wake: *here:* staying up during the last night before emigrating and sharing the grief of parting with friends and relatives
30/44 most *(AE, infml.)*: almost
31 save for: except for
39/40 road map: *here:* official plan
40 siliconized: *here:* used as a parallel indicating a development similar to 'Silicon Valley', a high-tech center in California, USA

49 moment: *here:* importance
50 polities: politically organized communities
54/55 Enterprise Unlimited: the name of the cross-border inter-city train service between Dublin in the Republic of Ireland and Belfast in Northern Ireland
58/59 Fintan O'Toole: Irish journalist and writer
60 Yeats, Synge, Joyce: great Irish writers: W. B. Yeats (1865–1939), poet and winner of the Nobel Prize for Literature 1923; J. M. Synge (1871–1909), dramatist; J. Joyce (1882–1941) novelist.

**Aufgabenstellung**

1. Point out the stages in the author's life and his relationship to Ireland.
2. Examine the images of the cross and the crossroads throughout the text with regard to their significance for Ireland.
3. "[…] I knew nothing about issues of civil rights and violence in the American South" (ll. 53/54). Explain what these issues were about. Refer to materials concerning the African-American experience studied in class.
4. Discuss in which way Henry Smart's life *(A Star Called Henry)* is characterized by "crossroads", too. Support your arguments with examples.

---

## Lösungsvorschläge

1. *In the first task you have to point out the stages in A. Higgins-Wyndham's life and to summarize the main aspects of his relationship to Ireland. It is important to concentrate on the main points only and to leave out the details the author mentions in connection with the various places he has lived in.*
   - *life:*
     - *born in England, Polish father, Irish mother*
     - *age of 6: moved to Ireland (Dublin: traditional environment, Shannon: more international)*
     - *some years later: moved to Virginia, USA*
   - *relationship to Ireland:*
     - *often visits the country*
     - *follows its development closely*

   The author A. Higgins-Wyndham, who has written the preface to *Re-Imagining Ireland* in 2006, is the child of an Irish mother and a Polish father. He spent the first years of his life in England, where he acquired an English accent. At the age of six he moved to Ireland. First he lived in a traditionally Irish environment in Dublin. Then he moved to Shannon with his family, where the atmosphere was more international. Many of the author's friends at Shannon had foreign accents, but he went to a school in Limerick where he was taught a strongly accented Irish.
   A. Higgins-Wyndham's Irish mother Eileen, who loved her country, nevertheless encouraged her husband to leave Ireland and go to the USA. Since then Higgins-Wyndham has lived in Virginia in the South of the USA. He still visits Ireland regularly, closely observing the various changes the country has seen within the last decades.

2. *Here you have to examine the images of the cross and the crossroads the author uses in his text. You have to consider that these symbols are both characteristics of traditional Ireland and images of the changes in the country. Crossroads in particular refer to the contrasts between traditional and modern Ireland the author presents in his text.*
   *Note that the text was written in 2006, i. e. two years before a financial crisis hit Ireland and caused severe problems for the Irish economy.*

   In the first paragraph of his preface to *Re-Imagining Ireland* (2006) the author A. Higgins-Wyndham introduces the images of the cross and the crossroads. He explains to his readers that the word "cross" is not only used to describe the traditional Celtic Catholic cross, which you find in many Irish streets and which has been extensively used as a grave marker, but that this word also refers to "a crossroads, a place where people and traffic intersect" (l. 3). Throughout his text Higgins-Wyndham uses the word "crossroads" in a figurative sense, referring to Ireland's present situation between its traditional role as the country of Irish literature, family stories, beliefs, beautiful landscape and rich culture and its new role as a high-

ly-industrialized country representing globalisation, traffic and urban development. In this context the author mentions the "nascent industrial park" (l. 17) at Shannon. He explains to his readers that "the original plan for Shannon has become the road map for the 'siliconized' country" (ll. 39/40); it's a multicultural place where interaction – either face-to-face or online – between people from different parts of the world and from different regions in Ireland is commonplace.
When the author and his parents moved to Dublin, Ireland's capital was "at a kind of crossroads" (l. 15), becoming more and more international. Dublin was "beginning to scope out and implement plans to encourage foreign investment" (l. 16).
A few years later, when Higgins-Wyndham and his parents emigrated to the USA, Ireland was at crossroads again; "it was a place of modest intersections, encounters and change" (ll. 36/37). Higgins-Wyndham goes on explaining that Ireland today is at an "'interchange' on a freeway" (l. 37), which can be seen as a climax of the image "crossroads". It shows that Ireland has made a leap forward in development "emerging as the most globalized society in the world" (l. 38). The author's mother, who has always been hungry for the best the world had on offer (cf. l. 25), is coming back from the USA to stay in Ireland because you no longer have to leave Ireland to be able to benefit from these things (cf. l. 44). Moreover, the quarrels between Northern Ireland and the Republic of Ireland have mostly subsided and democratic solutions to long-lasting problems seem possible (cf. l. 51) – another reason why Ireland was at a crossroads at the time the text was written.
This new Ireland contrasts sharply with the vision of a very traditional, idyllic Ireland that those "who have read Yeats and Synge and Joyce" (l. 60) still think of and that those who come to Ireland on holiday with the romantic images from traditional stories or travel brochures have in mind (cf. ll. 60–62). However, this is not just a romantic idea: in spite of globalisation, industrialization and economic change Ireland still has this traditional side (cf. ll. 62–64).
In conclusion one can say that the images of the cross and the crossroads throughout the text symbolize Ireland's identity crisis at the time A. Higgins-Wyndham wrote his preface. Due to the rapid developments and the ensuing consequences in various fields (society, economy, politics, culture) Ireland is in a state of transition, the end of which is still uncertain.

3. *In task 3 you have to explain what the issues of civil rights and violence in the American South were about.*
*In class you probably discussed aspects of slavery and Ernest J. Gaines' novel* A Lesson Before Dying. *Since you are asked to explain the problems with civil rights in the South of the USA you should focus your attention on this topic and the events related to it. That means you have to leave out other aspects of the African-American experience, for example Gaines' novel, but elaborate on civil rights and the Civil Rights Movement in the USA.*
*The key points are:*
– *origin of the Civil Rights Movement: discrimination against African-Americans*

*in the first half of the 20th century, particularly in the American South*
- *attempts to improve the situation: NAACP (litigation, lobbying)*
- *the Civil Rights Movement tried to focus the authorities' attention on the problems by means of: civil disobedience and non-violent protests, for example:*
  - *Montgomery bus boycott, Rosa Parks*
  - *March on Washington for Jobs and Freedom: Martin Luther King's speech "I have a dream"*
- *divisions in the Civil Rights Movement*

When A. Higgins-Wyndham came to the USA he "knew nothing about issues of civil rights and violence in the American South" (ll. 53/54). Higgins-Wyndham was still a child when he and his family came to Virginia. At the time, he knew neither about the solutions that were discussed to solve the problems between Northern Ireland and the Republic of Ireland, nor about civil rights and the Civil Rights Movement in the South of the USA (cf. ll. 49–54).
The Civil Rights Movement had its origins in the injustices that the African-Americans were still suffering from in the first half of the twentieth century, even though Blacks and Whites had the same rights by law. However, in the workplace, in public transport, on TV and in many other fields of everyday life in the USA and in the American South in particular Blacks were still discriminated against. Organizations like the "National Association for the Advancement of Colored People" (NAACP) tried to improve the situation of African-Americans through litigation and lobbying attempts. Racial segregation, however, remained a characteristic of everyday life.
In the second half of the twentieth century, the so-called Civil Rights Movement tried to draw the attention of the authorities to the various forms of discrimination against Blacks in the USA. The methods of the movement included boycotts, for example, the famous Montgomery Bus Boycott in Alabama, which officially started on December 1st, 1955, when Rosa Parks, a well-respected black woman, refused to make more room in the white section of a city bus, for which she was arrested. At that time, Blacks in Montgomery as well as in many other cities in the American South were relegated to the back of the bus when a white person entered. From that day on, in response to Rosa Park's arrest, the Blacks in Montgomery decided to boycott the city buses until they could be allowed to sit anywhere they wanted, thus causing financial damage to the city's public transport system. On November 13th, 1956, the United States Supreme Court ruled that segregation was unlawful and that the city of Montgomery had no right to impose it on the people riding the city buses. This meant the end of the boycott. The fact that today American citizens of all skin colors can sit wherever they want on buses is mostly due to the courage displayed by Rosa Parks.
Another important event that is often associated with the Civil Rights Movement is the "March on Washington for Jobs and Freedom" (1963), one of several examples of non-violent protest against racial injustice. This march has become famous for various reasons. On the one hand, it was very difficult to bring together different leaders of civil rights as they were disunited. On the other hand, the

march is so well-remembered because Martin Luther King gave his famous "I Have a Dream" speech during this event. In it, King, the best-known leader of the Civil Rights Movement and an advocate of civil disobedience as a means of fighting racial segregation, voices his vision of an end of discrimination and of full racial equality between former slaves (Blacks) and former slave owners (Whites). At the age of 35, Martin Luther King was the youngest man to have received the Nobel Peace Prize, donating the prize money to the furtherance of the Civil Rights Movement. After his assassination in 1968, the divisions within the Civil Rights Movement increased. Nevertheless, the movement's aims and measures are, among others, responsible for many significant changes in US society in the 20th and 21st century.

4. *In task 4 you have to relate the image of the crossroads to the life of Henry Smart, the protagonist in Roddy Doyle's novel* A Star Called Henry. *You should choose significant points in Henry's life and explain why they can be called a turning point, a crossroads.*
*Major changes in Henry's life you could mention:*
- *leaves his mother together with his brother at the age of 5, lives on the streets, finds Victor dead when he wakes up one morning*
- *Easter Rising 1916: soldier of the Irish Citizen Army; meets Miss O'Shea again and has his first sexual encounter; witnesses the killings of several of his comrades, but shows no grief*
- *manages to escape from his impending execution; when he learns that this made him a hero, he joins the rebellion again*
- *after working for the rebellion for three years he realizes that he just plays a superficial role*
- *marriage with Miss O'Shea: assassins for the IRA; Henry is eventually disillusioned with the rebels' cause: abstract ideas like freedom and Irishness have been used as justifications for ruthless acts of violence*

A. Higgins-Wyndham uses the image of the crossroads to describe Ireland's situation between tradition and change. The same image can be applied to Henry Smart's life, which is also characterized by a number of crossroads.
The first change in Henry's life takes place when he is five years old. Henry leaves his mother and takes to the streets with his younger brother Victor. After a particularly cold night Henry wakes up to find that his brother is dead.
Six years after Victor's death the fourteen-year-old Henry fights in the Easter Rising (1916) as a soldier in the Irish Citizen Army. During this time of uprising Henry meets a woman who will play an important role in his future life: his former teacher, Miss O'Shea, with whom he has his first sexual encounter. Several days later, Henry and the other members of the new "IRA" make their way from the besieged General Post Office in Dublin to another building through a hail of bullets. Henry witnesses that several of his friends and colleagues are killed.

However, he does not show any grief. There is no evidence that Henry psychologically suffers from what he sees.
After the rebels' surrender, Henry is again at a crossroads. He manages to escape from the barracks and his probable execution. When Henry learns that his escape has made him a modern Republican hero, he joins the rebellion again, being once more ready to die for Ireland. After three years of enlisting volunteers for the rebel army, Henry realizes that his place in the inner circle of the famous Michael Collins is just superficial. This realization marks another crossroads in Henry's life.
When Henry meets Miss O'Shea again, they marry. Together they work as assassins for the IRA carrying out robberies and killings. When she and Henry are shot at, Henry decides to no longer take part in the killings. His wife, however, remains an active freedom fighter, even during her pregnancy. Henry realizes at that time how little the endless violence and the killing of innocent people have got to do with the concept of a free Ireland. Before Henry decides to leave Ireland, he spends a night at the brothel which was once his father's workplace. He kills his father's murderer, visits his imprisoned wife for one last time and goes away, leaving his wife and daughter behind.
Although Henry is presented as a rather brutal, unemotional fighter throughout the story, there is a kind of change taking place inside him at the end of the novel. He is disillusioned with the rebels' cause, realizing that abstract ideas like freedom and Irishness have been used as justifications for ruthless, often useless acts of violence. Therefore one could say that Henry is actually at a crossroads when the novel ends, although his character does not really change.

## Gymnasium Niedersachsen – Englisch
## Erhöhtes Anforderungsniveau 2011 – Abiturprüfungsaufgabe 2

### Text 1: Excerpt from Don DeLillo's novel *White Noise* (1984)

*After a railway accident in which a tank car has been damaged a huge toxic cloud has spread across the sky. The authorities are busy trying to contain the catastrophe, but the population of a small town somewhere in the east of the USA has to be evacuated. The Gladney family, like many other citizens, have fled the town and are being directed to a place called Iron City:*

We reached Iron City at dawn. There were checkpoints at all the road exits. State troopers and Red Cross workers handed out mimeographed instructions concerning evacuation centers. Half an hour later we found ourselves, with forty other families, in an abandoned karate studio on the top floor of a four-story building on the main street. There were no beds or chairs. Steffie refused to take off her mask.

By nine a.m. we had a supply of air mattresses, some food and coffee. Through the dusty windows we saw a group of turbaned schoolchildren, members of the local Sikh community, standing in the street with a hand-lettered sign: IRON CITY WELCOMES AREA EVACUEES. We were not allowed to leave the building. […]

At noon a rumor swept the city. Technicians were being lowered in slings from army helicopters in order to plant microorganisms in the core of the toxic cloud. These organisms were genetic recombinations that had a built-in appetite for the particular toxic agents in Nyodene D. They would literally consume the billowing cloud, eat it up, break it down, decompose it.

This stunning innovation, so similar in nature to something we might come across in the *National Enquirer* or the *Star*, made us feel a little weary, glutted in an insubstantial way, as after a junk food spree. I wandered through the room, […], moving from one conversational knot to another. No one seemed to know how a group of microorganisms could consume enough toxic material to rid the sky of such a dense and enormous cloud. No one knew what would happen to the toxic waste once it was eaten or to the microorganisms once they were finished eating. […]

At seven p.m. a man carrying a tiny TV set began to walk slowly through the room, making a speech as he went. He was middle-aged or older, a clear-eyed and erect man wearing a fur-lined cap with lowered flaps. He held the TV set well up in the air and out away from his body and during the course of his speech he turned completely around several times as he walked in order to display the blank screen to all of us in the room.

"There's nothing on network," he said to us. "Not a word, not a picture. On the Glassboro channel we rate fifty-two words by actual count. No film footage, no live report. Does this kind of thing happen so often that nobody cares anymore? Don't those people know what we've been through? We were scared to death.

We still are. We left our homes, we drove through blizzards, we saw the cloud. It was a deadly specter, right there above us. Is it possible nobody gives substantial coverage to such a thing? Half a minute, twenty seconds? Are they telling us it was insignificant, it was piddling? Are they so callous? Are they so bored by spills and contaminations and wastes? Do they think this is just television? 'There's too much television already – why show more?' Don't they know it's real? Shouldn't the streets be crawling with cameramen and soundmen and reporters? Shouldn't we be yelling out the window at them, 'Leave us alone, we've been through enough, get out of here with your vile instruments of intrusion.' Do they have to have two hundred dead, rare disaster footage, before they come flocking to a given site in their helicopters and network limos? What exactly has to happen before they stick microphones in our faces and hound us to the doorsteps of our homes, camping out on our lawns, creating the usual media circus? Haven't we earned the right to despise their idiot questions? Look at us in this place. We are quarantined. We are like lepers in medieval times. They won't let us out of here. They leave food at the foot of the stairs and tiptoe away to safety. This is the most terrifying time of our lives. Everything we love and have worked for is under serious threat. But we look around and see no response from the official organs of the media. The airborne toxic event is a horrifying thing. Our fear is enormous. Even if there hasn't been great loss of life, don't we deserve some attention for our suffering, our human worry, our terror? Isn't fear news?"

Applause. A sustained burst of shouting and hand-clapping. The speaker slowly turned one more time, displaying the little TV to his audience. *811 words*

*Edited and abridged from WHITE NOISE by Don DeLillo, © 1984, 1985 by Don DeLillo. Used by permission of Viking Penguin, a division of Penguin Group (USA) Inc.*

**Annotations:**

2 mimeographed: copied
5 Steffie: a daughter of the Gladney family
5 mask: gas mask
13 Nyodene D: an imaginary toxic chemical substance supposedly made up from byproducts of the manufacture of insecticide
13 to billow: to rise and move in a large mass G.: *in Schwaden aufsteigen*
16 *National Enquirer, Star:* celebrity news and gossip tabloid magazines
16 glutted: *here:* overfed, stuffed, having had too much of something
17 junk food spree: eating too much junk food in a very short time
29 Glassboro channel: local TV station
33 specter: something that people are afraid of because it may affect them badly
35 callous: cruel, unfeeling
45 lepers: people suffering from leprosy (G.: *Lepra*), outcasts because of this contagious disease

## Text 2:

"When it came to race issues the state [i. e. Mississippi] operated under a virtual media lockdown in the early 1960s. When James Baldwin was a guest on 'Today', NBC stations in Mississippi cut to an old movie. When Thurgood Marshall, then an N.A.A.C.P. lawyer, appeared on TV, a notice flashed: 'Cable Difficulty'". *52 words*

*From: "Mississippi Invaded by Idealism" In:* The New York Times, *18 July 2010.*

**Annotations:**

2 James Baldwin (1924–1987): famous African-American writer
3 Thurgood Marshall (1908–1993): famous African-American lawyer, prominent member of the Civil Rights Movement and the first African-American to serve on the Supreme Court of the USA
4 N.A.A.C.P.: National Association for the Advancement of Colored People

**Aufgabenstellung**

1. Outline the situation presented in the text.
2. Examine the speech (ll. 28–51) concerning the way the media is dealt with. Also pay special attention to the use of language and its effect on the audience.
3. Compare the situation in this text to that in the radio play *War of the Worlds* with regard to the impact of the media on human behavior.
4. "[…] don't we deserve some attention for our suffering, our human worry, our terror? Isn't fear news?" (ll. 50/51).
   Comment on both this quotation and text 2 with regard to the African-American experience. Also refer to texts and materials studied in class.

---

## Lösungsvorschläge

1. *In task 1 you have to outline the situation that is presented in the text. This means that you have to focus your attention on the central aspects of what characterizes the situation of the evacuees.*
   *The key points are:*
   - *reason the Gladneys are evacuees in Iron City: environmental disaster*
   - *rumours about attempts to contain and disperse the toxic cloud cause fear and insecurity among the evacuees*
   - *criticism about the lack of media coverage is supported by the whole group*

   In the excerpt from the novel *White Noise*, published in 1984, the author Don DeLillo describes what happens to the Gladney family and other people who have been evacuated from their hometown. The reason why the Gladney family and many other citizens have come to a place called Iron City is an environmental disaster, a huge toxic cloud which has contaminated the air. After the evacuees have been given some food and air mattresses, there is a rumor that attempts are being made by the authorities to contain and disperse the toxic cloud with the help of microorganisms which are meant to decompose the cloud. The rumor causes fear and insecurity among the people since the effects of this measure on human beings are incalculable. One of the evacuees, a middle-aged man carrying a TV set through the room, starts to make a speech. He strongly criticizes the lack of media coverage and asks what kind of accident actually has to happen to attract the TV stations' attention. The other people in the shelter shout and clap their hands to show that they support the man's criticism.

2. *The middle-aged man delivering the speech in front of the evacuees expresses an ambivalent attitude towards the media. This attitude is clearly reflected in the use of language. Both the choice of words and the stylistic devices underline the speaker's ideas and his feelings.*

*The key points are:*

- *feeling of loss and fear because of missing media coverage, evacuees crave for attention: rhetorical questions (cf. ll. 33/34, 40–42)*
- *criticism of sensationalist aspects of the media: vivid image, straightforward language (ll. 42–44)*
- *speaker shows his knowledge in the field of media: use of specialist words ("network", l. 28; "film footage", l. 29; "live report", ll. 29/30 or "cameramen and soundmen", l. 38)*
- *atmosphere of danger: use of adjectives like "terrifying" (l. 47), "horrifying" (l. 49) and "enormous" (l. 50)*
- *speaker creates feeling of togetherness: pronoun "we" (ll. 31/32)*
- *criticism of the absence of the media: contrasts (ll. 45–47), simile: "like lepers" (l. 45), negative phrases (ll. 28–30), anaphora (ll. 37–39), use of adjectives: "insignificant", "piddling", "callous" (ll. 34/35)*

At the beginning of his speech the man talking to the other evacuees states that people experience a feeling of loss and fear because there is no apparent media coverage of the environmental disaster the evacuees are so seriously suffering from. Therefore he asks rhetorical questions like "Is it possible nobody gives substantial coverage to such a thing? Half a minute, twenty seconds?" (ll. 33/34). The question "Do they have to have two hundred dead, rare disaster footage, before they come flocking to a given site in their helicopters and network limos?" (ll. 40–42) underlines that the evacuees crave attention for media coverage of what has happened to them, of their suffering. However, people also loathe TV because of the sensationalist side-effects. This aspect is underlined with vivid images and straightforward language when the man asks, "What exactly has to happen before they stick microphones in our faces and hound us to the doorsteps of our homes, camping out on our lawns, creating the usual media circus?" (ll. 42–44). The negative connotation of the expression "media circus" (l. 44) particularly stresses the speaker's criticism of the media.

The fact that the speaker uses a lot of media-related vocabulary intensifies the effect the speech has on the evacuees. Words like "network" (l. 28), "film footage" (l. 29), "live report" (ll. 29/30) or "cameramen and soundmen" (l. 38) convey the impression that the speaker knows how the "media circus" (l. 44) works. Adjectives like "terrifying" (l. 47), "horrifying" (l. 49) and "enormous" (l. 50) underline the seriousness of the disaster and the dangers resulting from the toxic cloud. They describe the fear the evacuees are feeling at the moment and therefore deeply touch their emotions.

To create a feeling of togetherness between the people in the evacuation center and himself the speaker repeats the pronoun "we": "We were scared to death. We still are. We left our homes, we drove through blizzards, we saw the cloud" (ll. 31/32). The message the man tries to convey can easily be understood because the parallel structure of the sentences (l. 32) is very simple.

The author's criticism of the absence of the media in such a situation is voiced with the help of a number of stylistic devices. The speaker uses contrasts to illus-

trate the enormously big differences between those who have been evacuated and those who are responsible for the evacuees (cf. ll. 45–47). The contrasting pronouns "we" and "they" in particular stress that the situation of those who have had to leave their hometown is not only completely different from those who support them, but that it is extremely humiliating. Especially the simile "like lepers in medieval times" (l. 45) underlines that the evacuees feel like outcasts who are not paid any attention.
This lack of interest in the fate of the evacuees is underlined by the speaker's using negative phrases like "nothing on network" (l. 28), "Not a word, not a picture." (l. 28), "[n]o film footage, no live report" (ll. 29/30). Thus the speaker strongly criticizes the absence of the media.
In combination with a number of rhetorical questions to win the support of the listeners the man uses anaphora to make his criticism clear: "Shouldn't the streets be crawling with cameramen and soundmen and reporters? Shouldn't we be yelling out the window at them, ..." (ll. 37–39).
Moreover, the man delivering the speech in front of the evacuees enumerates adjectives that underline how those who are responsible for what is shown on TV and what is not might feel about the situation of the people in the evacuation center: "insignificant", "piddling", "callous" (ll. 34/35). These questions in lines 34/35 evoke the consent of the audience. The enumeration of words with negative connotations like "spills" (l. 35), "contaminations" (ll. 35/36) and "wastes" (l. 36) serves the same purpose. The speaker wonders if the media is bored "by spills and contaminations and wastes" (ll. 35/36) and uses an imperative to tell them to direct their attention to the evacuation center: "Look at us in this place" (ll. 44/45). Furthermore, the speaker chooses nouns that underline the seriousness of the evacuees' situation to win their support: "fear" (l. 49), "loss of life" (l. 50), "suffering" (l. 51), "worry" (l. 51), "terror" (l. 51).
The man's speech comes to its climax in the end when he asks: "Even if there hasn't been great loss of life, don't we deserve some attention for our suffering, our human worry, our terror? Isn't fear news?" (ll. 50/51). The fact that the audience shout and clap underlines that they show signs of disorientation and loss when they are deprived of media exposure and coverage. At the same time he voices the above-mentioned criticism of the media.

3. *In task 3 you have to compare the situation in the extract from* White Noise *to that in the radio play* War of the Worlds *by Orson Welles, which you have studied in class. "Compare" means that you have to discuss both similarities and differences, particularly with regard to the impact of the media on human behavior as it is presented in the two texts.*
*The key points are:*
– White Noise:
  - *fictional text about a real danger*
  - *cloud is an anonymous danger from outside*
  - *people are evacuated because of this danger*

  - *fear and suffering is not covered in the media*
  - *evacuees remain relatively calm, no panic*
- War of the Worlds:
  - *fictional radio play which sounds like a news broadcast*
  - *danger: invasion from Mars*
  - *vivid presentation of seemingly real facts causes panic among the listeners*
- *Impact of the media:*
  - White Noise: *people are addicted to media representing reality*
  - War of the Worlds: *piece of entertainment is taken as real*
  - *both texts: media is able to establish or influence the perception of reality by its manipulative power*

In Don DeLillo's *White Noise* the people in the evacuation center have been forced to leave their hometown because of a toxic cloud. This cloud, a real, but anonymous threat from outside, is the reason why the evacuees are afraid, "scared to death" (l. 31). Despite their fear and suffering there is no media coverage of what has happened to them, which makes them angry and leaves them with a feeling of disorientation. Although the evacuees are angry and afraid, particularly because they don't know any details about the toxic cloud, they do not panic. They applaud the man delivering his critical speech about the lack of media coverage, but they remain relatively calm. They try to keep their primeval fears, which mostly result from rumors concerning the toxic cloud, under control. They want to be mentioned in the media hoping to get both attention and information. There is, of course, the danger that the interest of the media in the toxic cloud and the ensuing reports might cause even more worries and insecurity among the population in general and among the evacuees in particular. But the evacuees crave attention for media coverage.

In Orson Welles' radio play *War of the Worlds*, broadcast on 30th October, 1938, the reaction of the listeners to what is reported in the play is in many respects different from that described in the extract from *White Noise*. In most of its parts the radio play sounds like a news broadcast about an invasion from Mars. Thus Welles tries to heighten the dramatic effect on the audience. Only at the beginning of the play and after 40 minutes are the listeners informed about the fictional character of what is being broadcast. As the play unfolds, dance music, for example, is interrupted by fake news bulletins saying that an invasion force from Mars is landing and destroying the United States. An actor in a studio plays a news reporter in a field describing the emergence of one of the aliens from a spacecraft. The vivid presentation of these seemingly real facts, supported by various sound effects, caused panic among the listeners. Uncontrollable rumors spread very quickly; a kind of mass hysteria broke out among parts of the American population. There were reports about evacuations, although there was no actual reason for them. Several people called their relatives and friends or even police stations. Some people are said to have committed suicide in reaction to the events that were broadcast on the radio. The fact that the reaction was so strong has also got to do

with the political situation in those days. Hitler had seized power in Germany and there was the danger of a second world war.
In *White Noise*, however, people are evacuated because there is a real danger, a toxic cloud threatening their lives. In this dangerous situation it becomes clear that the people are addicted to media representing reality. In *War of the Worlds*, by contrast, people react to a program that was intended as entertainment, yet interpreted as a realistic event. Both fictional texts underline that media is able to establish or influence the perception of reality by its manipulative power directed at the imagination of humans causing fright, panic, a generally uneasy atmosphere, suspicion etc. This is true of both the media in the 1930s and media today.

4. *In task 4 you have to comment on a quotation taken from the excerpt of* White Noise. *Both this quotation and text 2, which also has to be considered in your comment, deal with the influence the media has on human behavior. Therefore you should give your personal opinion on this aspect with regard to the African-American experience. It is important to support your comment with arguments based on what you have studied in class.*
*The key points are:*
   - *media's indifference to people's suffering was also felt by African-Americans*
   - *19th century: hardly any media, the few abolitionists who criticized the Whites' behaviour (e. g. Frederick Douglass) didn't get much attention*
   - *20th century: Civil Rights Movement could use media to make their problems and their demands known to a larger audience; Martin Luther King's speeches were broadcast on the radio; problem: radio and TV stations were owned by Whites, they had the power to decide what was aired and what wasn't (cf. text 2)*
   - *conclusion: enormous influence and manipulative power of the media becomes obvious both in the quotation from* White Noise *and in text 2.*

The quotation "[…] don't we deserve some attention for our suffering, our human worry, our terror? Isn't fear news?" (ll. 50/51) underlines the wish of the evacuees for media attention in their desperate situation. The man delivering the speech in front of the people in the evacuation center criticizes the media's indifference towards the despair and the helplessness of the evacuees.
Many African-Americans probably felt much the same in the course of their history. In the times of slavery most white Americans did not take any interest in the living conditions of Blacks. There was hardly even any media in those days and only very few abolitionists criticized the behavior of the white masters towards their slaves. One of them was Frederick Douglass, who was born into slavery and managed to become a well-known critic of the Whites' behavior. Frederick Douglass and other African-American writers of those days, for example W. E. B. DuBois and Booker T. Washington, tried to influence their fellow blacks in such a way that they become aware of the injustice that was done to them. Their chances, however, were very limited in the 19th century. In *A Soul in Chains* Douglass describes how he managed to become more and more educated. How-

ever, despite his education he could not do anything against the injustices that were done to Blacks.
During the times of the Civil Rights Movement, in the 1960s, Martin Luther King became the most prominent spokesman for the African Americans. His speeches against racism and for equality between Blacks and Whites turned him into the United States' most famous civil rights activist. Unlike Frederick Douglass, Martin Luther King could profit from the radio and partly from TV. Since some of his speeches were broadcast on the radio, Martin Luther King managed to inform large numbers of US citizens about the Civil Rights Movement and its aims. However, the owners and chief executives of many radio and TV stations in those days were white and could deliberately curtail media coverage of the movement. This fact becomes particularly clear in the excerpt from *The New York Times* (text 2). When James Baldwin, a famous African-American writer who supported the Civil Rights Movement, was a guest on the TV show 'Today', many TV stations in Mississippi decided to switch to an old movie, thus banning the author from the TV. So Baldwin was not given any "attention" (ll. 50/51); the interests of the African-Americans, their "suffering" (l. 51) and their "worry" (l. 51) were not what the Whites wanted to show in their programs. The aims of the Civil Rights Movement were thus prevented from being aired.
In conclusion you can say that both the quotation from *White Noise* and text 2 underline the enormous influence, the manipulative power that media can have. This influence can be fatal for those humans who need the media to draw people's attention to their "suffering, [their] human worry, [their] terror" (l. 51) in order to get help or support or to change their situation for the better.

## Text: Phillip Jackson, "The Big Divide" (2010)

The lack of response to globalization by Black America is frightening and troubling. While much of the world has adapted to the new-world economy and new-world standards of existence, most of Black America is still operating much the same way it did in the 1950s and 1960s. But now, throughout Black communities in America, there is a whisper campaign by Black people who don't know each other and Black people who live in different parts of the country, saying to each other, "We are in trouble!" We know it and the rest of the world knows it! Black America, as we know it, is in danger of not surviving globalization.

In the 21st century, there are only two kinds of people. Not Black or White, or rich or poor, or foreign or national. The two kinds of people in the world today are those who are educated and those who are not. Although education has become the new <u>currency of exchange</u> in the 21st century, the old American educational <u>paradigm</u> stopped working decades ago for Black Americans. Simply sending Black children to American schools without a clear purpose or goal has contributed to the <u>demise</u> of the Black community. Black America watched formerly third-world countries catapult over America to become educational super powers while America rested on its old, stale educational laurels and fell way behind much of the world in educational performance. And because Black America unthinkingly depended on the American education system to educate its children, we have fallen way behind.

The horrific educational, social, health, economic and criminal justice indicators in much of Black America predict a meltdown of <u>gargantuan</u> proportions in the near future for the Black community. But still, the thing that is most remarkable and unbelievable is the lack of response by Black Americans to this impending doom! Without numerous positive changes, practical well-thought-out ideas, massive mobilization and immediate action, the fate of many Black Americans is sealed. We will not be able to prosper in the cities of America or possibly in any city in the world where the new currency for existence is access to global information, higher-order critical thinking and advanced technological skills. There used to be a time when it was better to be poor in America than rich in other countries. Now it might be better to be poor in some other countries than to be poor in America.

Black people in America must immediately disengage from the diversions of mind-deadening entertainment, useless sports, hyper-sexuality, excessive social celebrations, pointless conversations and debates, meaningless media and the civil rights issue <u>de jour</u> approach to managing our problems. We must focus on the most important issue in our communities – making education the highest priority. We must create a culture of literacy and learning that replaces intellectual apathy and resistance to educational progress. Somehow, we must re-inspire our children to want to learn and to love to learn. But having educated children is not enough. We must have educated families and educated communities. Every Black man, woman and child must become part of this new community of learners.

Black America must take education out of the schools and universities and root it in our homes, our workplaces, our communities, our churches and even in our streets and prisons. […]

The ability of a people to survive in changing times is not magic, nor is it by chance. Success depends on people being able to change to survive in a new environment! And new environments demand new skills for survival. Equipped for the Future tells us that without certain basic skills, survival will be extremely difficult for Black people, or any people, in the 21st century. These essential skills are the ability to read with understanding; convey ideas in writing; speak so that others can understand; observe critically; listen actively; solve problems and make decisions appropriately; plan and put those plans into action effectively; use math to solve problems and to communicate; cooperate with others; guide others; advocate and influence; resolve conflict and negotiate; take responsibility for life-long learning; learn through research; reflect and evaluate; and use information and communication technology. These are the skills necessary to survive in the 21st century.

The solution to the issue of Black America's poor response to globalization is to 1) Deconstruct value systems that have caused Black people to arrive at the precipice of non-existence; 2) Construct value systems that will rebuild the Black family as a purveyor of positive values, cultures, mores and education, and re-establish the Black family as the primary and most important social unit of our culture and society; 3) Embrace education as the highest value in the Black community; 4) Effectively manage the negative cultural influences that hugely impact the thinking and actions of Black boys; and 5) Understand that for the rest of existence, change is a required part of the living process. The faster Black America is able to put this plan into action, adopt these new principles and manage change, the more likely we will survive.

Today, many Black people seem to be having "cosmic flashbacks" to our time in slavery, which was the first crude effort at globalization that helped to set the stage for today's globalization. For years, Black America was buffered from modern globalization by political boundaries and economic barriers. Now globalization has come to our country, our cities, our communities, onto our blocks and into our homes, schools and workplaces. Globalization has happened, whether Black America is ready for it or not. We still have time to make the necessary changes that will guarantee that Black people will survive into the 21st century and that we will thrive in this global economy. But there is not much time. With globalization, Black America has entered into the "Educate or Die" era. In this era, there are only two questions worth answering: "Will we change? Can we survive?" How we emerge from this era is up to us.

*992 words*

*From: http://www.thenewblackmagazine.com/view.aspx?index-2350*

**Annotations:**
Phillip Jackson is the executive director of The Black Star Project
12 currency of exchange, G.: *Währung*
12 paradigm: model, system

14 demise: ruin, downfall
21 gargantuan: enormous, colossal
34 de jour: G.: *aktuell*
46/47 Equipped for the Future: educational improvement initiative for adult basic education
59 purveyor: supplier, provider
68 to be buffered from: to be shielded from

## Picture printed as an illustration of the article

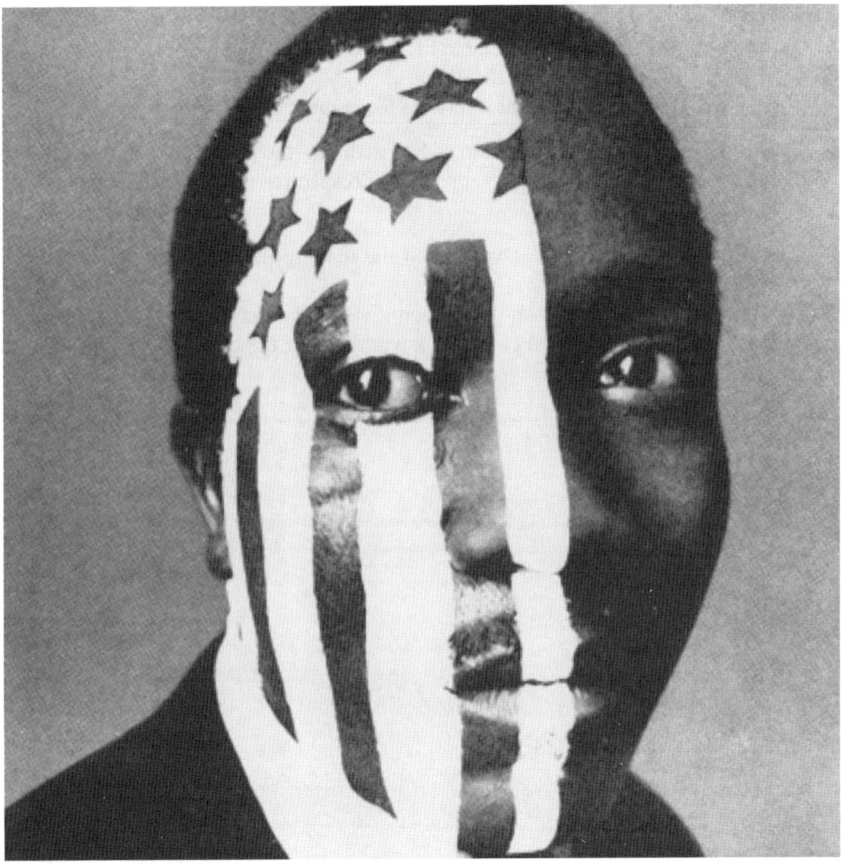

*© Lou Dorfsman; designed for a CBS News series on black history*

**Aufgabenstellung**

Imagine you are taking part in a school project on the challenges of globalization. You focus on the topic "Globalization and African Americans". The article "The Big Divide", a picture and materials you dealt with in class are your references. The paper you are asked to write will be published on your school's website.

1. You outline the problems Black America faces according to Phillip Jackson and the measures he suggests.

2. To find out if the picture is a suitable illustration of the article
   a) you describe the picture in detail and
   b) you examine to what extent it reflects the content of the text.

3. For both Phillip Jackson and Thomas L. Friedman, the concept of change is crucial in a globalized world. You compare their respective views of what change implies for each of them.

4. The novel *A Lesson Before Dying* is on the reading list of numerous American high schools.
   Having dealt with Jackson and Friedman's views, you comment on the question whether this novel is a good choice in a world facing the challenges of globalization.

## Lösungsvorschläge

1. *In this task you must consider that you have to do two things. Firstly you are asked to outline the problems Black Americans face in the era of globalisation according to Phillip Jackson's article, "The Big Divide":*
   - *African Americans have not responded to globalisation adequately, stagnation (cf. ll. 1–4)*
   - *no true interest in education or career planning (cf. ll. 36/37); instead: only interested in entertainment (ll. 31–33)*

   *And secondly you have to explain the measures he suggests to solve them:*
   - *promoting education as the most important value (cf. ll. 35, 61); must be deeply rooted inside families and communities (cf. ll. 41–43, 58–60)*
   - *developing the skills that are necessary to succeed in a globalised world (cf. ll. 48–55)*
   - *spreading the acceptance of a necessity for change (cf. ll. 63–65)*

   The article "The Big Divide" written by Phillip Jackson and published online deals with the problems African Americans face in the era of globalisation and possible measures that can be taken to solve them.
   The author expresses his worries that African Americans are currently in real danger of not being able to cope with globalisation successfully. He argues that they have failed to respond adequately to a globalised economy, still act the same way they did in the 1950s and 1960s and do not see the necessity for change. In his opinion, the biggest problem is that most Black Americans are not truly interested in education and career planning, but in activities that are for mere pleasure and could even be called destructive. According to Jackson, many African Americans waste too much of their time on parties, meaningless media and entertainment instead of activities with an educational benefit.
   Regarding the solution to the issue of the African Americans' poor response to globalisation, he makes some suggestions. In his view, the highest importance should be attributed to education. According to him, it is most important to arouse a zest for learning in children and make them aware of the importance of a good education. In this context, he also points to the fact that this is only possible if this value of education is generally accepted, in families and communities as well as at schools and in companies. There are several skills children have to develop to be able to succeed in a globalised world: Beside reading, writing, arithmetic and IT skills they must be able to work together and to communicate with other people successfully, to deal with conflicts and to solve problems. Moreover, he holds the view that African Americans have to accept the necessity for change and to adapt to the new situation of a globalised world in order to survive.

2. *You can write one text that covers both task 2 a and b.*
*You should give a brief description of the picture first:*
- *portrait of an African American*
- *formally dressed (dark suit, white shirt); short hair, scar on his face, moustache*
- *one side of his face is covered with white stripes, stars on his forehead: US flag*
- *right eye not covered with stripes*

*Then relate the picture to the article about the situation of African Americans in the era of globalisation. You could either come to the conclusion that there are links that reflect the content of the text or that there are not. It is only important that you give convincing reasons for your opinion. This sample solution assumes that there are fairly obvious links to the article:*
- *stripes on his face: prison bars, opportunities for African Americans are still limited*
- *protruding eye: symbolizes possibility of an unrestricted view on the present situation in a globalised world and the measures that have to be taken to cope with it*
- *stars on his forehead (= brain): realizes the necessity for change and for developing the essential skills for life in a globalised world*
- *formal attire: looks like an educated man, maybe a successful businessman*
- *serious expression: reflects urgency of the matter that allows no delay*

The picture shows a portrait of an African American man. He is formally dressed and wears a dark suit and a white shirt. His hair is short and he has a moustache and a scar on his face. One side of his face is covered with white stripes and stars that are irregular and depict the American flag. His right eye, however, is not covered with stripes and seems to protrude from behind the stripes. The stars of the American flag are located on the man's forehead.
In my view the picture reflects the content of the article fairly well. In the article it is said that African Americans still focus too much on the 1950s and 1960s, which seems to be the reason why one side of the black man's face is covered with stripes looking like bars that seem to indicate that the opportunities for Black people are still sharply limited. The protruding eye, however, is not covered at all and seems to symbolise hope that African Americans will finally begin to realise that it is important to have an unrestricted view on the current events in the world in order to cope well with globalisation. In addition, the stars on the man's forehead – which might stand for his brain – seem to represent Black people's successful response to globalisation by making them achieve the essential skills that are decisive for a successful life in today's world according to the author of the article. This is reinforced by the formal attire of an educated and successful businessman. Furthermore, the uncovered side of his face suggests that there is still hope for blacks to succeed in a globalised world. Nevertheless, he looks quite serious, which alludes to the urgency of the matter that bears no delay.
The picture thus exactly mirrors the current situation of African Americans in my view.

3. *Comparing Phillip Jackson's view to Thomas L. Friedman's attitude (as expressed in his non-fiction book* The World is Flat*) concerning why change is crucial in a globalised world you will find similarities: e. g. the essential willingness to change and adapt to new conditions in order to survive in a globalised world. You will also spot differences because Jackson's views are restricted to African Americans in the US only. In addition, make sure that you write a well-structured text and also include examples and reasons to support your explanations.*

Taking into account Phillip Jackson's view and Thomas L. Friedman's attitude – as expressed in his non-fiction book *The World is Flat* –, it can be said that there are similarities as well as differences with regard to the changes that are necessary in order to survive in a globalised world.
Similarities are that both consider it necessary for people to be really willing to change and to adapt to new conditions, and see this as a basic requirement for their survival. Additionally, both note that there must be a central focus on education to improve future-orientated skills as the unskilled and under-educated will find it hard or even impossible to be employed in this new world.
Differences between Jackson's and Friedman's approach mainly result from Jackson's one-sided focus on the education of African Americans, which makes it necessary in his view to start a joint campaign to tear down barriers and leave behind old attitudes that should be replaced by those required today. Moreover, cultural influences which have an effect on young African Americans must be redesigned and new values are supposed to be instilled in their communities.
In contrast to Jackson, Friedman's concept of change is a global one with positive connotations that include terms like progress, innovation, diversity and empowerment. He suggests that if people are willing to meet challenges and cultivate a spirit of entrepreneurship, global, local and individual economic conditions can be optimised. According to Friedman, the change itself is just the result of the ability and willingness to be well-prepared for the future.

4. *You are asked to write a personal comment on the question of whether the novel* A Lesson Before Dying *by Ernest G. Gaines is a good choice to deal with the challenges in a globalised world. Take into account Jackson's and Friedman's views and write a comment. First, you should outline the pros and cons in a structured text. You can mention the following aspects with regard to Gaines' novel:*
   - *pros:*
     - *good example to show what life was like for African Americans in the past*
     - *example that change is possible*
     - *stresses the importance of education*
   - *cons:*
     - *only refers to the past*
     - *very limited number of changes*

   *Then present your own views and finally write a concluding sentence.*

Thinking about the challenges for African Americans in a globalised world the question arises whether a novel like Ernest G. Gaines' *A Lesson Before Dying* can help young people to deal with this situation.

First of all, the novel, which is set in the late 1940s, can show young people what life was like for African Americans in those days. It will certainly be helpful for students to keep in mind the history of African Americans when dealing with the challenges of their present situation.

In the novel, Jefferson, a 21-year-old African American, was accidentally in the wrong place at the wrong time. Although innocent, he is accused of having killed three people in a robbery. In court his attorney pleads for mercy, saying Jefferson is not a man but a fool with little intelligence, a "hog" that is not worth executing. Nevertheless, he is sentenced to death by an all-white jury. However, Miss Emma, Jefferson's godmother, does not want him to crawl but to stand and die as a human being. She puts pressure on Grant Wiggins, a teacher at the local church school, to visit Jefferson in jail and "teach him a lesson" and turn the hog into a man. Before being executed, he is finally transformed and regains his dignity and self-respect by walking upright like a man. Thus, he protests against being treated as an inferior, second-class citizen.

In this way the novel can also serve as an example that change is possible. Moreover, the novel is a convincing illustration that blacks have no real chance in life if they are uneducated and only enjoy the simple pleasures of life as Jefferson did. In addition to that, the novel shows that strong support and the teaching of the "right" values within a family or black community might change the situation of African Americans for the better by generating respect and developing self-esteem.

On the other hand, the novel focuses on the past and on racial issues that have now mostly been overcome in many fields of life. Furthermore, it depicts only a very limited number of changes that have to be made, for example, to die like a human being rather than an animal.

To sum up, I think the novel is worth reading as Jefferson shows a lot of courage in the end and is a shining example of a man who dares to rebel and challenge the system in order to get things changed.

## Text 1: Excerpt from Philip Batty, "Saluting the dot-spangled banner" (1998)

The closing ceremonies of the Atlanta Olympics [1996] were watched by a fifth of the world's population. At the very end of this global spectacle, just before the billion or so viewers had time to switch to another channel, Australia was given a brief TV spot to invite the world to Sydney for the next Olympic Games in the year 2000.

This was arguably the most expensive piece of air-time on the planet at that moment; filling it with a slick bit of advertising would of course be a routine matter for the average transnational corporation – they speak the lingua franca of consumerism – but how does one go about representing a 'nation' in a short television message that encapsulates what might be called a 'unique national essence' and communicates in a language that is broadly comprehensible to a global audience?

What the world saw of 'Australia' in that brief moment of planetary exposure were the signs not of the 'progressive modern state' (as seen at the festivities surrounding the Melbourne Olympics in 1956), nor was it exactly a fragmented assortment of disparate elements trying to look 'post modern' [...], rather, it was an odd mixture of both; a kind of work in progress.

Gone were the stockmen, the circles of stumbling sheep, the show ponies, the wood-chopping, the prize bulls, the tractors, the wheat harvesters, and the brand new Holden cars fresh off the production line. Instead, the organisers chose to represent 'Australia', through a pageant of the 'indigenous', heavily laced with the associated signs of the 'primordial' and the 'natural'.

Rising up in the centre of what looked like a mass of flames (long red streamers blown upwards by hidden fans), a group of painted Aboriginal musicians blew into their amplified didgeridoos, while all around them danced an odd assemblage of female performers dressed in knee-length, see-through dresses.

Other actors disguised as sulphur-crested cockatoos and a troop of cyclists carrying blow-up plastic kangaroos on their backs (decorated with the dots and lines of Australian Aboriginal art), also appeared. Towards the end of the performance, as if in an awkward glance back to the days when Australia was secure in its modernity, (and Aboriginal culture represented nothing more than a curious footnote in the pages of national advancement), a plastic replica of the billowing sails of the Sydney opera house rose up in the background. [...]

So how did we get from the 'dying race', or 'the most backward and wretched' race on earth, or the 'evolutionary relic' to the performance at the Atlanta Olympics? How did Aboriginal culture become so transformed that it can now be represented, on the global stage, as symbolising a kind of essential Australian? Indeed, we now find signs of the 'indigenous' in any number of nationalist representational strategies – the 'national carrier', QANTAS, for instance, recently covered two of its jumbo jets in a montage of 'indigenous' designs and Aboriginal artists are regularly presented at international events as purveyors of a uniquely 'Australian' art. Ironically, a recent design for Australia Post corporate uniforms was awash with the dots and circles of central Australian Aboriginal iconography. […]

Australia continues to seek a sense of identity through yet another reinvention of Aboriginal culture, but this time it is constituted not as a problem to be eradicated, or assimilated – but as a site of national redemption, where Australia can reaffirm its most cherished beliefs about itself; that is, as a fair-minded, just, and compassionate global citizen. […] *578 words*



**Annotations:**

2 billion: *here:* a very large number
8 to go about sth.: G.: *etwas angehen, etwas in Angriff nehmen*
12 progressive modern state: referring to progress and modernity up to the 2nd half of the 20th century
14 post modern: mixing traditional and modern styles
19 pageant: a colourful show or public entertainment in which people dress in historical costumes and give performances of scenes from history
20 the primordial: the very first, the original
25 sulphur-crested cockatoo: a white bird with a striking sulphur yellow crest
32/33 'dying race', 'the most backward and wretched' race, 'evolutionary relic': quotations referring to the Australian Aboriginals by scientists from the 19th and 20th century, among them Charles Darwin and Sigmund Freud
39 purveyor: supplier
41 iconography: the use of images and symbols in art

## Text 2: Excerpt from Therese-M. Caiter, "The Other Side of Us"

*Therese-M. Caiter, then a Ph.D. student at the University of Tuebingen, Germany, has commented on Batty's paper. She concludes:*

[…] This leads to the folkloristic aspects of the new discovery of Aboriginal art, to the dots on post office uniforms made to look like Central Australian bark paintings, to the permanent display of Uluru photos and didgeridoo sounds, and to other, stranger manifestations. It does, however, also confine Aboriginal culture in a new racism, a limbo of eternal pristine primitivity and permanent opposition to civilisation. In this ecological construction of the "real Australians" (yet again), there is little space for Aboriginal reality in the 20th century. […] *86 words*



**Annotations:**

2 bark: G.: *Borke, Baumrinde*
4 manifestation: a sign that sth. exists or is happening
5 limbo: originally this word referred to the edge of Hell; in a more general sense it is a situation in which you are stuck and are not certain what to do next or cannot take action because you are waiting for sb. else to make a decision

**Book Covers:**

1. **1964**

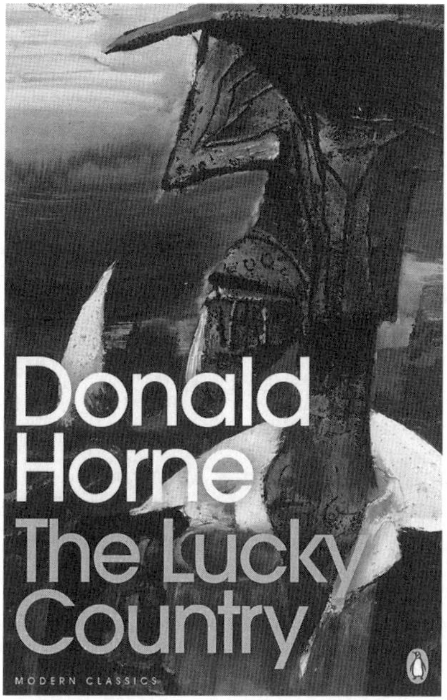


This Australian Classic has been a bestseller since the 1960s. Its title has even become a nickname for Australia itself. And the picture has become a national icon.

*From: The Lucky Country by Donald Horne*
*© Penguin Group (Australia) 2008*

2. **2007**

This book was published in 2007.

*From: Catriona Elder, Being Australian: Narratives of National Identity*
*(Crows Nest: Allen & Unwin, 2007)*
*Courtesy of Allen & Unwin Australia*

**Aufgabenstellung**

You have won a scholarship to the Centre for Indigenous History and the Arts at the University of Western Australia. For the course "Australia's Image at Home and Abroad" you have to submit a structured paper.
Make use of the materials at hand and the knowledge gained in your English classes.

1. First, you outline the different elements of Australian identity as presented in text 1, and give the gist of Ms Caiter's criticism in text 2.

2. Secondly, you analyse the book covers. In which way do they add to the images of Australia presented in the texts?

3. "[…] how does one go about representing a 'nation' […]?" (l. 8).
   The Australian short stories you studied in your English class have given you an insight into this question.
   Choose **two** of these stories and examine their relevance in this respect.
   Also refer to other materials studied in class.

4. In text 2 Ms Caiter states that there is a new racism towards Aboriginals.
   Considering the general development of racial matters in Australia, would you agree with this? Would you say the same for African-Americans in the US?
   Discuss.

---

## Lösungsvorschläge

1. *This task consists of two parts referring to two different text excerpts.*
   *Main aspects text 1:*
   - *not typical elements of modern Australia (like scenes from sheep or cow stations, or products and landmarks that are usually associated with Australia)*
   - *but mainly elements from Aboriginal culture (Aboriginals with painted bodies: musicians, dancers, actors)*
   - *= atonement for injustice that has been done to indigenous people, Australia wants to appear as an unprejudiced, just and sympathetic global citizen*

   *Main aspects text 2:*
   - *Ms Caiter criticises Batty's view: new form of racism against Aboriginals*
   - *Aboriginal culture seen as primitive and in contrast to civilisation*

   *Make sure that you avoid irrelevant information and structure your text according to the task. Your answer might read like this:*

   The excerpt from Philip Batty's article "The dot-spangled banner" deals with the representation of Australian national identity in the brief TV spot that was broadcast after the closing ceremonies of the Atlanta Olympics in 1996 to invite the world to Sydney for the next Olympic Games in the year 2000. What is actually shown in this spot are not elements that allude to a typical state in the second half of the 20th century with scenes from Australian sheep or cow stations, industrial

products like Holden cars or the image of Sydney Opera House that are often associated with modern Australia. Instead signs of an end-of-century Australia are shown with many elements from Aboriginal culture to represent Australian culture. It is, for example, Aboriginal musicians with the typical Aboriginal body painting, dancers and actors who are the focus of attention. Thus, Australians are presented as unprejudiced, just and sympathetic global citizens who want to atone for all the injustice that was done to Aboriginals in the past. Aboriginal art can now be seen everywhere in Australia, for example on Qantas aeroplanes or on the uniforms of Australia Post. Thus, Australia presents itself as a nation that is committed to human rights.
Ms Caiter, however, sees things differently and criticises Philip Batty's view in her article "The Other Side of Us". In her opinion the use of elements from Aboriginal culture does not really value this culture for what it is, but merely uses it as folklore. Once again Aboriginal culture is seen as primitive and not part of modern civilization. According to Caiter this is nothing but a new form of racism.

2. *You should give a brief description of the two book covers first:*
   - The Lucky Country:
     - *background: sails of boats*
     - *foreground: weathered face of a man; looks as if it is chiselled out of wood*
     - *man: wearing an old hat with a feather, a black jacket with a playing card in his breast pocket, a white shirt with an open collar; holding a cup/glass*
     - *illustration of the archetypal Australian: male, rugged, independent, hardened by life in the outback*
   - Being Australian:
     - *empty sandy beach, cloudless blue sky, clothes line with different shirts, flip-flops in the foreground (facing the sea)*
     - *picture conveys the idea of freedom, relaxation, fun and enjoyment*

   *Then relate the book covers to the images of Australia presented in the texts:*
   - The Lucky Country: *may correspond to Australia as presented at the Melbourne Olympics in 1956; no references to Aboriginal culture*
   - Being Australian: *no hints of Aboriginal culture*

The first book cover from 1964 shows a man with a very weathered face which looks as if it has been chiselled out of wood. He is looking off to the left but the viewer cannot see his eyes, which are shaded by the brim of his old hat. The hat has a feather in it. The man is wearing a black jacket with a playing card in the breast pocket, and the open collar of his white shirt mirrors the shape of the sails of the boats in the background. In his right hand he is holding a cup or glass.
The picture seems to represent the archetypal Australian – male, rugged, and hardened by life in the outback, spending his free time drinking and gambling. He knows who he is and leads an independent life. The book title, "The Lucky Country", seems to underline Australia's view of itself as a good country to live in, because of its nature, its people and its good social and economic conditions.

Referring to the first text this book cover may correspond to Australia presented as a progressive modern state at the festivities surrounding the Melbourne Olympics in 1956. However, it does not contain clear references to Aboriginal culture in any way.

The second picture, the book cover for "Being Australian" by Catriona Elder, shows an empty sandy beach under a cloudless, blue sky. In the picture you can also see a clothes line holding four different shirts. In the foreground there is a pair of flip-flops standing neatly next to each other and facing the sea. They give the impression that somebody has gone swimming in the sea. The viewer is reminded of sun, sea and fresh air and the relaxation and enjoyment of a holiday. Being Australian in 2007 is closely connected with being free and having fun.

This picture contains no references to issues of Australian identity as mentioned in the texts, nor is there any hint of Aboriginal culture.

3. *In this task you are expected to choose two of the Australian short stories you studied in class and examine how far they represent the nation of Australia. Do not forget to refer to the two texts and book covers at hand as well as to other materials studied in class. Draw a conclusion at the end of your text.*

   *For this sample answer the short stories "The Drover's Wife" by Henry Lawson and "Neighbours" by Tim Winton were chosen:*
   - *Representation of Australia in "The Drover's Wife": shows hard living conditions in the Australian outback in the past; strengthen people's character = historic image of (white) Australian identity*
   - *Representation of Australia in "Neighbours": shows conflicts between different ethnic minorities in Australia that can be overcome once people get to know each other = harmonious image of multicultural Australia*

The short story "The Drover's Wife" deals with life in a remote place in the bush. The landscape described in the story is very monotonous as it does not change for miles and miles. The drover's wife, a tough bushwoman, is all alone most of the time and has come to rely on herself in order to survive in the outback. She accepts her life in the bush, which is extremely hard and primitive. It becomes obvious that this kind of life strengthens her character.

The same holds true for many Australian women in the outback who had to do physical and manual work without the help of machines or other people in the past; very few people (if any) lived nearby and medical help was often out of reach. Therefore, "The Drover's Wife" can be taken as a historic image of Australian identity in those days.

With reference to further material studied in class, it can be said that the image of the outback conveyed in the story matches reality to a great extent. The outback covers about 80 % of Australia's entire territory and living conditions have mainly been hostile for people. It is extremely hot and dry and agriculture is restricted due to the climate. Whereas the children in the story could not attend school at all, nowadays students living in the outback are taught via computer in most cases.

There are parallels between this story and picture 1, although the image paints a much more desirable picture of life in the outback than in the story where the living conditions seem harder. Gambling and drinking are certainly not an issue for the drover's wife and her children. Picture 2 stands in marked contrast to the life of the drover's family, as work was no pleasure at that time and they might never have seen the ocean.

The short story "Neighbours" is about an Australian couple that moves to a new neighbourhood which is mainly inhabited by European immigrants. At first the husband notices that he earns lots of scornful looks from his new neighbours, as he stays at home while his wife goes to work. In contrast to them, the immigrants from Poland or Macedonia in their neighbourhood still live a very traditional life with traditional gender roles.

On the other hand, the Australian couple is not used to so many different sounds, such as the loud conversations or hammering next door. Although they disapprove of their neighbours' apparently strange customs at first, they get used to their new surroundings after some time. The couple's feelings and behaviour towards the immigrants slowly change, especially when the woman gets pregnant and receives lots of help and attention from her neighbours. The couple is pleasantly surprised. As a result it can be said that the author of this short story depicts a very harmonious image of Australia's multicultural society. Values such as helpfulness and friendliness can help people to appreciate and like each other and make Australia a good place to live for immigrants from different cultures. This harmonious image of Australia is in contrast to other texts we read in class which depicted racial tensions between different ethnic minorities in Australia.

A connection can be made between the story "Neighbours" and the final sentence in text 1 in which Australia is described as a "fair-minded, just, and compassionate global citizen" (ll. 45/46).

In both stories, however, Aboriginal culture is not an issue. To represent the Australian national identity as a whole, elements from Aboriginal culture as shown in the TV spot for the Sydney Olympic Games must be considered.

To sum up, it is not easy to describe and represent something abstract as national identity. There are lots of different ways to present the nation of Australia in all its many facets and there is certainly no one 'correct' way of doing this.

4. *You can start your discussion by stating the general development of racial matters for both Aboriginals in Australia and African Americans in the US. Then draw your own conclusions and say if you agree or disagree with Ms Caiter's statement that there is a new racism towards Aboriginals.*
   *The following sample solution considers racism to have been largely overcome:*
   - *Australia: general regret for past mistreatment of Aboriginals (e. g. fate of the "stolen generation"); National Day of Remembrance*
   - *USA: civil rights movement (Rosa Parks, Montgomery bus boycott) led to the abolition of the Jim Crow laws ("separate but equal")*

In the past, Aboriginals were subjected to racism as they were often seen and treated as inferior human beings. Their culture was widely considered primitive and equal rights were refused to them. Many people today still think that Aboriginals are disadvantaged economically, politically and socially.

However, I do not consider this to be completely true and I think that things have changed in the meantime. Aboriginals have achieved equality, at least on paper. Maybe they are still disadvantaged in the ways mentioned above, but they have also gained influence in those spheres. In Australian society the regret for the past mistreatment of Aboriginals such as the attempted genocide and the fate of the "stolen generation" is widespread. This can be seen, for example, in the National Day of Remembrance (formerly called "Sorry Day"), which is celebrated annually to commemorate these past events. So, I think that traces of racism have largely been overcome today.

The same applies to African Americans in my opinion. The so-called Jim Crow laws, which were state and local laws in the United States between 1876 and 1965, have long ceased to be in force. They conferred a "separate but equal" status on African Americans in all public facilities in the southern states of the former confederacy. The result was that public schools, public places and public transportation were segregated. It was not until 1964/1965 that the Jim Crow Laws were completely overruled by the Civil Rights Act and the Voting Rights Act. An important incident in 1955, which led to the emergence of the civil rights movement, was Rosa Parks' refusal to let a white person take her seat in a public bus. This incident caused a bus boycott in Montgomery that lasted for 381 days. The civil rights' movement that developed as a result helped African Americans to gain equal rights and overcome racism in the USA.

The American society is not totally free of racism against African Americans but times have changed for them as well. In contrast to Aboriginals in Australia they are already well represented in American politics – with Barack Obama as the first African American to become President of the USA –, economy, culture and sports. Overall, racism both in Australia and in the US has largely been overcome. Both societies are headed in the right direction.

## Leseverstehen

### Task 1: True/False + Evidence and Multiple Choice (12 points)

*The following text is an excerpt from black teacher E. R. Braithwaite's autobiographical novel* To Sir With Love, *in which he describes his time teaching in a run-down, working-class neighbourhood in East London after World War II. Towards the end of Braithwaite's first year at the school, the mother of Seales, who is one of Braithwaite's students, dies. The class collects some money to buy a flower arrangement for the funeral, which then needs to be taken to Seales' home.*

Then I remarked:

"Which of you will take it over to his home?"

Their reaction was like a cold douche. The pleasantly united camaraderie disappeared completely from the room, and in its place was the watchful antagonism I had encountered on my first day. It was as if I had pulled a thick transparent screen between them and myself, effectively shutting us away from each other.

It was ugly to see; I felt excluded, even hated, but all so horribly quickly.

"What's the matter with you?" My voice was loud in my ears, "What's suddenly so awful about the flowers?"

Moira stood up, "We can't take them, Sir."

"What do you mean, Miss Joseph? Why can't you take them?"

She looked quickly around the room as if pleading with the others to help her explain.

"It's what people would say if they saw us going to a coloured person's home." She sat down.

There it was. I felt weak and useless, an alien among them. All the weeks and months of delightful association were washed out by those few words.

Nothing had really mattered, the teaching, the talking, the example, the patience, the worry. It was all as nothing. They, like the strangers on buses and trains, saw only skins, never the people in those skins. Seales was born among them, played with them; his mother was white, British, of their stock and background and beginnings.

All the hackneyed clichés hammered in my head. A coloured boy with a white mother, a West Indian boy with an English mother. Always the same. Never an English boy with a Negro or West Indian father. No, that would be placing the emphasis on his Englishness, his identification with them.

It was like a disease, and these children whom I loved without caring about *their* skins or *their* backgrounds, they were tainted with the hateful virus which attacked their vision, distorting everything that was not white or English. […]

I turned and walked out of the classroom, sick at heart. […]

I walked into the Head's office. He listened, his face mirroring the deep humanity and sympathy which were so truly part of him.

"I'm glad this has happened, Braithwaite, for your sake, especially."

"Why, Sir?"

"Because I think you were setting too much store by quick results. After all, we are not concerned here merely with academic effort; our idea is to teach them to live with one another, sharing, caring, helping. It's not easy for them."

Here we go again, I thought. Everything those little bastards do is right, even this. Was he never prepared to see any point of view except that which supported their case? [...]

I was feeling angry with him for his attempt to excuse their conduct.

"You have been taking too much for granted, because of your success in the classroom. I am sure they all like Seales very much, but once outside the school things are different, and I think Seales would be the first to appreciate that."

"But Mr. Florian ..."

"You must be patient, Mr. Braithwaite," he continued, rising. "You've been here, how long? From May to now, nearly seven months, and you've done a great deal with them. Be patient. Maybe next year, the year after – who knows? Go back to them and show them some of the same tolerance and patient goodwill you hope to get from them." [...]

They were quiet in the classroom. I wanted to say something, but no words came. Jacqueline Bender rose.

"Sir, I don't think you understood just now. We have nothing against Seales. We like him, honest we do, but if one of us girls was seen going to his home, you can't imagine the things people would say. We'd be accused of all sorts of things." She sat, evidently overcome by this long speech.

"Thank you for making that so clear, Miss Bender. [...]" *729 words*

*From: E. R. Braithwaite:* To Sir With Love. *Englewood Cliffs: Prentice-Hall 1960, pp. 165–167.*

**Annotation:**
34 to set too much store by sth.: to find sth. too important

**Aufgabenstellung**

Read the text and the statements (1–11). Tick whether the statements are true or false. Quote 1–15 words as evidence to confirm or disprove the idea in each statement. There is one example (0).
Furthermore, there is an overall statement at the end (12).
Choose the answer and tick the correct box (a, b or c).

| Statements | True | False | Evidence (1–15 words) |
|---|---|---|---|
| 0. The students' reaction to their teacher's request takes him totally by surprise. | ☑ | ☐ | Their reaction was like a cold douche. |
| 1. The teacher has got along well with his students from the very beginning. | ☐ | ☐ | |
| 2. The students' reaction to his request about taking the flowers makes the teacher feel like an outsider. | ☐ | ☐ | |
| 3. It is easy for Moira to explain to her teacher why the students do not want to go to Seales' home. | ☐ | ☐ | |
| 4. The teacher thinks that his efforts as a teacher have been without effect. | ☐ | ☐ | |
| 5. The teacher realizes that a coloured boy is by definition not called "English". | ☐ | ☐ | |

| | | | |
|---|---|---|---|
| 6. The students' problem is that Seales' parents are black. | ☐ | ☐ | |
| 7. The headmaster thinks his school's students should just focus on learning facts. | ☐ | ☐ | |
| 8. The teacher criticizes the fact that the headmaster supports the students' behaviour. | ☐ | ☐ | |
| 9. The teacher is advised not to expect results from his students after a short time. | ☐ | ☐ | |
| 10. The headmaster tells the teacher to respond to his students with the openness and understanding he expects from them. | ☐ | ☐ | |
| 11. Jacqueline confirms that the students have warm feelings towards Seales. | ☐ | ☐ | |

12. According to Braithwaite, how do typical British kids look at the coloured children in their community?

a) ☐ They dislike all children from mixed marriages.

b) ☐ They define someone's ethnic background by focussing on the non-English parent.

c) ☐ They include children from mixed marriages in their definition of English people.

## Task 2: Multiple Choice **(10 points)**

### "Tiger Daughter" (2011)

*An American in Shanghai reports: I'm glad my kid has a tiger mom*
by Bill Powell

I sat in our suburban home in Shanghai and read online the excerpt from Amy Chua's *Battle Hymn of the Tiger Mother* that appeared in the *Wall Street Journal*. My reaction to it was straightforward: Maybe a little over the top, but yeah, that's about right. My wife's reaction: "I guess I'm not the toughest Chinese mother after all."

Our daughter, age 6, is in first grade. She's bilingual (Mandarin and English). She takes violin and ballet lessons. And she does two or three hours of homework a night, seven days a week. She is not Superkid. The fluency in English excepted ("An accident of birth," I remind her every time she comes home boasting about acing her latest English quiz), she's a normal kid. Pretty much every other child in her class at her Chinese school does the same stuff.

American passport holder Abby Cui-Powell, in other words, is living a typical Shanghai childhood. That doesn't mean all work and no fun. She goes out to play with the kids in our neighborhood. And she watches movies. In fact, one of the reasons Abby's English is so good is that she spends time watching *The Lion King* and *Toy Story*. That's more freedom than Chua's kids were allowed, according to her book.

Chua may be extreme in the discipline she tries to impose, even by Chinese standards. But where she is not extreme is in the intellectual and emotional underpinnings of *why* she does what she does. The most important assertion she makes in the piece, in my view, is this: "Chinese parents assume strength, not fragility."

This is exactly right. The assumption undergirding my wife's attitude toward Abby's education at home is that life is tough, you have to be educated to get through it, and what we're doing is aimed toward that end. You may not like it very much now, but it'll be worth it.

So she takes the lead. My role is pretty much limited to English; I read to Abby often and help correct her spelling mistakes. Joyce does the heavy lifting. Each night, she drills Abby relentlessly in math and Chinese. (Joyce and I both were lousy in math as kids, so we're assuming that Abby's gene pool is missing a few chromosomes when it comes to numbers.) Sometimes Abby cries and mopes. But every single night, she does the work. If she gets it wrong, she does it over until she gets it right. And I see no evidence that she's turning into a tortured, malfunctioning kid.

Mind you, this is only the first grade. The competitive pressure of the Shanghai school system intensifies as students get older and closer to the fateful college-entrance exam that determines which university they can attend. We had lunch recently with friends whose daughter, a 10th-grader in an elite high school here, is frequently up until midnight doing homework. "It's too much," her father said. "Something has to change." This attitude is growing among middle-class Chinese parents, and the government is looking at ways to foster more creative thinking in schools.

But what you'll never see here is an adoption of what Chua calls the obsessive concern in the U.S. with a kid's self-esteem, which from my expatriate viewpoint has practically become a form of dementia among some parents: the Little Leagues in which they don't keep score, for example, lest the kids on the losing team get their feelings hurt.

There are things that are not quite right with Chua's piece. "What Chinese parents understand," she asserts, "is that nothing is fun until you're good at it." That's not only wrong, it's ridiculous. Kids – even Chinese kids! – enjoy sports at all levels, not just the Olympics. Abby unprompted, loved to draw from an early age, and like everyone else, she started with stick figures.

But the bottom line, to me, is the studies Chua cites reporting that Chinese parents spend approximately 10 times as long every day as Western parents "drilling academic activities." Even if it's only three times as long, that's still a lot. Whatever Chua's excesses – and don't worry, we don't call Abby "garbage" if she flubs a math problem – when it comes to a child's education, having a Chinese mother is a big advantage; I'm very glad my daughter has one. *719 words*

*From: Bill Powell: An American Dad on Raising a Tiger Daughter. From:* TIME Magazine, *Jan 20, 2011.*

**Aufgabenstellung**

Read the text and complete the statements (1–10) by ticking the right answer (a, b, or c). There is one example (0).

0. Bill Powell explains that he …
   a) ☑ agrees with Amy Chua's basic theories.
   b) ☐ sees no sense in Amy Chua's statements.
   c) ☐ finds it hard to understand Amy Chua's ideas.

1. The author describes his daughter as …
   a) ☐ an ordinary schoolgirl.
   b) ☐ a very talented child.
   c) ☐ a girl with unusual hobbies.

2. As one basis for Abby's very good English the author explains that she …
   a) ☐ speaks English with both her parents.
   b) ☐ watches English films.
   c) ☐ avoids the neighbours' children.

3. According to the author, the Chinese view that children are strong is …
   a) ☐ a central statement in Chua's book.
   b) ☐ criticized as a prejudice in Chua's book.
   c) ☐ a point of small importance in Chua's book.

4. The author's wife believes that her daughter has to be …
   a) ☐ protected by her parents from difficulties in life later on.
   b) ☐ trained to face difficulties although her life will very probably be easy.
   c) ☐ prepared by her parents for difficult challenges in her later life.

5. Abby's drilling at home is mostly in …
   a) ☐ her mother's hands.
   b) ☐ her father's hands.
   c) ☐ both her parents' hands.

6. Abby's reaction to the pressure of drilling is that she …
   a) ☐ gives up on difficult tasks.
   b) ☐ shows abnormal behaviour.
   c) ☐ completes the tasks given to her.

7. As they grow older, students in Shanghai face increasing challenges because they …
   a) ☐ have to get used to changes in the school system.
   b) ☐ want to get a place at the university of their choice.
   c) ☐ are forced to develop a more open way of thinking.

8. There are government plans to …
   a) ☐ reduce the emphasis on drilling activities.
   b) ☐ keep up the present methods of teaching.
   c) ☐ take the focus away from more imaginative activities.

9. Powell believes in children …
   a) ☐ doing things just for fun.
   b) ☐ having to perform well before they enjoy something.
   c) ☐ being protected from pain and pressure.

10. When the author compares Chinese and Western parents, he …
   a) ☐ sees little difference in the effect on their children's education.
   b) ☐ praises the positive educational influence of Chinese mothers.
   c) ☐ attacks Western parents for neglecting their children's education.

## Task 3: Multiple Matching (6 points)

**"#Revolutionwhatrevolution?" (2003)** by Simon Kuper

**0** […] When I recently discovered Twitter, I went from contemptuous to addicted in about three days. But one thing still puzzles me about the world's 10th most popular website: the notion that it's a revolutionary medium. The failed Moldovan rebellion of 2009 was probably the first to be dubbed the "Twitter revolution", but since then, Twitter has been credited with launching the Iranian uprising, Arab spring and London riots. Now it has supposedly prompted the African Union to hunt for the Ugandan warlord Joseph Kony, after an anti-Kony propaganda film spread through social media and was watched more than 100 million times. I confidently predict that the next revolution anywhere on earth will be dubbed "the Twitter revolution".

**1** Non-tweeting readers may have formed the impression that the Twittersphere is devoted to summoning people to demonstrations in grey repressive capitals. In fact, "trending" items are usually celebrity deaths, goals in football matches or anything to do with the teenaged singer Justin Bieber. And what's true of Twitter appears true of computers in general. They are antirevolutionary devices. The global addiction to computers is helping keep the world quiet and peaceful.

**2** Every now and then, of course, social media do contribute to change. The Facebook page "We are all Khaled Said", named after a young Egyptian who died in police custody, helped galvanise protesters in Cairo's Tahrir Square last year. And bad activists use YouTube and Twitter too. "On the web one can proselytise for the jihad all day and night with friends from around the world," writes Jytte Klausen, an expert on terrorism at Brandeis University, and colleagues.

**3** Mostly, though, computers produce quietism. […] a striking fact of the great recession in developed countries has been the passivity of young people. Historically, revolutions are made by the young: […] And today's youth ought to be rebelling. About a fifth of under-25s in western countries are unemployed. Their luckier peers are mostly either studying something that won't lead to much, working as underpaid interns or waiting tables. The best-educated generation in history is ceasing even to think in terms of careers anymore: entry-level positions in sought-after industries such as fashion and media are now typically unpaid. If that were me, I'd be angry.

**4** True, there was a wave of rebellion: by one estimate, 900 occupations of urban public space have taken place in western countries since last spring. However, from Oakland to Auckland the wave died. This was not 1968. Only in the much less internet-penetrated Arab world did the young demonstrators persist. Of course, few western youths quite want to topple their regimes, but there was an additional force keeping them off the streets: computers. Computers are the perfect narcotic, even better than TV, because you rarely sit around a computer with your friends. Occupy Wall Street quickly grasped that to keep its customers satisfied, it needed to install free WiFi in New York's Zuccotti Park. The authorities quickly grasped that to deflate the occupation, they needed to seize the WiFi gear. […]

**5** If you're watching a screen, you're probably not making revolution. The 300 million Chinese microbloggers are arguably the greatest antirevolutionary force on earth. Where were they a year ago, when the Communist party was worrying about uprisings? In their bedrooms, blogging. Some of them blogged about politics. It didn't change much. Sarah Nouwen, a law lecturer at Cambridge who studied the viral campaign against Kony, believes that, for many people, sending a political tweet is an end in itself. "It's something you can use to strengthen your moral CV," she says. "So if you tweet about Kony, you look and feel good." The tweeter may not fret much about what happens in Uganda afterwards. This is what is known as "slacktivism": lazy support for causes.

**6** Perhaps we should be grateful to screens. Some social scientists puzzling over the recent fall in violent crime in western countries have formulated a new theory: many potential criminals are too addicted to their screens to go outside. After all, mugging, fighting in pubs and storming the presidential palace are leisure-time activities. When you can spend your leisure-time inside with a computer, why stand in the rain and harass passers-by? The economists A. Scott Cunningham, Benjamin Engelstätter and Michael R. Ward argue that though violent video games make people feel more violent, the net effect of those games is to reduce violence because they keep potentially violent people home. […] *738 words*

*From:* The Financial Times, *30 March 2012. By Simon Kuper.*
*http://www.ft.com/intl/cms/s/2/0e072330-7940-11e1-9f0f-00144feab49a.html# axzz1uHzfiA7k*

**Annotation:**
to proselytise: um Anhänger werben

**Aufgabenstellung**

Read the paragraphs (1–6) and match them with the statements: You may use each letter only once. There are more statements than you need. There is one example (0).

| | According to the author … |
|---|---|
| A | it is surprising that Twitter is believed to bring about radical change. |
| B | young people in the west spend a considerable part of their days in front of the computer with their friends. |
| C | joining an online campaign makes many people feel better but does not lead to action. |
| D | social media can be used anywhere to recruit followers of revolutionary ideas anytime. |
| E | virtual aggression and brutality seem to work as a substitute for anti-social behaviour in reality. |
| F | one would expect young people to rise against the system just as in the past. |
| G | social networks are needed to start riots and demonstrations around the world. |
| H | obsession with IT news about entertainment leads to people staying calm. |
| I | protest movements have survived longer in regions with limited access to the internet. |

| 0 | 1 | 2 | 3 | 4 | 5 | 6 |
|---|---|---|---|---|---|---|
| A | | | | | | |

## Task 4: Multiple Matching **(3 points)**

**Text 1:**

LONDON: Priti Patel, an Indian-origin Conservative MP in the UK has been racially attacked by a convicted killer who is leading a campaign to give prisoners the right to vote.

According to a report in the Mail, John Hirst, who served 25 years in jail for killing his 69-year-old landlady with an axe, unleashed a stream of vitriol against Patel, branding her a "Paki", a "foreign import" and even insulting her looks.

60-year-old Hirst wrote: "Unlike the foreign import Patel, I am a Brit born and bred". Born in London, Patel is the child of Ugandan Indian immigrants.

On his blog, Hirst said: "If Patel wasn't so stupid she would understand that passing another bill trying to establish the UK's supremacy on how it treats prisoners is a non-starter.

If Patel was an honest woman instead of being corrupt then she would not be calling for the government and parliament to stand up to Europe, she would be condemning them for their abuse of the most vulnerable group in society – prisoners," he said. […]

Patel said last night: "These comments are beneath contempt. My argument on votes for prisoners is based on principle, not inaccurate slurs and racist abuse".

She said, "I believe that people are in prison for a reason. You lose the right to vote once you commit a crime". […]

*From: PTI: Indian-origin MP faces racist attack in UK. In:* The Economic Times, *Feb 6, 2011.*

**Text 2:**

A Carlisle restaurant boss fears that a spate of vandal attacks on his business over more than two years may be racially motivated.

The award-winning Indigo Indian restaurant in Denton Street has had its sign damaged and obscene words spray painted on the front of the building in the latest attack at 7.20 a.m. on January 10.

The attack is just the latest in a series which date back to January 2010. […]

In October, in a similar incident, vandals covered the same restaurant in unsightly graffiti using red paint. Eggs were also lobbed at the windows and the sign outside the restaurant was damaged.

Some staff believe the same group of people is responsible for all of the vandalism over recent years. They point out that their restaurant has been the only business targeted.

Ata Miah, one of the managers at the restaurant, said yesterday: "The police say they can't recognise the people who are seen on the video images of the incident. We would like to pay to have the images improved so that there is a better chance of recognising these people. I believe what is happening may be racist because they are only targeting our restaurant.

"This latest attack happened at 7.20 a.m., and there were people around but so far nobody has come forward." […]

*From:* News & Star, *25 January 2012. "Racist" Attack on Carlisle Indian Restaurant. By Phil Coleman.*

**Text 3:**

An Indian man who claimed he was set on fire in a racist attack has received a suspended jail sentence for lying to police.

Jaspreet Singh, 28, pleaded guilty in the Melbourne Magistrates Court to making a false report to police and criminal damage. Singh suffered burns to 30 per cent of his body while setting his car alight in Essendon in January to claim insurance. He told police he had been the victim of a racist attack and was set upon by four men.

The magistrate told Singh he had made a serious and cynical decision to "feed into racism" and sentenced him to eight months' jail, suspended for two years.

The fire occurred a week after Indian national Nitin Garg was stabbed to death on his way to work in West Footscray. The incidents sparked outrage in India and among Indians in Melbourne who claimed racist attacks were on the rise.

*From: Indian man avoids jail over alleged racist attack. In:* ABC News, *May 3, 2010.*
*Reproduced by permission of the Australian Broadcasting Corporation and ABC Online.*


*590 words*

**Aufgabenstellung**

Read the texts (1 to 3) and match them with a suitable heading (A to E); there are two more headings than you need.

| | **Headings** |
|---|---|
| **A** | Police have so far failed to fully investigate racist attacks |
| **B** | Policymakers withdraw funding after racist attacks |
| **C** | Indian avoids jail over alleged racist attacks |
| **D** | Indian-origin politician does not back down despite racist attacks |
| **E** | Police hunt mob after racist attack on Indians |

| 1 | 2 | 3 |
|---|---|---|
| | | |

## Textaufgabe

Der Prüfling hat **eine** Textaufgabe seiner Wahl zu bearbeiten.

### Textaufgabe I

**David McCullough Jr.'s commencement address, "You're Not Special" (2012)**

[…] commencement is life's great ceremonial beginning, with its own attendant and highly appropriate symbolism. Fitting, for example, for this auspicious rite of passage, is where we find ourselves this afternoon, the venue. Normally, I avoid cliches like the plague, wouldn't touch them with a ten-foot pole, but here we are on a literal level playing field. That matters. That says something.

And your ceremonial costume … shapeless, uniform, one-size-fits-all. Whether male or female, tall or short, scholar or slacker, spray-tanned prom queen or intergalactic X-Box assassin, each of you is dressed, you'll notice, exactly the same. And your diploma … but for your name, exactly the same.

All of this is as it should be, because none of you is special.

You are not special. You are not exceptional. […]

Yes, you've been pampered, cosseted, doted upon, helmeted, bubble-wrapped. Yes, capable adults with other things to do have held you, kissed you, fed you, wiped your mouth, wiped your bottom, trained you, taught you, tutored you, […].

But do not get the idea you're anything special. Because you're not.

The empirical evidence is everywhere, numbers even an English teacher can't ignore […].

Even if you're one in a million, on a planet of 6.8 billion that means there are nearly 7,000 people just like you. Imagine standing somewhere over there on Washington Street on Marathon Monday and watching sixty-eight hundred yous go running by. And consider for a moment the bigger picture: your planet, I'll remind you, is not the center of its solar system, your solar system is not the center of its galaxy, your galaxy is not the center of the universe. In fact, astrophysicists assure us the universe has no center; therefore, you cannot be it. […]

"But, Dave," you cry, "Walt Whitman tells me I'm my own version of perfection! Epictetus tells me I have the spark of Zeus!" And I don't disagree. So that makes 6.8 billion examples of perfection, 6.8 billion sparks of Zeus. You see, if everyone is special, then no one is. If everyone gets a trophy, trophies become meaningless. […]

No longer is it how you play the game, no longer is it even whether you win or lose, or learn or grow, or enjoy yourself doing it … Now it's "So what does this get me? […]"

It's where you go from here that matters.

As you commence, then, and before you scatter to the winds, I urge you to do whatever you do for no reason other than you love it and believe in its importance. Don't bother with work you don't believe in […].

Develop and protect a moral sensibility and demonstrate the character to apply it. Dream big. Work hard. Think for yourself. Love everything you love, everyone you love, with all your might. And do so, please, with a sense of urgency, for every tick of the clock subtracts from fewer and fewer; […].

The fulfilling life, the distinctive life, the relevant life, is an achievement, not something that will fall into your lap because you're a nice person or mommy ordered it from the caterer. […]

Climb the mountain not to plant your flag, but to embrace the challenge, enjoy the air and behold the view. Climb it so you can see the world, not so the world can see you. Go to Paris to be in Paris, not to cross it off your list and congratulate yourself for being worldly. Exercise free will and creative, independent thought not for the satisfactions they will bring you, but for the good they will do others, the rest of the 6.8 billion – and those who will follow them. And then you too will discover the great and curious truth of the human experience is that selflessness is the best thing you can do for yourself. The sweetest joys of life, then, come only with the recognition that you're not special.

Because everyone is.

Congratulations. Good luck. Make for yourselves, please, for your sake and for ours, extraordinary lives.

*658 words*

*From: David McCullough Jr.'s commencement address, "You're Not Special".*
*In:* The Swellesley Report, *June 5, 2012.*

**Annotations:**
2 auspicious: promising
5 level playing field: equal opportunity, state of equality
25 Walt Whitman: American poet (1819–1892)
26 Epictetus: Greek philosopher (c. AD 50–c. AD 138)

## Aufgabenstellung

David McCullough's commencement speech (delivered 2012) caused a vivid and broad discussion. Your American partner school has invited you to contribute to the debate by writing a comment for their yearbook, which is read by students, teachers and parents.

1. As a first step you study the speech in detail. To do so, you
   - outline McCullough's main ideas.
   - examine the structure of his speech and its effect on the reader. *(40 %)*
2. On the basis of your findings, write your comment. To support your arguments also refer to materials studied in class. *(60 %)*

## Textaufgabe II

**Paul Laverty, *Ae fond Kiss* (excerpt from movie script, 2005)**

*Casim and his sisters Tahara and Rukhsana are second generation Pakistanis living in Glasgow. Their parents are devout Muslims and plan for Casim to marry his cousin, who is soon to arrive in the UK. Plans go awry when Casim falls deeply in love with a white girl. He is trying hard to keep this relationship secret because he knows that, even if he wasn't due to marry, his parents would never accept a white girl. Only his sister Tahara knows about it.*
*In the following scene, Tahara is standing close to her mother, who is at the sink doing the dishes.*
*Tahara's father, Casim and Rukhsana are sitting at the kitchen table.*

TAHARA: Er … I've got some really good news today. I've been offered an <u>unconditional place</u> at Edinburgh University. Look, Dad.

*[Tahara moves nearer to her father to give him the letter she has in her hand, looks at her mother, then turns back to her father. Tahara's father starts reading the letter.]*

TAHARA: There's twenty students chasing every place.

FATHER: Wait a minute. What's going on here? Why Edinburgh?

*[Tahara steps forward and sits down at the table.]*

TAHARA: Um, because the course I want to do, um, is in Edinburgh.

FATHER: Listen, dear, there are four or five universities in this bloody city. What the <u>community</u> is gonna say?

TAHARA: It's a good university, it's the only course I want to do …

FATHER: Your brother … Your sister went to Glasgow University, and your brother went to university in Glasgow. Is that not good enough for you?

TAHARA: No, Dad, it's not that … It's just …

FATHER: It says you were there for an interview. You never asked us. You never mentioned and got permission in the house … to go for an interview!

TAHARA: Look, I've got an unconditional place, it's amazing for someone my age.

FATHER: If you could go for an interview without <u>intimating</u>, without getting permission, what could you do there when you're there?

RUKHSANA: Dad, one second. *[addressing Tahara]* Can't you just commute or something?

TAHARA: What's the point then? I might as well stay in Glasgow. The whole part of this is so I can …

FATHER: What's more important to you? Education or staying away from home?

*[Tahara looks at Casim and mouthes "Please, please, …"]*

CASIM: There's unis here in Glasgow as well.

RUKHSANA: Can't you just commute there?

TAHARA *[addressing Casim]:* How can you say that! *[addressing her father and Rukhsana]* No, I can't, it's not fair. I'm going to be missing out on a whole different life. I don't want to do that.

*[Tahara gets excited and angry. She starts shouting.]*

TAHARA: Why, why did you even get married and come here and have kids? Why? What's the point in having kids here? We're Western … I'm sorry, but we're not from Pakistan.

FATHER: Listen! Don't change the subject. You are going to study in Glasgow. You can't go there.

TAHARA: I'm not changing the subject. It's the same bloody subject!

FATHER: And don't look at me like that, hey!

*[He gets angry, too, raises his voice, bangs his fist on the table, gets to his feet, tears up the letter.]*

FATHER: T'is not right. Enough is enough. Is this the way we've got you educated?

*[Tahara starts crying.]*

FATHER: That this day had to come? You cannot go. And that's final.

*[Tahara's father leaves the room. Tahara bursts into tears.]*

TAHARA: I'm sorry. It's really hard. It means so much. Do you know how much you want to come …

*[Tahara's mother goes over to her and tries to calm her down by hugging her. Tahara refuses her mother's hug.]*

TAHARA: Do you know how much you work for that … No, Mum, please! I've worked my arse off …

RUKHSANA: You're just overdramatic.

TAHARA: Oh, just fuck off!

*[Rukhsana gets up and starts leaving the room.]*

RUKHSANA: Don't you ever talk to me like that again.

*[Tahara violently pokes Casim's arm with her finger.]*

TAHARA: You're such a hypocrite. Casim, look at me. Look at me. What's wrong? You're such a fucking hypocrite. Look at me.

*[Tahara's mother tries to hug her, but Tahara tries to shrug her off again.]*

TAHARA: I'll never forgive you for this.

MOTHER: I'm here for you. You're only upset.

*[Tahara allows her mother to lead her out of the room.]* *616 words*

*From: Paul Laverty.* Ae Fond Kiss. *Icon Film Distribution.*

**Annotations:**

1/2 unconditional place: Tahara has met all academic requirements (grades, projects, …), and the university is happy to accept her

11 community: *here:* the community of Pakistani families living in Glasgow

19 intimating: making known

**Aufgabenstellung**

You take part in an international seminar dealing with the impact of immigration on second generation migrants. Participants are required to find out how fiction (novels, short stories, drama, film, ...) deals with this issue.
You have been given the task to analyse a part of the movie script *Ae fond Kiss* and to present your findings in a letter that the main character writes to a friend.

1. As a first step, you study the text at hand. You
   - describe Tahara's plans as well as her family's reactions.
   - compare Tahara's experience in this scene with the experience of characters portrayed in materials studied in class. *(40 %)*

2. Imagine yourself in Tahara's situation. Write her letter to a non-Pakistani friend, in which she reflects on her situation. *(60 %)*

## Lösungsvorschläge

### Leseverstehen

### Task 1: True/False + Evidence and Multiple Choice

*Go through the statements first. Next, search the text for keywords (or their synonyms or opposites) that you have come across in the statements. The sentences appear below in chronological order, following the arrangement of information in the text. When you have found a passage that seems suitable, compare it with the statement again and make sure that it does match. Then decide whether the statement is true or false taking into consideration the contents of the passage to which it refers. Do not use any background knowledge you may have, but refer only to the text.*
*Possible keywords in the statements:*
*1) very beginning, to get along with*
*2) student, reaction*
*3) to explain, Moira, easy*
*4) without effect, effort as a teacher*
*5) coloured boy, English*
*6) black, parents*
*7) headmaster, learning (facts)*
*8) behaviour, to criticize, to support*
*9) not to expect results, short time*
*10) openness, understanding*
*11) to have warm feelings, Seales*
*For the additional question (number 12) you need to look at the corresponding text passages. Then decide which statement is correct. Hint: Take a look at lines 22 to 28.*

| Statement | True | False | Evidence (1–15 words) |
|---|---|---|---|
| 1. The teacher has got along well with his students from the very beginning. | ☐ | ☑ | the watchful antagonism I had encountered on my first day |
| 2. The students' reaction to his request about taking the flowers makes the teacher feel like an outsider. | ☑ | ☐ | a thick transparent screen between them and myself *OR*<br>(effectively) shutting us away from each other *OR*<br>I felt excluded *OR*<br>I felt … an alien among them |
| 3. It is easy for Moira to explain to her teacher why the students do not want to go to Seales' home. | ☐ | ☑ | as if pleading with the others to help her explain |

| | | | |
|---|---|---|---|
| 4. The teacher thinks that his efforts as a teacher have been without effect. | ☑ | ☐ | I felt … useless *OR*<br>All the weeks and months of delightful association were washed out by those few words. *OR*<br>Nothing had really mattered, (the teaching,) (the talking,) (the example,) (the patience,) (the worry). *OR*<br>It was all as nothing. |
| 5. The teacher realizes that a coloured boy is by definition not called "English". | ☑ | ☐ | Never an English boy with a Negro (or West Indian) father. |
| 6. The students' problem is that Seales' parents are black. | ☐ | ☑ | his mother was white (, British) *OR*<br>A coloured boy with a white mother *OR*<br>a West Indian boy with an English mother *OR*<br>It's what people would say if they saw them going to a coloured person's home. |
| 7. The headmaster thinks his school's students should just focus on learning facts. | ☐ | ☑ | we are not concerned merely with academic effort *OR*<br>our idea is to teach them to live with one another (, sharing) (, caring) (, helping) |
| 8. The teacher criticizes the fact that the headmaster supports the students' behaviour. | ☑ | ☐ | Everything those little bastards do is right *OR*<br>Was he never prepared to see any point of view except that which supported their case? *OR*<br>I was feeling angry with him for his attempt to excuse their conduct. |
| 9. The teacher is advised not to expect results from his students after a short time. | ☑ | ☐ | You must be patient *OR*<br>Be patient. (Maybe next year, the year after …) |
| 10 The headmaster tells the teacher to respond to his students with the openness and understanding he expects from them. | ☑ | ☐ | (show them) the same tolerance and patient goodwill you hope to get from them |
| 11. Jacqueline confirms that the students have warm feelings towards Seales. | ☑ | ☐ | We like him, honest we do, … |

12. According to Braithwaite, how do typical British kids look at the coloured children in their community?
   a) ☐ They dislike all children from mixed marriages.
   b) ☑ They define someone's ethnic background by focussing on the non-English parent.
   c) ☐ They include children from mixed marriages in their definition of English people.

## Task 2: Multiple Choice

*Look for matching passages in the text. They follow the order of information in the text. If you have trouble finding them, use the following hints:*
*1) ll. 5–10*
*2) ll. 11–15*
*3) ll. 16–19*
*4) ll. 20–23*
*5) ll. 24–26*
*6) ll. 28–30*
*7) ll. 31–33*
*8) ll. 35–37*
*9) ll. 43–47*
*10) ll. 48–53*

1. The author describes his daughter as …
   a) ☑ an ordinary schoolgirl.
   b) ☐ a very talented child.
   c) ☐ a girl with unusual hobbies.
2. As one basis for Abby's very good English the author explains that she …
   a) ☐ speaks English with both her parents.
   b) ☑ watches English films.
   c) ☐ avoids the neighbours' children.
3. According to the author, the Chinese view that children are strong is …
   a) ☑ a central statement in Chua's book.
   b) ☐ criticized as a prejudice in Chua's book.
   c) ☐ a point of small importance in Chua's book.

4. The author's wife believes that her daughter has to be …
   a) ☐ protected by her parents from difficulties in life later on.
   b) ☐ trained to face difficulties although her life will very probably be easy.
   c) ☑ prepared by her parents for difficult challenges in her later life.

5. Abby's drilling at home is mostly in …
   a) ☑ her mother's hands.
   b) ☐ her father's hands.
   c) ☐ both her parents' hands.

6. Abby's reaction to the pressure of drilling is that she …
   a) ☐ gives up on difficult tasks.
   b) ☐ shows abnormal behaviour.
   c) ☑ completes the tasks given to her.

7. As they grow older, students in Shanghai face increasing challenges because they …
   a) ☐ have to get used to changes in the school system.
   b) ☑ want to get a place at the university of their choice.
   c) ☐ are forced to develop a more open way of thinking.

8. There are government plans to …
   a) ☑ reduce the emphasis on drilling activities.
   b) ☐ keep up the present methods of teaching.
   c) ☐ take the focus away from more imaginative activities.

9. Powell believes in children …
   a) ☑ doing things just for fun.
   b) ☐ having to perform well before they enjoy something.
   c) ☐ being protected from pain and pressure.

10. When the author compares Chinese and Western parents, he …
   a) ☐ sees little difference in the effect on their children's education.
   b) ☑ praises the positive educational influence of Chinese mothers.
   c) ☐ attacks Western parents for neglecting their children's education.

## Task 3: Multiple Matching

*First of all, you need to read the statements. Next, go through the text paragraph by paragraph. Underline keywords. Then match the statements to the right paragraph. Be careful: there are two sentences that do not match any passage in the text. When you have finished the task, double-check your answers in order to ensure that you have not made any mistakes.*
*There are some keywords that can help you find the right statements for the paragraphs. Concentrate on synonyms or opposites of those expressions:*
*1) "trending" items, global addiction to computers, quiet and peaceful*
*2) to contribute to change, to proselytize for jihad*
*3) passivity of young people, historically, revolutions are made by the young*
*4) less internet-penetrated Arab world, demonstrators persist*
*5) sending a political tweet is an end in itself, strengthen you moral CV, lazy support for causes*
*6) recent fall in violent crime, to keep violent people home*

| 1 | 2 | 3 | 4 | 5 | 6 |
|---|---|---|---|---|---|
| H | D | F | I | C | E |

Distraktoren: B, G

## Task 4: Multiple Matching

*Concentrate on reading the headlines first. Then read the three texts and match them to the most suitable heading. Watch out for keywords and be careful, as there are two headings that cannot be matched with any of the texts.*
*1) Indian-origin (l. 1), MP (l. 1), racially attacked (ll. 1/2), abuse (l. 17)*
*2) vandalism over recent years (ll. 10/11), police (l. 13), can't recognise people (l. 14)*
*3) Indian man (l. 1), claimed racist attack (l. 1), suspended jail sentence (ll. 1/2), lying to police (l. 2), false report (l. 4)*

| 1 | 2 | 3 |
|---|---|---|
| D | A | C |

Distraktoren: B, E

## Textaufgabe

### Textaufgabe I

1. *As the task is subdivided by bullet points, it might be a good idea to focus first on the main aspects of the speech and then look at the structure. Otherwise, important points might be overlooked or not fully considered.*
   *The main aspects of the text are:*
   - *students' claim to individuality as an impossible demand*
   - *actions in later life as indicator of being special dependent on the contribution made to society*
   - *encouragement to live consciously and independently*

   *When analysing the text, you should focus first on the overall structure of the speech (e.g. by dividing it up into units and labelling them with specific headings). Then refer to the effect on the reader/the audience. Express your findings in your own words, but remember to add evidence from the text.*
   *Structure of the text:*
   - *first part (ll. 1–31): opinions voiced to catch the audience's attention*
   - *second part (ll. 32–54): advice on how to live a fulfilling life*

   *Effect on the audience:*
   - *making listeners eager to learn more about his point of view*
   - *leaving listeners feeling understood*

Asked to contribute a comment to the debate on Mr McCullough's commencement speech for the yearbook of our partner school, I would like to examine the text more closely before evaluating it. As the title already suggests, the idea of being special is the crucial point of Mr McCullough's argument. He claims that, despite the students' constant striving to be individual, they are not special, since they are all at exactly the same stage in life. According to him, it will be their future actions both in the public and the private sphere that make them unique – if they take things into their own hands and work for society rather than individual interests, are enthusiastic and passionate about what they do, and think for themselves. If the students learn to live life to the full and care for their fellow humans, they will realise that everyone counts. It is this insight that will enable them to live special lives.

Having outlined McCullough's main ideas, I would now like to examine how those aspects are put across. Firstly, the speaker shocks the audience to get their full attention. McCullough achieves this by employing various methods: the students are addressed directly (cf. ll. 6–9); hitting on stereotypical ways of high-school life, the speaker shows that he is well informed about high-school hierarchies. Students will realise this and are therefore more likely to feel understood and to both listen and believe him. However this trust is lost as he enumerates the many ways in which the students have been spoilt (cf. ll. 12–14). He thus both tickles the students' pride and also captures the parents' attention by implying that

they have been overprotective. The teachers are reeled in by references to famous writers and thinkers (cf. ll. 25/26). Secondly, McCullough impresses his audience by taking the idiom "[being] one in a million" (l. 18) literally. He breaks the number down in terms of the world population and thus proves his point with the help of statistics (cf. ll. 18–21).
Then the speech reaches a turning point (cf. l. 32). The whole second part shows McCullough giving advice to the students on how to live a fulfilling life (cf. ll. 33–54). The speech becomes more solemn, there are no jokes or other humorous devices anymore. The sentences get shorter, and the tone of the speech becomes more commanding, using a lot of imperatives (cf. ll. 36–39). McCullough takes the students on a journey full of metaphorical language meant to demonstrate what is to be called special (cf. ll. 43–46) and that some effort has to be made to achieve this goal (cf. ll. 40–43). By the end of his speech, he is finally able to resolve the paradox created in the beginning: "[...] you're not special. Because everyone is." (ll. 51/52) and can thus resolve the tension present throughout. The whole structure of McCullough's speech is designed to capture the attention of the audience and it thus creates the constant desire to know more about his point of view. As only the very last sentences complete the picture, the listeners who at first strongly disagree with the speaker will now feel encouraged to follow his advice, the argumentation being quite plausible.

2. *A comment is a written presentation of arguments and should feature an introduction, a main part and a conclusion. You should use formal language and support what you write with sound evidence. It is essential that you arrange your arguments convincingly. Bear in mind that you need to refer to materials covered in class.*
*Points in favour of McCullough's position:*
- *learning as a lifelong process*
- *references to Thomas Friedman's attitude in* The World is Flat
- *references to Al Gore's argumentation in* An Inconvenient Truth

*Points against McCullough's position:*
- *references to* The Prime of Miss Jean Brodie *and her way of influencing students*
- *"you're not special" as a drastic opening for a graduation speech*

McCullough's speech has caused a heated discussion. We therefore have to ask ourselves which aspects of the speech are so controversial to inspire such a discussion. A distinction has to be made between the content and the methods employed in the speech.
As to the latter, I do not see anything outrageous in them. I rather like the way the text is crafted. First of all, McCullough put his ideas across plausibly, making it easy to follow his line of argumentation. Being a student, I know how important it is to explain matters in a way that is once exciting, informative, and easy to understand. Using sarcasm, anecdotes, metaphors, and witty examples, the speak-

er immediately manages to capture the listeners' attention. Recently we talked about the documentary film *An Inconvenient Truth*, in which Al Gore, a successful politician and environmentalist, convinces the viewers by using the same techniques as McCullough does. He offers examples; his story is full of humorous anecdotes and sound empirical evidence designed to put his message across. The issue of sustainability was once only discussed by experts, but it has now received huge public attention thanks to Al Gore and his plausible argumentation.
However, when it comes to the contents of McCullough's speech, I can understand that the speech did not only inspire praise, but also caused irritation. The speaker has a rather philosophical way of defining goals in life and also uses his words in quite a drastic way. To grab the attention of his audience, he starts the graduation speech by claiming "You are not special." (l. 11). This might seem unconventional in a world of global competition, assessment centres, and the resulting pressure. I partly wonder whether it might have been better if he had given the students more practical advice, e. g. on what subjects to study. What is more, only students who are really mature would be able to take his meaning. This quite personal way of addressing his students reminds me of the heroine in *The Prime of Miss Jean Brodie*, a novel by Muriel Spark. There the teacher does not simply teach the curriculum, but tries to impose her own view of the world on her students. The difference between her and McCullough is that he is prepared to let go of his students and does not try to influence them further. Still, there are some facts that support and justify McCullough's view of the world. One could argue that Thomas Friedman's thesis, presented in the chapter on education in his book *The World is Flat*, supports McCullough's approach to a fulfilled life. Friedman claims that it is more important to do something you truly love rather than just pursuing a career.
It is this argument that fuels my support for McCullough. Every human being has his or her particular talents. Doing things that run contrary to our abilities and interests can only be unwise and must certainly result in unhappiness. For this reason, I believe that the students should be glad to have been given such valuable advice.

## Textaufgabe II

1. *This task is split in two parts. In the first you need to describe Tahara's plans and her family's reactions to them. The following points should be mentioned:*
   - *Tahara's secret application for a place at Edinburgh University*
   - *her father's wish to have her study in Glasgow as normally expected of community members*
   - *her mother's silent but caring behaviour towards Tahara*
   - *her brother's and sister's refusal to interfere*

   *Next, you should compare Tahara's experience in this scene with the situation of other characters studied in class. As the story involves second-generation immigrants, it seems obvious that especially the protagonist of* The Black Album, *Sha-*

*hid, should be considered here. Possible points of comparison could be the family background in terms of religion and social life, preferred lifestyle, and reactions of the family to changes in their teenager.*

In preparation for the seminar on second-generation immigration, I was asked to analyse a scene from the film script *Ae fond Kiss*. I shall first briefly introduce the dramatis personae and the film's main issue.
The scene in this excerpt is about the protagonist Tahara's wish to move out of the family home and study in Edinburgh. Tahara's parents emigrated to Britain from Pakistan, whereas their children Tahara, Casim, and Rukhsana were born and raised in Glasgow. Presenting a letter with the offer of an unconditional place at Edinburgh University, to which she had applied secretly, Tahara's plan does not meet with her parents' approval. The main opponent is her father, while her mother and her siblings just do not dare to interfere. At first, her father seems to react calmly and wants to know why she prefers the university in Edinburgh to the ones in Glasgow. But it soon becomes clear that his main worry is his reputation within the Pakistani community. He gets angry and takes the argument to a more personal level, implying that Tahara thinks too highly of herself and accusing her of keeping secrets. Tahara tries at first to convince her father with facts, but loses her temper when her sister suggests commuting as a compromise. To Tahara, that would deprive her of the opportunity to enjoy the freedom of student life in Edinburgh. On top of all that, Casim agrees with his parents, in spite of the fact that he is having a secret love affair with a white girl and therefore also fails to behave in a traditional way. With Tahara insisting on the same rights as other British teenagers have, her father finally loses his temper and destroys the letter. Only after he has left the kitchen, does her mother, who has remained totally passive throughout the conflict, try to console Tahara and calm her down. However, she is unsuccessful at first, as Tahara is still furious with her siblings.
The little evidence we have (the patriarchal hegemony, an arranged marriage, the devout Muslim community) seems to suggest that this is not merely a conflict between father and daughter, but also a conflict between different ways of life – the Western lifestyle and the one based on Muslim traditions. Tahara's situation seems typical of a second-generation immigrant: Although the teenager wants to break free of her parents' influence, family ties prevent her from doing so.
In this respect, Tahara's situation can be easily compared to the position of Shahid, the protagonist of *The Black Album*, who also is the child of a Pakistani family and a second-generation immigrant. Brought up in a rather "Westernised" way, Shahid's liberal background differs significantly from Tahara's, as his family represents no obstacle to his self-determination. At university Shahid gets drawn into a Muslim circle of second-generation immigrants who have a fundamentalist mindset and violently reject "Western" culture. When Shahid changes his outward appearance, his siblings openly mock him and the group. But thanks to his rather hedonistic, open-minded lecturer Deedee, Shahid rejects the fundamentalist ideals in the end.

The most important difference between the two protagonists is that Shahid's family does not actually prevent him from living the life he considers suitable. Instead, it is Deedee who challenges the group's ideology. Of course, both Tahara and Shahid are presented stereotypically as suffering from a conflict of identity, torn as they are between the culture of their Western host society and their Muslim origin. What distinguishes the two teenagers is the different approach they take towards solving this problem.

Furthermore, it can be claimed that Shahid also faces a conflict with his family. Yet whereas Tahara's parents want to prevent her from living a "Western" life, Shahid's family rejects his transformation into a Muslim fundamentalist. The important difference is that Shahid's family does not actually forbid him to become a fundamentalist but tries to make him see what he has turned into. In fact it is Deedee, who plays the most crucial role in causing Shahid to turn his back on the group. Tahara's father on the contrary imposes his will on his daughter.

The fundamentalist group also hosts a set of characters that are worth comparing. In the main, the group appreciates everything Tahara dislikes. Whereas Tahara finds her Muslim environment suffocating and considers her heritage a burden, the fundamentalists Hat, Chad, Riaz and Tahira consider traditions their safe haven. All of them seem traumatized by their past and therefore appear lost in a multicultural society. With its principles and moral codex the group provides a structure for the second-generation immigrants who struggle with their multicultural background: repulsed by scantily-clad women, Tahira is happy being an obedient and dedicated wife, whereas Trevor, alienated from his father, changes his British Christian name into Chad.

Despite the tendency in literature to present clichés, it needs to be said that such cases do exist in reality. The Boston Marathon bombings are just one example. The bombers were second-generation immigrants who were disillusioned with their host society and so decided to take revenge for its wars in Muslim countries. This shows that there is still much to be done if we want to have a tolerant and open-minded multicultural society, one in which both the immigrant community and the host population stick to democratic principles when trying to sort out the problems.

2. *For this task you may use informal language, since teenagers are more likely to use colloquial expressions in this type of situation. Remember that a letter requires an addressee. Furthermore, your version of Tahara should be plausible and needs to keep her original characteristics, such as being rather impulsive. You are free to add new information to the story or to refer in more detail to aspects already mentioned there. Do not simply copy from the original text or rephrase the whole dialogue. Make sure, however, that your letter has some overlap with the original story.*

Dear Kanta,

How are things? I haven't heard from you since you moved to Oxford. I cannot e-mail you because I am grounded at the moment and not allowed to use the family computer. That's why I am writing a letter. I guess you are probably just a bit short on time, having to squeeze in your lectures between parties and chatting away with friends. That'll be why I haven't heard from you for ages, right?
I really miss you. You've always been my idol. You're the bravest person I know – and the only Bangladeshi girl to be offered a place at Oxford last year. And you even convinced your parents. Honestly, I urgently need to know how you've talked them round. I could use a strategy like that right now.
Today I was offered an unconditional place at Edinburgh uni. I admit its biggest advantage is that it's far away from our precious Muslim environment. I just want to break free from those lies and this whole pretense. When I told my father he almost had a fit. He wants me to study in Glasgow so he can keep me on a tight rein. What would be the point of studying in the first place then? Looking at Ma, I really don't see it. If I get a higher education, it will make me more self-confident. I'm not going to sit there silently, married to a man who won't hear me out, let alone ask me what I think about my child's unconditional place.
Well, Dad tore up the letter and he's forbidden me to go to Edinburgh. Ma didn't say anything – as usual – and Rukhsana suggested some rotten compromise: commuting to Edinburgh – just how daft would that be? I had counted on Casim, who, by the way, is going out with a white girl. Of course, he let me down as well, that two-faced coward. Now I'm at a crossroads: I could hide for the rest of my life, just like my brother (who is actually going to be married soon, an arranged match, of course), and then have a secret life nobody knows about. Or I could pull myself together and rebel.
But this is what I am really scared of – being an outcast shunned by my family and all my old friends. And I honestly love my family, even my Dad. I would miss Ma so much. But I feel British, not Pakistani, and I've certainly been brought up in a world where everybody can try to achieve what they want. You know perfectly well what I'm talking about, don't you? After all, it was my Dad who tried to prevent yours from sending you to Oxford. But he did not convince him. What is the difference between you and me? Is it our country of origin? Is it that your father is more tolerant or more proud of you? Are you more patient or am I less eloquent than you are? Please tell me!
You see, I am sitting on a fence here. It would mean the world to me if you sent me a text so we could talk on the phone secretly. I am afraid I can't go through all this by myself. And of course, I'd love to help you too, if there's anything I can do for you – get in touch with old friends, for example?
I hope I'm not imposing myself too much on you. It is just that I'm really out of my depth just now and need some sensible advice from an understanding friend.

Take care,
T.

**Gymnasium Niedersachsen – Englisch**
**Erhöhtes Anforderungsniveau – Abitur 2014**

## Sprachmittlung

### Text: Moritz Koch, „Computer am Steuer ist noch ungeheuer“ (2012)

Die Geisterhand sitzt oben auf dem Autodach, eingezwängt in eine Büchse aus Metall. Das Konstrukt sieht seltsam aus – wie eine fahrende Kaffeemühle. Tatsächlich aber handelt es sich um ein Hightech-System, das den Straßenverkehr revolutionieren könnte: Die Metallbüchse soll Autos ohne Fahrer ans Ziel bringen, vorbei an Staus und Unfallstellen, sicher, pünktlich, spritsparend. Wie von Geisterhand geführt.

Das „autonome Auto“, wie es in Fachkreisen genannt wird, klingt nach Science-Fiction, doch auf den Straßen von Nevada ist es schon Realität. Seit ein paar Wochen dürfen die Bordcomputer dort das Steuer übernehmen, nicht nur auf der Teststrecke, sondern im normalen Berufsverkehr. Der Führerschein für die Geisterhand ist ein Novum in der amerikanischen Verkehrsgeschichte. Einzige Bedingung der Behörden Nevadas ist die Präsenz eines menschlichen Beifahrers, der einspringen soll, falls die Systeme verrückt spielen. Ein Tritt auf die Bremse oder eine Bewegung des Lenkrads genügt, um den Autopilot auszuschalten.

Hinter dem Projekt stehen Ingenieure aus dem Hause Google, allen voran der deutsche Computerwissenschaftler Sebastian Thrun. Als 18-Jähriger verlor Thrun seinen besten Freund bei einem Autounfall. Er entschloss sich, den Rest seines Lebens darauf zu verwenden, gegen den tödlichen Alltag auf den Straßen anzukämpfen. Thrun studierte in Hildesheim und Bonn, dann wanderte er nach Kalifornien aus. Dort lehrt er an der Universität Stanford und widmet sich als Google-Fellow den Forschungsarbeiten am autonomen Auto.

Acht Prototypen aus den Laboratorien des Technologiekonzerns haben nun in Nevada eine Zulassung erhalten. Sechs Toyota Prius, ein Audi TT und ein Lexus RX 450h. In allen Fahrzeugen übernehmen Lasersysteme und GPS-Ortung die Rolle der menschlichen Sinnesorgane. Computerprogramme verarbeiten die Datenströme und lenken die Google-Mobile durch den Wüstenstaat […].

Sogar ein eigenes Kennzeichen für die autonomen Autos gibt es in Nevada schon. Eine liegende Acht, das Symbol für Unendlichkeit, auf einem roten Hintergrund, dazu der Schriftzug: „Autonomous Vehicle“. Bruce Breslow, der Chef von Nevadas Zulassungsbehörde, findet das Unendlichkeitssymbol würde am besten passen zum „Auto der Zukunft“. Aber macht sie wirklich das Auto der Zukunft aus, die auf dem Dach aufmontierte Geisterhand?

Es ist kaum vorstellbar, dass Autokäufer in ein paar Jahren bereit wären, auf computergesteuerte Autos umzusteigen. Viele Menschen beschleicht ein ungutes Gefühl, wenn die eigene Möglichkeit zur Kontrolle der versprochenen Sicherheit eines IT-Systems geopfert wird. Und selbstverständlich verlöre Autofahren die emotionale Qualität, auf die Konzerne in ihrer aufwendig produzierten Werbung so gerne abheben.

Solche Fragen beschäftigen Thrun nicht. Für ihn geht es vor allem um eines: die Sicherheit. Im Autoland Amerika sterben jedes Jahr 30 000 Menschen im Straßenverkehr. Und menschliches Versagen ist mit großem Abstand die Unfallursache Nummer eins. [...] Die Akzeptanzprobleme sind [jedoch] gewaltig. Menschen vertrauen eben lieber ihren eigenen Fähigkeiten; das Gefühl, sich einem Computersystem auszuliefern, schürt hingegen Angst. [...]

Eine vielleicht noch wichtigere Hürde für die Einführung der neuen Technologie als die psychologischen Vorbehalte gegen Computer ist der Einwand, dass führerlose Fahrzeuge im Straßenverkehr enorme Verwirrung stiften würden. Beispielsweise an Kreuzungen, an denen Menschen ihr Fahrverhalten oftmals nach Zeichen anderer Fahrer richten.

Sie geben einander Signale, eine Handbewegung, ein Blick in die Augen reicht zur Verständigung. Menschen wissen, wie sich andere Menschen orientieren. Was in einem Computer vor sich geht, wissen sie nicht. Dieses Problem ließe sich nur lösen, wenn alle Autos auf Autopilot umstellen würden – was einstweilen noch vollkommen unrealistisch erscheint. Doch vielleicht werden die Vorteile autonomer Verkehrsmittel die Skeptiker irgendwann überzeugen, schließlich gehen sie über den Sicherheitsaspekt hinaus. Computersysteme im Auto dienen schließlich auch dem Umweltschutz. Die Programme lassen sich so einstellen, dass sie den Spritverbrauch minimieren. Anders als mancher menschliche Fahrer haben die Bordcomputer keine Freude an heulenden Motoren und quietschenden Reifen. Und auch darum geht es: um verlorene Zeit. Staus sind eine massive Produktivitätsbremse in modernen Volkswirtschaften. Stunden, die für die Arbeit genutzt werden können, verstreichen mit stumpfsinnigem Warten, wenn wieder mal eine Unfallstelle die Autobahn blockiert.

[...] Zwar sind die Aussichten gering, dass das autonome Google-Mobil demnächst in Serienproduktion geht. Der Computerkonzern kann aber darauf hoffen, Technologien und Patente an Autohersteller zu verkaufen. *645 words*

*Quelle:* Süddeutsche Online, *12. 6. 2012. Von Moritz Koch.*
*http://www.sueddeutsche.de/auto/fahren-ohne-fahrer-computer-am-steuer-ist-noch-ungeheuer-1.1380556.*

**Aufgabenstellung**

Gemeinsam mit einer englischen Schule nehmen Sie an einem internationalen Projekt zum Thema *„The Technology of Tomorrow, Today“* teil. Ihre Aufgabe besteht darin, auf der Grundlage des folgenden Textes einen englischsprachigen Artikel für den Internetauftritt des Projekts zu verfassen. Darin beschreiben Sie die Funktionsweise des autonomen Autos und stellen die möglichen Auswirkungen seiner Nutzung dar.
Ihr Text soll etwa 250 Wörter umfassen.

## Textaufgabe

Der Prüfling hat **eine** Textaufgabe seiner Wahl zu bearbeiten.

### Textaufgabe I

#### Excerpt from H. M. Naqvi, *Home Boy* (2009)

*The novel is about the experiences of three young Americans of Pakistani origin shortly before and after 9/11. At the end of the novel, Shehzad, the narrator, phones his mother in Karachi, Pakistan.*

The phone rang. A crosstown bus thundered past. "Hello?" I said.

After a pregnant pause, Ma replied, "Beta?"

"Ma –"

"Is everything all right?"

"Well … everything wasn't all right … but now it is … so don't worry –"

"Shehzad," Ma interrupted, "it is nearly one in the morning. I am a little slow, and you are talking a little too fast. Now tell me again: why should I not worry?"

"Me," I replied. "You shouldn't worry about me."

"You are calling at one in the morning just to tell me that I should not be worried about you?"

Taking a deep breath, I attempted to organize my thoughts. "Yes," I began, "kind of. I actually have something to tell you. About three months ago, in the first week of July, I was let go, you know, fired. There were companywide layoffs. There's been a downturn in the market, an economic recession, and after 9/11, well, companies have mostly stopped hiring."

I could hear Ma breathing. I could see her massaging her eyes. She was probably sitting up by now, hunched and cross-legged.

"But don't worry, Ma. About fifteen minutes ago, I was offered a job. It's with this research house. I like the people. They want me to write financial reports. It's something I can do and do well. They told me I'm a 'great fit.' It's very promising. It's a wonderful opportunity."

My disclosure was met with silence, and for a moment I thought the line had dropped. Then Ma said, "If it is such a wonderful opportunity, beta, why do you sound unhappy?"

"I do?"

"Are you?"

"I don't know," I said, then blurted, "yes, yes, I am. I would have been okay, but there's more."

"More?"

"More I haven't told you," I replied, clearing my throat. "Last week Jamshed, Ali, and I were arrested on terrorism charges –"

"What?"

"We were arrested, interrogated, thrown into solitary confinement. It was crazy. They kept saying we were *in possession* of bomb-making manuals, terrorist literature. They kept telling us that we were *in for life*. I was certain that I wouldn't see the light of day. But somehow, somehow, they let Jamshed and me go –"

"*Thank God!*"

"Then Khan Sahab had a heart attack –"

"*Oh God!* –"

"Don't worry. He's okay. I went to see him and he sends you his salam. He's recovering –"

"Inshallah!"

"But Ali, he's still inside. […] I've been feeling so helpless. There's nothing I can do. What can I do?"

"Why didn't you tell me, beta?"

"What do you want me to tell you, Ma? That life's changed? The city's changed? That there's sadness around every corner? There are cops everywhere? You know, there was a time when a police presence was reassuring, like at a parade or late at night, on the street, in the subway, but now I'm afraid of them. I'm afraid all the time. I feel like a marked man. I feel like an animal. It's no way to live. Maybe it's just a phase, maybe it'll pass, and things will return to normal, or maybe, I don't know, history will keep repeating itself …"

I stopped. I was talking to myself. Ma had fallen silent. She was probably standing, regarding the city lights through the lattice circumscribing the balcony. Although the brightest blazed from the Dentonic-Once-A-Day-Everyday billboard welded to our building, our balcony offered a panorama of the old city, from the great white modernism dome of Jinnah's mausoleum in the north to the spire of the grand neo-Gothic colonial relic, Empress Market, in the south. Bandar Road cut past below, connecting the landmarks and ferrying traffic to and from the sea. I could hear the purl of rickshaws over the clamor of crosstown buses; I could almost smell the smog, feel the breeze against my cheek. I heard myself say, "I want to come home, Ma."

*652 words*



**Annotations:**

2 beta: *(Kosename für) Sohn*
30/31 Jamshed, Ali: the narrator's best friends, Americans of Pakistani origin
38 Khan Sahab: Jamshed's father
40 salam: Arabic: a salutation meaning "peace"
55 Dentonic …: advertisement of a dental care provider
57 Jinnah: Pakistan's founding father
60 purl: *here: dichte Reihe*

**Aufgabenstellung**

An educational publishing house is planning to compile a reader with the title *Literary Responses to 9/11* including extracts from Mohsin Hamid's novel *The Reluctant Fundamentalist.* Wishing to take into consideration the viewpoints of young adult readers, the editors have asked your English class to submit articles commenting on the suitability of further literary extracts. You have been asked to write an article commenting on the quality of an excerpt from H. M. Naqvi's novel *Home Boy.* Your article will be posted on the internet platform of the publishing house.

1. As a preparation for your article you
   - outline the content of the conversation between Shehzad and his mother.
   - examine the language used to express Shehzad's feelings. *(50 %)*

2. With reference to your findings, to Mohsin Hamid's novel and possibly other materials studied in class, you write your article commenting on the suitability of this extract for young adult readers.
   Consider if the excerpt
   - contains attitudes towards or reactions to 9/11 which are different or similar to those depicted in Hamid's novel.
   - is well-written from your point of view.
   - provides topics for lively class discussions. *(50 %)*

## Textaufgabe II

### Yasmin Alibhai-Brown, "Shakespeare and Love" (2012)

No one has ever captured the joy and lunacy and power of love better than William Shakespeare, and no one ever will. We know that well enough, and hear his evocations at many a modern wedding, sweet notes for happy ever-afters. However, I'm more beguiled and intrigued by his transgressive depictions of love, the audacity of rebellious couples reaching out to each other across thorny borders, the colour line, the culture line, the faith line, old enemy lines. […]

Let me take you to lush Kampala, Uganda, in the 60s, to my school, cheap shacks in hot tin roofs. We performed Shakespeare's plays, sometimes under the Jacaranda tree, its violet flowers shedding petals over our heads. Many pupils, those who went on to be millionaire businessmen, couldn't see the point, and were surly and usually cast as villains. For me Shakespeare was my furtive *enamorato,* a tempter who took me to exciting, edgy places. […] I fell in love with his idea of love, mutinously cast aside, at least in my head, the strict codes of female behaviour and rigid conventions. Asians who had migrated to East Africa during the glory days of the British Empire were old Elizabethans. Girls were possessions. We had no autonomy, only bartering value. Cross-communal marriages between Asians of different faiths were taboo. Those who dared lost. Black African men, though, were the more deadly imagined threat to Asian female virtue. […] With this backdrop I was cast as Juliet in a school play with Romeo, whose skin was jet black. Our teacher from England was an idealist. Made sense in our world then. Word got out that I'd kissed a black man on stage. My father cut me out of his life and never spoke to me again till he died. […]

In the *Merchant of Venice* […] Shylock is malevolent, the archetypal Jew, as labelled through the centuries. The play's anti-Semitism has been much debated. His child Jessica secretly marries the Christian Lorenzo, steals away, steals the family jewels, too, including a precious ring given by her mother Leah to Shylock. The final cuts: she forfeits her family and community, commits religious patricide. Those leaps from faith and those dilemmas are with us today. Jessica is deeply troubled about self-hatred: "What heinous sin is it in me to be ashamed to be my father's child". Shylock speaks for many fathers when he can't understand how she could betray him and her people. […] Does Jessica give up Judaism for an easier life? She sells her mother's ring for a monkey, is ready to do anything to be accepted by the other side […].

Finally to *Romeo and Juliet,* which is not about lovers crossing race, religion, or ethnicity, yet has become just that, and defiantly. I was commissioned by the Royal Shakespeare Company to enact my personal Romeo-and-Juliet story on stage. When I take the show to schools, I find illicit love, even the acting of it, is still forbidden in contemporary Britain. So-called multiculturalism doesn't extend to the body or the bed. Asian and Arab Juliets are bullied, burnt, beaten, driven to suicide, killed or compelled to marry within the tribe. In every conflicted location of the world they perform *Romeo and Juliet* to divest themselves of inherited hate, the worst sort. […] In these plays there is so much more to love than love. […]

Apparently, Britain now has the highest number of mixed-race couplings in the world, and children, too. Their compulsions and fears, joys and sorrows, were so consummately showcased by Shakespeare 400 years ago that there is little more left to say. *595 words*

*From: Transcript of essay on BBC Radio 3 by Yasmin Alibhai-Brown.*
*http://www.bbc.co.uk/programmes/b01g4vrx*

**Annotations:**

title Yasmin Alibhai-Brown: British journalist and writer of Pakistani origin; grew up in Africa and moved to England in the 1970s
4 beguiled: *here:* fascinated
4 transgressive: going beyond acceptable limits
4 audacity: *Wagemut*
10 surly: bad-tempered
11 furtive *enamorato: here:* secret love
12 mutinously: rebelliously
15 were old Elizabethans: *here:* they thought like people in Shakespeare's times
15/16 bartering value: *Tauschwert*
22 archetypal: most typical
25/26 final cuts: *die letzte, endgültige Trennung*
26 to forfeit: *here:* to give up, to abandon
26 patricide: *Vatermord*
44 consummately: perfectly

## Aufgabenstellung

You are doing an internship with "Playing Shakespeare", an educational project that stages *Romeo and Juliet* as well as *The Merchant of Venice* at the Globe Theatre in London. You have been given the following text to prepare an article in which you comment on the challenges of "Love Across Borders" in literature or film as your contribution for the project brochure.

1. In order to write your article you
   - outline Yasmin Alibhai-Brown's personal experience and her attitude towards Shakespeare and his plays.
   - compare the behaviour parents and ethnic or religious communities show towards young people in the text at hand with that in the Shakespeare play you studied in class:
     **either** *Romeo and Juliet*
     **or** *The Merchant of Venice*. *(50 %)*

2. On the basis of your findings, write your article "Love Across Borders", in which you comment on the challenges lovers may face when crossing "the colour line, the culture line, the faith line, old enemy lines" (ll. 5/6). Also refer to **one** of the following materials: *The Reluctant Fundamentalist, Outsourced, Four Weddings and a Funeral.* *(50 %)*

**Lösungsvorschläge**

## Sprachmittlung

*This task follows a rather classic mediation pattern. You are asked to write an article that should be directed towards a broad public readership to inform them about the recent invention of an "autonomous" car. Do not forget that this article needs to have a heading as well as a brief introductory statement in which you present the key information and a short conclusion at the end of your text to round it off.*
*Your text should contain the following aspects:*
- *Ersatz eines Fahrers durch moderne Technologien wie GPS- und Lasersysteme*
- *menschliches Eingreifen in die vollautomatische Technologie jederzeit möglich*
- *Bedenken gegenüber dem autonomen Auto:*
  - *Unvermögen der Autos, Reaktionen menschlicher Verkehrsteilnehmer richtig einzuschätzen*
  - *mangelndes Vertrauen in die neuen technischen Möglichkeiten*
- *Vorteile des autonomen Autos:*
  - *umweltfreundlicheres Fahrverhalten*
  - *sinkende Zahl von Unfällen*
  - *Steigern der Produktivität durch Verringern der Staus auf den Straßen*

**The car of the future – the future of the car?**
What was once science fiction has now turned into reality: Thanks to the inventive genius of scientists from Google, the first "autonomous" cars are cruising the streets of Nevada. The only condition is that there has to be a person on board in case of a technical malfunction. Touching the brake or turning the steering wheel overrides the system and hands back control to the human driver. Laser systems and GPS replace the sensory organs and computer programmes process the data thus making it possible for the car to drive.
Putting safety in the hands of technology, however, might deter potential customers from buying one, especially as many people still trust their own driving skills more than a computer system. In addition, autonomous cars cannot understand human gestures used at intersections, for example, where people use hand signals and eye contact to interact – not to mention the missing fun factor once a computer operates the accelerator.
They might not excite you, but autonomous cars can help to protect the environment because they can minimise fuel consumption. Moreover, these cars increase road safety, as human failure is the main reason for fatal road accidents. The economy also profits from them because the number of people stuck in time-consuming traffic jams could be reduced, therefore having a positive impact on productivity. The chances of seeing these cars on our roads in the near future are slim, but Google hopes to sell the technology to car manufacturers.

## Textaufgabe

### Textaufgabe I

1. *One possibility of dealing with the two-in-one task is to write two separate parts for each subtask, which is demonstrated in the following sample solution. Bear in mind that you should write a fluent, coherent, well-structured text, stating the contents in your own words.*
   *The following aspects should be mentioned in your outline of the conversation:*
   - *Shehzad informs his mother about his past and current job situation*
   - *he lets her know that he and two friends have been arrested in connection with potential terrorist attacks*
   - *he tells her about the changes he has experienced since 9/11 and how he feels about this*

   *Then focus on the language used to express Shehzad's feelings. Provide evidence from the text in the form of quotes. However, these references only support your findings on the use of language and need to be explained.*
   *These points should be covered in your analysis:*
   - *Shehzad is confused, afraid, and desperate because he does not know what to do and how much he should tell his mother about his problems*
   - *his feelings are shown in the way he speaks: mixture of short and long sentences, use of rhetorical questions, repetition and comparisons that indicate his inferior social position in New York since 9/11*

The excerpt taken from H. M. Naqvi's novel *Home Boy*, published in 2009, is about a phone call between the narrator Shehzad, who lives and works in New York City, and his mother in Karachi, Pakistan. He tells her about changes in his professional life as well as his growing feeling of unease since the terrorist attacks of 9/11.
When Shehzad calls, it is late at night in Pakistan, but he tries to placate his mother by emphasizing that there is nothing to worry about. He then explains that he had lost his job a few months earlier due to the economic downturn after 9/11, but that he has just been offered a new position that he is very pleased about. His mother, however, senses her son's discomfort, so Shehzad has to admit that he and two Pakistani friends of his had been arrested on the suspicion of terrorist activities and threatened with the prospect of life-long imprisonment. One of his friends is still in custody. Shehzad is confused about how he and other Asian immigrants have been treated since 9/11 and expresses his wish to return to Pakistan.

When reading the excerpt, the reader gets the strong impression that Shehzad is caught up in some sort of emotional crisis. He appears very confused and is not sure about his feelings as well as the extent to which he wants to tell his mother about his situation in New York or about what is going on in his mind.

In the beginning of the telephone conversation, it is noticeable that Shehzad pauses a lot and breaks off his sentences. This indicates that he is very unsure of what to say. For example, he falters in mid-sentence (cf. l. 5), which leads the reader (and his mother) to believe that nothing is going as well as he pretends it is. Furthermore, his mother mentions that Shehzad is “talking a little too fast” (l. 7), which is a clear sign of his nervousness and shows that he has probably been under pressure for some time. It is also a common symptom for someone who wants to get something off his chest. This is made even more obvious when Shehzad lets the reader know: “Taking a deep breath, I attempted to organize my thoughts.” (l. 11). It becomes clear that it is hard for him to talk about the arrest, which is why he has to collect his thoughts before speaking.
Moreover, one can deduce that he is confused from the contradictory way in which he acts: he wants to talk about his current problems, but does not want to burden his mother – who knows that something is wrong, or else her son would not have phoned her in the middle of the night. When put on the spot, he gradually starts opening up. Talking about his arrest, he speaks in a mixture of short and long sentences (cf. ll. 27–36). The anaphora “They kept saying […]. They kept telling us” (ll. 34/35) show his helplessness and despair.
Once the whole truth about his situation has surfaced, he takes refuge in a series of rhetorical questions (cf. ll. 46/47), thus highlighting his feeling of confusion. This is further emphasised by the anaphoric use of comparisons: “I feel like a marked man. I feel like an animal” (l. 50). The same applies to the repetition of “I'm afraid” (l. 49). The comparisons illustrate that Shehzad sees himself less and less like an equal or even human being in Western society, which is why he wants to return to his native country Pakistan. To recapitulate, it can be said that the author makes very effective use of language to illustrate the protagonist's feelings of insecurity and confusion.

2. *Your article is supposed to be based on your findings in assignment 1 as well as on references to Mohsin Hamid's novel* The Reluctant Fundamentalist. *Be sure to produce a coherent and well-structured text that is suited to its intended readership: aim for a neutral style, as it will be published on the website of a publishing company and read by a wide variety of people. The article should also have a suitable heading. Besides your judgment of* Home Boy *concerning its suitability for English classes, the following points could be part of your argumentation:*
   - *similarities:*
     - *both protagonists have their native country and status as expats in common*
     - *Shehzad and Changez experience a changing US society in the aftermath of 9/11*
   - *differences:*
     - *concerning their attitude towards 9/11: Changez' triumph and radicalisation versus Shehzad's fear and frustration over the events that followed*
     - *different reasons for leaving the US: Changez' political engagement and Shehzad's longing for safety*

**Dazed and Confused in New York after 9/11**

In comparison with Mohsin Hamid's novel *The Reluctant Fundamentalist*, I found this excerpt from H. M. Naqvi's *Home Boy* to represent a somewhat familiar, but also slightly different view of the events of September 11, 2001. Suitability as reading material in English classes depends on several aspects, such as content, readability, and food for thought, in short: in how far a book "speaks" to young adult readers. Belonging to this target group myself, I have taken a closer look at these two texts.

One very striking similarity between the novel and the excerpt is the experience the protagonists, Changez in *The Reluctant Fundamentalist* and Shehzad in *Home Boy*, make in the aftermath of 9/11: In both cases, people of Asian or Arab appearance are regularly stopped and searched. Changez finds himself being apprehended and strip-searched at the airport on his return from Manila, where he had witnessed the attacks on television. He is held and interrogated for so long that his colleagues have long left the airport by the time he is finally released. This experience is similar to Shehzad's account of his – seemingly random – arrest and the treatment he has experienced in prison (cf. ll. 33–36).

The more obvious differences can be found upon comparing the reactions of the two protagonists to the attacks. While we are not told about Shehzad's immediate reaction in the excerpt given, he seems to have been living in constant fear since 9/11 and, despite his frustration about the treatment he receives, he does not seem to have developed an anti-American attitude. Instead, he rather sees himself as an accidental victim of the fallout of 9/11. Changez' immediate reaction on seeing the Twin Towers collapse on television is to smile. This reaction suggests approval and even triumph. He later describes it as a feeling of awe for this act of destruction. He starts to reject the values of the concept of the American Dream, such as status, money, and power. This is particularly striking as he seems to be living this dream himself: Changez is very successful in his high-paying job with a prestigious firm and has just been offered a promotion. He develops a new-found patriotism for his native country Pakistan and starts growing a beard after a trip home, thus actively singling himself out.

Moreover, both protagonists wish to leave the US, but for different reasons. Changez starts a new life in Lahore because he completely rejects everything connected with the US. He lectures at a university in his home town, imparting to students his idea of a "Pakistani Dream", a strong country with no interference from the US. By contrast, Shehzad's reasons for leaving are solely personal and a result of his fear and insecurity. He wants to escape and to feel at home again (cf. l. 61).

To sum up, the extract from *Home Boy* complements Hamid's work nicely, showing some different approaches to the events of September 11. Moreover, the text is very well written. Naqvi's characters come across as very authentic because of their complex and conflicting emotions. At the same time, the text is easy to understand.

Regarding its suitability for class discussions, I can well imagine that the excerpt from *Home Boy* would lend itself to the in-depth discussion of several interesting topics (e. g. questions such as "Who can you trust with your problems?" or "Is leaving the US Shehzad's only option?"). Current issues, such as the matter of the US Patriot Act, which basically allows organisations like the National Security Agency (NSA) to infringe on citizens' personal and privacy rights, can be discussed in the context of the treatment Shehzad and his friends experienced at the hands of the police.

All in all, I personally can highly recommend this text, together with Mohsin Hamid's novel, for young readers as both texts shed light on various aspects of life for young Pakistanis in the US after 9/11, all presented in a way that young adult readers will find easy to relate to.

## Textaufgabe II

1. *The first assignment contains some hints that can help you structure your outline and decide what is important. For the first bullet point task, only gather information that is related to the author's personal experiences and her opinion on Shakespeare and his plays. The aspects listed below should be contained in your text:*
   - *the author loved Shakespeare's plays at school because they made her question her role in society*
   - *her father ignored her after she was said to have kissed a black boy while performing* Romeo and Juliet *on stage*
   - *in her Shakespeare workshops, she has the impression that intercultural relationships are still an issue in British society*
   - *she believes Shakespeare's perspective on the power of love to be very special*
   - *the issues Shakespeare's plays deal with are still up to date*

   *In the second part of the assignment, you are asked to compare the article at hand to one of Shakespeare's plays that you have read in class. The sample text will concentrate on* Romeo and Juliet. *Only focus on the reactions of parents or ethnic or religious communities young people have to deal with. Provide suitable quotes from the text to support your findings.*

   *You need to cover the following aspects:*
   - *girls are considered a commodity and have to obey to their parents*
   - *relationships or marriages are only accepted within one's own social group*
   - *failure to obey social norms might result in severe consequences*

Due to her origins and upbringing, Yasmin Alibhai-Brown has encountered many interpersonal borders. In her 2012 radio broadcast "Shakespeare and Love", she comes up with ideas that are most definitely worth sharing as her personal experiences and opinions are comparable to the ones displayed in *Romeo and Juliet.*

Alibhai-Brown is of Pakistani origin, but grew up in Uganda in the 1960s. Shakespeare has played an important role for her from her early life up to the present. In school in Uganda, Alibhai-Brown loved to act. Introduced to a different view of the world by Shakespeare, she soon started to question the rules of her own society. Once she played Juliet which involved kissing a black Romeo. Because of the harsh social norms inherent in African society, where ethnic communities were strictly divided, this kiss resulted in her being ignored by her father for the rest of his life. Despite this incisive event, her attitude towards Shakespeare has remained positive throughout. She states that, in her view, the poet's ability to capture the emotional upheaval and consequences of true love are unparalleled, and she is especially fond of his depiction of love across borders. According to her, his plays are still relevant today: in *The Merchant of Venice*, decisions between community and love interests have to be made, while *Romeo and Juliet* also retains its modernity as forbidden love is still an issue today. This is what Alibhai-Brown experienced herself when staging *Romeo and Juliet* in British schools.

Both the behaviour of Alibhai-Brown's father and the attitude of the Asian community in which she grew up can be related to the world Shakespeare created. Firstly, the attitude that "[g]irls [are] possessions" (l. 15) can be found in *Romeo and Juliet* too. This is largely due to the age from which the play originates. In Elizabethan times, women's rights were not as far advanced as in most Western societies today. Just like Asian girls in Uganda in the 1960s, Juliet does not have the right to decide for herself, which becomes especially clear at the beginning of the play. In the first act, she is told that her parents have chosen Paris, a young nobleman, as husband for her, which she seems to accept without complaint. When she later tries to rebel against her parents and refuses to marry Paris, her father demands her to be obedient by threatening to disinherit her. Alibhai-Brown's own father does something similar: he ignores her after she is said to have kissed a black boy in a school play (cf. ll. 20/21). Both examples demonstrate how serious the consequences of going against social conventions are taken in communities that couple parental love and absolute obedience.
The same is true of the view concerning marriages befitting one's social status. Alibhai-Brown explains that "[c]ross-cultural marriages between Asians of different faiths were taboo" (l. 16), which clearly implies that the community would interfere in relationships it did not consider suitable. This practice shows that love can come only after community requirements have been met, and this is also true of Juliet's life. Her choice of men is limited to those who belong to the Capulets' social circle. This is why she is very upset after finding out about Romeo's background, knowing that this relationship will cross a border: the enmity between their families, the Capulets and the Montagues, is so strong that neither of them ever considered telling their story to their parents to seek their approval. Thinking about a solution to their problem, Juliet can only come up with the suggestion that Romeo should abandon both his family and name, which is out of the question for him. Thus two teenagers keep their relationship secret to avoid losing the life they have.
The examples Alibhai-Brown provides from her own experience are not limited to her upbringing, but also to those of second-generation immigrants in contemporary Britain, above all girls. Their communities have a variety of punishments for intercultural digressions, ranging from being "bullied, burnt, beaten, driven to suicide, killed" (l. 38) to being "compelled to marry within the tribe" (ll. 38/39).

Romeo and Juliet have to deal with the same "inherited hate" (l. 40). In several scenes, Juliet beseeches Romeo to leave her family's property because she fears for his life if her parents or guards should find out about them. To put it in a nutshell, one can say that Shakespeare's *Romeo and Juliet* still accurately depicts the conflicted love lives of many young people.

2. *Here you are asked to write an article entitled "Love Across Borders" in which you refer to material covered in class to illustrate the challenges facing lovers who start a relationship that is considered unsuitable. You only need to include one of the listed works of literature or film in your article. Choose the one you feel most confident about. Make sure that you also meet the requirements of a proper article (headline, neutral to formal speech register, logical structure and line of argumentation). You could use the quote from the text (cf. ll. 5/6) as a starting point by incorporating it into your introduction.*
*The following aspects could be part of your article:*
   - *choosing love over family as a common trend thanks to agencies which rescue desperate couples in India*
   - *choosing family over love out of duty in the case of Asha in* Outsourced
   - *the ruling of Sharia Courts versus democratic principles in Western societies*

**Love Across Borders – The Challenges Facing Today's Romeos and Juliets**
More than 400 years after their creation, Romeo and Juliet, "the star-cross'd lovers" (prologue), still number among the world's most popular fictional characters. They are compelling because of their passion, courage, and tragic love story, but that is not the only thing which makes them so special. The Elizabethan author William Shakespeare created the timeless tragedy of Romeo and Juliet, two young people who cross a line drawn by their community, but cannot avoid doing so because of the depth of their love for each other. Even today, lines of colour, culture, religion and hate (cf. ll. 5/6) pose challenges for young lovers which are no less tragic than those you find in the works of famous poets. Different ways of dealing with the dilemma of family versus love will be shown in the following.
In our Western world, we hope that such restrictions on personal freedom have ceased to exist; however, this, sadly, is not the case. Immigrant families in particular try to preserve their cultural heritage and identity by setting up a "culture line" (l. 5) their children should not cross. If they do, the consequences can be harsh punishments, as Alibhai-Brown explains (cf. ll. 38/39). By setting up such divisions, the parents ultimately force their children to choose between love and family. In India, secret agencies have recently been established to rescue desperate couples, find them a hiding place, and help them start a new life in another part of the country without any contact with their families. These agencies are in great demand. Finally couples are at least provided with a trustworthy alternative to accepting their fate.

The feature film *Outsourced* casts a different light on the borders love has to overcome. The American protagonist Todd has been sent to India to improve the performance of his company's call centre, where he meets Asha, one of the employees. She seems to be the embodiment of emancipation, being bright and quick-witted, and she helps Todd understand Indian mentality better. It is her efforts that lead to motivating the Indian workforce and prevent further misunderstandings. When she falls in love with Todd, she refuses to live out their relationship openly as her parents have already arranged a marriage for her. To her, family is the central focus in life, and she does not want to lose it. The arranged marriage is a requirement she is happy to meet, since it is a common belief in India that love will come with the wedding. Consequently, Todd returns to the States alone when his job is finished, leaving her behind. However, the film ends with a phone call from Asha that could mean that she revised her decision. If this were the case, she and Todd would now have to decide where and how to live and how to raise children should they have any. Maybe Todd would also have to convert to Hinduism in order to satisfy Asha's parents.

Contemporary Britain has "the highest number of mixed-race couplings in the world, and children too" (ll. 42/43) which shows that more and more people from different ethnic backgrounds dare to decide in favour of love and leave old barriers behind. A trend may be unfolding: cultural, parental and religious challenges may diminish, and free, individual choices might become possible. However, there also is a growing number of Sharia Courts in Britain, and their traditional rulings sometimes contradict existing law and even basic human rights. To save couples from the execution of such dangerous legislation, Western societies need to take action in support of young people who no longer wish to obey old traditions any more. The development towards an open-minded, multicultural society might then experience a further boost.

Personally, I think that free choice in matters of the heart should be guaranteed to young people by their parents as a sign of love and acceptance. On the stage, love hindered by borders as shown is Shakespeare's plays will never fail to touch and entertain us; in real life, however, one can only hope that the barriers love encounters will shrink in the future and vanish as the multicultural society becomes a worldwide reality.

# Ihre Meinung ist uns wichtig!

Ihre Anregungen sind uns immer willkommen. Bitte informieren Sie uns mit diesem Schein über Ihre Verbesserungsvorschläge!

| Titel-Nr. | Seite | Vorschlag |
|---|---|---|
| | | |
| | | |
| | | |
| | | |
| | | |
| | | |
| | | |
| | | |
| | | |

Bitte hier abtrennen

Lernen • Wissen • Zukunft
STARK

Bitte hier abtrennen

**Zutreffendes bitte ankreuzen!**

**Die Absenderin/der Absender ist:**

- ☐ Lehrer/in in den Klassenstufen: ____
- ☐ Fachbetreuer/in
  Fächer: ____
- ☐ Seminarlehrer/in
  Fächer: ____
- ☐ Regierungsfachberater/in
  Fächer: ____
- ☐ Oberstufenbetreuer/in
- ☐ Schulleiter/in
- ☐ Referendar/in, Termin 2. Staatsexamen: ____
- ☐ Leiter/in Lehrerbibliothek
- ☐ Leiter/in Schülerbibliothek
- ☐ Sekretariat
- ☐ Eltern
- ☐ Schüler/in, Klasse: ____
- ☐ Sonstiges: ____

**Unterrichtsfächer:** (Bei Lehrkräften!)

____

**STARK Verlag**
**Postfach 1852**
**85318 Freising**

24-V_Abi

Bitte ausfüllen und im frankierten Umschlag an uns einsenden. Für Fensterkuverts geeignet.

**Kennen Sie Ihre Kundennummer? Bitte hier eintragen.**

## Absender (Bitte in Druckbuchstaben!)

Name/Vorname ____

Straße/Nr. ____

PLZ/Ort/Ortsteil ____

Telefon privat ____ Geburtsjahr ____

E-Mail ____

## Schule/Schulstempel (Bitte immer angeben!)

*(Bitte blättern Sie um)*